DEFYING JIM CROW

DEFYING JIM CROW

African American Community Development and the Struggle for Racial Equality in New Orleans, 1900–1960

DONALD E. DEVORE

Louisiana State University Press
Baton Rouge

Published by Louisiana State University Press
lsupress.org

Copyright © 2015 by Louisiana State University Press
All rights reserved. Except in the case of brief quotations used in articles or reviews, no part of this publication may be reproduced or transmitted in any format or by any means without written permission of Louisiana State University Press.

Louisiana Paperback Edition, 2022

Designer: Laura Roubique Gleason
Typefaces: Georgia (text), Eveleth Dot (display)

Cover photo from the Louis C. Hennick collection. Used with permission.

Library of Congress Cataloging-in-Publication Data
DeVore, Donald E.
  Defying Jim Crow : African American community development and the struggle for racial equality in New Orleans, 1900–1960 / Donald E. DeVore.
     pages cm
  Includes bibliographical references and index.
   ISBN 978-0-8071-6037-4 (cloth) — ISBN 978-0-8071-7736-5 (paperback) — ISBN 978-0-8071-6038-1 (pdf) — ISBN 978-0-8071-6039-8 (epub)
    1. African Americans—Louisiana—New Orleans—Social conditions—20th century. 2. Community development—Louisiana—New Orleans. 3. African Americans—Segregation—Louisiana—New Orleans—History—19th century. 4. Race discrimination—Louisiana—New Orleans—History—20th century. 5. African Americans—Louisiana—New Orleans—History—20th century. 6. African Americans—History—1877–1964. 7. New Orleans (La.)—Race relations—History—20th century. I. Title. II. Title: African American community development and the struggle for racial equality in New Orleans, 1900–1960.
  F379.N59N437 2015
  305.896'0730763350904—dc23

2014043015

CONTENTS

Preface   vii

1. The Rise and Decline of Black Equality   1
2. Higher Education and Individual Initiative   31
3. The Religious Dimensions of Community Development   62
4. The Secular Dimensions of Community Development   92
5. Public Education   122
6. Business and Labor   151
7. Jim Crow Attacked   174
8. Freedom Now   214

Notes   229
Bibliography   251
Index   267

PREFACE

New Orleans's brief participation in the Civil War provided free blacks and former slaves an early opportunity to seek personal advancement and racial equality, and they possessed little doubt that they could succeed. The New Orleans black community was fortunate to have a large number of African Americans who had been free before the Civil War. Many of them were black Creoles already familiar with group protest and a tradition of fighting to maintain or expand individual civil and economic rights. Indeed, much of the early African American leadership in New Orleans came from the black Creole community. Black Creole leaders helped infuse the entire black community with an ideology that stressed racial equality and justice, community development, and individual initiative. And that community continued to grow as African Americans from rural parishes and other states moved to New Orleans. Most of the new arrivals were former slaves and lacked formal education, but they brought with them a worldview that was democratic and aspirational in its orientation. Like the black Creoles they found in the city, they, too, believed in racial equality and justice, community development, and individual initiative. Slavery, of course, had made those goals difficult to obtain but not invisible to them. When congressional Reconstruction produced opportunities for suffrage, education, and economic improvement, the aspirations of African Americans soared.

Many of the gains New Orleans's African Americans achieved during Reconstruction, however, were constantly challenged, and many were eventually eroded. The almost total loss of political influence that started in the 1880s and the complete loss of political influence by 1900 effectively closed electoral politics to African Americans in New Orleans and throughout the South. White leaders and citizens assumed that after reversing Reconstruction policies that had made some black progress possible, the "Negro Question" was settled. Whites believed that *Plessy v. Ferguson* fully sanctioned the numerous racial segregation and exclusion laws that local and state governments passed after the Supreme Court decision. And the climate of racial segregation, disfranchisement, violence, and police brutality made many types of protest dangerous, with little chance of success. African Americans and their leaders, however, worked to improve their status and refused to accept as permanent a South structured by white superiority and black inferiority. Throughout the period of legalized racial segregation and exclusion, the voices of black dissent expanded. How African Americans achieved group and individual goals and made progress in New Orleans during the Jim Crow period is the focus of this book.

Defying Jim Crow explores the various ways black New Orleans adjusted to the Jim Crow South from 1900 to 1960, with an emphasis on the aspirations, goals, and activities of African Americans. It examines but does not emphasize the legal and extralegal efforts by whites to maintain white supremacy. African American historiography has moved beyond a tendency to see the African American experience through the lens of dichotomies such as slave resistance or acceptance, house slave and field slave, industrial education or academic education, and accommodationist leadership or militant leadership. This book continues that trend and argues that black southerners constructed their lives and activities around the three themes of racial equality and justice, community development, and individual achievement. Black southerners realized the complexity of their social and political environment and knew they needed to employ different strategies to achieve their goals; metaphorically, they drank from the ideological font of both W.E.B. Du Bois and Booker T. Washington. It took a "Talented Tenth" to build the community institutions (even the vocational schooling) advocated by Washington, just as it required a robust network of interlocking institutions, sacred and profane, to nurture a Talented Tenth. This book also examines the endurance of African American protest in New Orleans during the Jim Crow period, adding further evidence to the argument that there was indeed a "long civil rights movement." Between 1900 and 1960 African Americans in New Orleans made important gains in their long quest for racial equality and justice, community development, and individual achievement. The civil rights victories of the 1950s and 1960s were possible in part because African American communities such as the one in New Orleans defied Jim Crow and built stronger communities.

DEFYING JIM CROW

1

The Rise and Decline of Black Equality

After the Confederate attack on Fort Sumter, citizens in both the North and the South rallied to support their respective governments, and many of them rushed to volunteer their services. From Virginia to Texas southerners joined the growing Confederate army. Confederate leaders believed not only that victory would be theirs but that the war would last only a short time. Initial army strength was set at one hundred thousand and required enlistees to serve for one year. Confederate leaders such as Secretary of War Leroy P. Walker were not alone in thinking that this new war would resemble past wars and that a decisive battle would bring the war to an early end. Federal government leaders shared that view as well. Indeed, President Abraham Lincoln and his military leaders established initial Federal troop levels at seventy-five thousand. Lincoln's general-in-chief at the start of the Civil War, Winfield Scott, entered the conflict confident of a Union victory but not as convinced as many other military and civilian leaders that victory would be easy or achieved quickly. Scott's Anaconda Plan reflected his views and encompassed defending the nation's capital, applying military pressure on Richmond, Virginia, the Confederate capital, and maintaining a blockade along the Atlantic and Gulf coasts. Another part of Scott's plan, however, would have profound repercussions for the city of New Orleans and its African American population: securing control of the important transportation arteries of the Cumberland, Mississippi, Ohio, and Tennessee Rivers.[1]

Building an effective naval force proved a more daunting task for the new Confederate government than raising an army. The task was difficult because a smaller percentage of naval officers defected to join the Confederacy than army officers, and the Confederate states had a modest number of merchant ships and a more limited shipbuilding capacity. Nonetheless, Confederate secretary of the navy Stephen R. Mallory and commanders Raphael Semmes and James D. Bulloch managed to build a navy and sustain a naval campaign using tugboats, steamboats, revenue cutters, and ships. At the start of the war Confederate leaders committed considerable resources to make New Orleans a key shipbuilding site. And Confederate leaders had success, despite Great Britain's neutrality laws, in obtaining ships from Britain. But as one scholar has shown, although the Confederate nation "built and bought abroad numbers of swift blockade-runners they were better adapted . . . to making fortunes for their owners than to denting the barrier the North erected around the South's coasts." Nonetheless, Confederate ships such as the *Alabama, Florida,* and *Shenandoah* destroyed or disrupted millions of dollars of maritime commerce. These naval efforts, though important to the overall war effort of the Confederacy, had much less of a bearing on the Civil War military experience of New Orleans.[2]

Participation by New Orleans in the Confederacy was brief. In April 1862, a year after the start of the Civil War, union military forces under the command of Capt. David G. Farragut captured the important Confederate port city of New Orleans. The Confederacy's "patchwork flotilla composed of needlessly expensive intermediate type vessels" offered little resistance to Farragut's superior naval forces.[3] The fall of New Orleans to Union control had different meanings for different people, but jubilation or despair fell primarily along racial lines. The brevity of their city's participation in the war chagrined most New Orleans's whites and astonished its blacks. The majority of whites acknowledged the surrender, but having supported the Confederate war effort, few of them conceded that the surrender entailed an end to white dominance. Most African Americans, no matter what their pre–Civil War status, believed a certain way of life had ended and anticipated a new social order. It took longer for President Lincoln and Congress to transform the conflict—from a war to preserve the Union to one that also aimed to secure black freedom—than it took for Union forces to capture New Orleans. But a few months after the fall of New Orleans, Congress gave President Lincoln the authority to accept African Americans, both enslaved and free, into the military. So, when President Lincoln issued his Preliminary Emancipation Proclamation on September 22, 1862, the war's goals started to mirror the position of abolitionists such as Frederick Douglass, who had insisted since the beginning of the conflict that the Civil War should be fought to end slavery.[4]

Although historians and researchers continue to analyze and debate Lincoln's views on race and slavery, there is widespread consensus on his motivation for arming African Americans. Lincoln's assessment of the North's military situation in the summer of 1862 convinced him that preserving the Union entailed using African Americans soldiers. Lincoln may have exaggerated when he wrote to the governor of Tennessee Andrew Johnson that "the bare sight of 50,000 armed and drilled black soldiers upon the banks of the Mississippi would end the rebellion at once," but his appreciation for the military contribution of African Americans increased throughout the war. As early as August 1863, in a lengthy letter to James C. Conkling, a lawyer, friend, and fellow Republican from Springfield, Illinois, Lincoln disclosed that commanders had started to acknowledge the contributions of African American soldiers. "I know as fully as one can know the opinions of others," he maintained, "that some of the commanders of our armies in the field who have given us our most important successes, believe the emancipation policy, and the use of colored troops, constitute the heaviest blow yet dealt to the rebellion; and that, at least one of those important successes, could not have been achieved when it was, but for the aid of black soldiers."[5] In addition, black military participation helped to legitimate the transformation of the Civil War into a war to both save the Union and end slavery.

African American soldiers from New Orleans and Louisiana made important military contributions to Lincoln's positive assessment of the worth of black troops. "Not only did Louisiana earn the distinction of providing more black troops — 24,000 — than any other Southern state," one scholar observed, "but its black troops were also the first units tested under fire."[6] In May 1863 members of the First and Third Louisiana Regiments participated in a battle at Port Hudson, the first major battle employing African American soldiers. The two regiments fought well in the Union's unsuccessful effort to capture the Confederate-held fort.[7] The lack of military success did not prevent observers and opinion leaders from noticing and commenting on the conduct of the African American soldiers during the battle. A northern newspaper maintained that after Port Hudson it was "no longer possible to doubt the bravery and steadiness of the colored race when rightly led." Less than two weeks after the Port Hudson battle, African American soldiers, mostly former slaves from Louisiana and Mississippi, helped repulse a Confederate attack at Milliken's Bend.

Again national opinion leaders expressed favorable comments. Assistant Secretary of War Charles Dana believed "the employment of negro troops has been revolutionized by the bravery of the blacks in the recent Battle of Milliken's Bend."[8] African American military service in the Civil War did change the racial attitudes of some Americans, including some in New Orleans, but failed, of course, to produce significant changes in race relations. President Lincoln understood this as he considered not just issues of war but also issues of peace and national restoration.[9]

The fall of New Orleans helped bring the problem of normal relations between the federal government and the Confederacy to the fore. President Lincoln had pondered the question even before the first shots at Fort Sumter. Lincoln had rejected the right of states to secede and considered the Confederate states to be fomenting rebellion. The spring of 1862 was still too early to consider a general or comprehensive policy of relations with the eleven seceded states, so he addressed the conquest of New Orleans and parts of Louisiana on an ad hoc basis. Using the power contained in the July 1862 Confiscation Act to pardon or give immunity to individuals who had rebelled against the United States, Lincoln brought enough white Louisianians back into the Union to enable the state to send representatives to Congress from the First and Second Congressional Districts. These early political developments suggested that little had changed to disrupt New Orleans's traditional centers of political power. Lincoln's Proclamation of Amnesty and Reconstruction, outlined in his Annual Message to Congress in December 1863, suggested that he still possessed a limited view of the citizenship status of African Americans. His enthusiastic embrace of the "Christian principle of forgiveness" that enabled him to support policies that made it easy for most Confederates to regain their citizenship and for their states to reenter the Union was matched by a very tepid response for calls for black suffrage. And Lincoln's eloquence clarified rather than masked his views on southern race relations: "The proposed acquiescence of the national Executive in any reasonable temporary State arrangement for the freed people is made with the view of possibly modifying the confusion and destitution which must, at best, attend all classes by a total revolution of labor throughout whole states." This was not the first nor would it be the last time that a national leader stood ready to sacrifice African American equality for civic peace and racial harmony.[10]

Lincoln's Proclamation of Amnesty and Reconstruction was not related to conducting the war but, rather, to dictating the terms of peace. Congressional leaders had surrendered powers to Lincoln to allow him to conduct the war, but they now sought to recover them so they could control or influence the peace. Congress spent the first several months of 1864 debating the proclamation but also considered fundamental questions of the legality of secession, the function of the American presidency, and the role of Congress. The debates and discussions produced the first comprehensive congressional plan of reconstruction, the Wade-Davis Bill. The bill's sponsors, Henry Davis and Benjamin Wade, and supporters believed it a fair and just one. Wade-Davis, if passed, would have made it decidedly more difficult for Confederate states and their citizens to reenter the Union. But like the Proclamation of Amnesty and Reconstruction that members of Congress had criticized and denounced, Wade-Davis was silent on the question of black suffrage, leaving the post-fighting and postwar citizenship status of black southerners in doubt. Lincoln vetoed Wade-Davis and maintained his plan, which left the pre–Civil War levers of power in the South in the hands of white leaders, levers that they intended to use to maintain the racial status quo.[11]

The entire social, economic, and political fabric of the New Orleans community, however, eventually experienced the effects of the victorious Yankees, who had condemned slavery and other facets of southern society. The northern critique of the South had extended to its economy, which they considered stagnant; the social structure, which they considered rigid; and its politics, which they believed to be the bastion of slave-owning elites. After the fall of New Orleans, white citizens had started to adjust to the end of slavery but remained determined to preserve a social and economic order that had been erected on the rock solid foundation of white domination and supremacy. They expressed their determination to maintain the antebellum status quo in various ways that included the relatively benign, such as the refusal to observe federal holidays, and the politically significant, such as the establishment of so-called Black Codes, which restricted black freedom and thwarted the efforts of black leaders in several areas that African Americans considered crucial to a successful transition from slavery to freedom. To give meaning to their change in status, African Americans sought tangible indices of freedom: land, jobs, suffrage, education, and improved race relations, among others. Despite the obstacles, many of them embraced the challenge with vigor and optimism.[12]

As the dreams and aspirations of white southerners and Confederates for independence and a nation secure for slavery faded and died under the assault of Union armies in 1864 and 1865, the fruits of Lincoln's "awful arithmetic" produced dreams and aspirations of a quite different kind for black southerners. And when the Civil War came to its bloody and fitful end during the long spring of 1865, unlike most other southern cities, New Orleans possessed a significant number of educated and prosperous African Americans who were determined to win full equality. From their ranks would emerge many of New Orleans's black leaders. In the main these men had been free men of color before the Civil War and heirs to what historian Caryn Cossé Bell considers an Afro-Creole protest tradition. Although possessing wealth and intelligence, they had endured the status of second-class citizenship during the antebellum period. After the war, not surprisingly, they emerged as some of the most outspoken and relentless champions of political and social equality. They realized that the attainment and retention of both forms of equality would depend on gaining suffrage.[13] African American leaders and some white leaders throughout the nation shared similar views. And no national black leader was more resolute in support of suffrage than Frederick Douglass. For Douglass the psychological benefits of black suffrage were as important as the political and civic ones. "By depriving us of suffrage," Douglass insisted, white Americans "declare before the world that we are unfit to exercise the elective franchise, and by this means lead us to undervalue ourselves, to put a low estimate upon ourselves, and to feel that we have no possibilities like other men."[14] But getting the vote would prove a challenge because most whites in Louisiana and the South shared the political view of J. P. Montanot, a state representative from New Orleans. Montanot vowed that "when this state extends to the Negroes the right of suffrage, I shall leave it forthwith." Although no records exist to show that Montanot made good on his threat, his sentiment found expression in continued white resistance to black suffrage.[15]

One of the ablest black advocates of suffrage in New Orleans was Dr. Louis Charles Roudanez, who understood the depth of white resistance to racial change in New Orleans. In September 1862 he was a member of the leadership group that started the black newspaper *L'Union*. Written almost entirely in French, the newspaper made its antislavery position clear in the inaugural issue. And before its demise in May 1864, the newspaper had joined the fight for both black suffrage and racial equality. Shortly after the demise of *L'Union,* however, Roudanez spearheaded another newspaper effort that was designed to reach a wider audience. The new publication, the *New Orleans Tribune,* was written in French and English and was, according to one historian "perhaps the most brilliant newspaper to appear in the entire South during Reconstruction." Editorials and articles in the *Tribune* constantly called for black suffrage and criticized early reconstruction policies that continued to deny suffrage to African Americans. To those who opposed suffrage or counseled gradualism, the newspaper argued: "We can compromise with interests, but we cannot compromise with principles. Assured of the sound basis of our rights, we proclaim them, we uphold them fully and completely, and we will hear nothing of sacrificing them."[16] Despite the efforts of national black leaders and local ones such as Dr. Roudanez, African Americans made little progress toward full citizenship before 1868. The lack of suffrage and of an overall improvement in southern race relations was especially troubling events to African Americans, who had donned Union blue to save the Union, end slavery, and extend democracy. Black veterans believed their military service gave them and their race rightful claims for full citizenship, or, as many viewed it, "the same rights as white men."[17]

The refusal of white leaders to extend suffrage and civil equality to wealthy and educated African Americans eventually forced free blacks into a political alliance with the former slaves. In the 1860s white racism and solidarity helped to unite the black community; thirty years later segregation institutionalized black community solidarity well into the next century. New Orleans's antebellum free black population linked, in part out of necessity, its political and civil liberation with that of the former slaves. That is not to say, however, that cleavages did not exist within the black community. African Americans, both formerly free and newly freed, carried experiences and certain cultural traits into post–Civil War New Orleans, not least of which was a language difference. Many free blacks spoke French exclusively or were bilingual. Indeed, their first newspaper appeared in French. Their relative wealth also separated free blacks from freedmen. Some of that wealth had been accumulated through the ownership of slaves, making suspect any initial appeals to solidarity based solely on race. Edmonia Highgate, a black woman who came to New Orleans to teach, recognized the challenge shortly after her arrival, observing: "Of course some of them are wealthy but do not feel in the least identified with the freed men or their interest. Nor need we wonder when we remember that many of them were formerly slaveholders."[18] And as scholars have demonstrated, skin color also separated segments of black New Orleans. Free blacks' initial attempts to distance themselves from the former slaves, however, had less to do with skin color than perceived status based on wealth and education. Free blacks had no more inclination to associate with poor whites than they had to associate with poor blacks. In the main wealth, education, and social relations determined leadership in the black community during Reconstruction (and, of course, in the white community as well). Many light-complexioned Creoles worked and associated with black Anglos without discord related to skin color. Disagreement over tactics, strategy, and conflict over the spoils of victory eventually contributed more to disunity among African Americans than color prejudices.[19]

During one of Louisiana's many constitutional conventions, this one in 1867–68, African Americans from New Orleans participated for the first time. The meeting, convened under congressional oversight, included a total of ninety-eight delegates. African Americans constituted a slight majority of fifty, with twelve of these delegates from New Orleans. As a group, the African American delegates possessed talent and diverse backgrounds but were all staunch supporters of the Republican Party. In the main they were educated, intelligent, ambitious, and courageous. Some had served in the military. What they did not share, however, were the same ideas and beliefs about political goals and tactics. Those differences became more important in the late 1870s and early 1880s. But in 1867 and 1868 the prospect of participating as founders of a new era in New Orleans produced more political unity than disagreement among African American leaders.[20] The convention met in New Orleans on 23 November 1867 and completed its work approximately fifteen weeks later. The delegates, both black and white, brought certain ideological and pragmatic objectives to Mechanics Institute Hall, the site of the convention. They hoped to put a definite imprint on Louisiana's future. Ninety-six of the delegates were Republicans, but events during the course of the convention demonstrated that not all Republican members pursued the same goals.

Historian Roger Fischer has argued that the convention contained three distinct factions. Sixteen members from the country parishes he considered white Unionists, and approximately thirty, mostly nonnative whites, he labeled Radicals. The fifty African American delegates formed a third faction. Yet it would be a mistake to suggest that any of the factions, including the African American group, were homogeneous.[21] Generally, however, African American delegates united to support universal suffrage and elimination of legal distinctions based on race. What the black delegates, and many white ones as well, lacked in political experience they compensated for with a keen understanding and appreciation of basic democratic values. And as one researcher of the subject observed, their political "limitations did not prevent them from establishing a workable structure of government."[22] African American delegates played an important role during the convention, chairing or sitting on all of the various committees. They helped to produce one of the more enlightened and democratic constitutions in the state's history. In addition, as historian Rebecca J. Scott has observed, "the draft Louisiana Constitution phrased its guarantees in an explicit, expansive, and positive language of rights," including "public rights and privileges." And "the roots of such a commitment," she argues, "lay in a combination of Christianity with French and American revolutionary ideologies, sometimes accompanied by an acknowledgment of the Haitian struggle and the Republican creed of the 1848 Revolution in France."[23] Including such lofty ideals in the new draft constitution represented an important first step in cleansing the stain of slavery from Louisiana and New Orleans society.

Although the provisions granting suffrage to African Americans and ensuring them equal treatment alarmed many members of the white community, given the mood of the new Congress, expressed through the Reconstruction Acts and visible in the form of federal troops, many whites realized black enfranchisement was inevitable. Then, too, some whites in New Orleans had heeded the words of the former Confederate war hero Gen. Pierre G. T. Beauregard, who "urged Louisianians to accept the facts that blacks would vote and work at influencing that vote."[24] Despite the cries of "Africanizing" the state, many whites resented the increasing political power and leadership of white northerners at least as much as the potential voting strength of black voters. Many African Americans were also interested in leadership, or rather in having a say in who would lead, but were most concerned with securing "radical" legislation to promote civil and political equality. Before and during the constitutional convention, the *New Orleans Tribune* urged the black community and its leaders to remain focused on the stated objectives of universal suffrage and equality before the law. Commenting on the potential of the convention as a means for change, a *Tribune* editorial stated: "In a community where we have been so long laboring under a denial of justice, in a community where customs rather than laws perpetuate a constant discrimination between White and Colored children, it is a matter of necessity to provide in the new Constitution for the enforcement of impartial treatment to all men, women and children."[25]

In April 1868 Louisiana voters went to the polls and voted 51,737 to 39,076 in favor of the ratification of the document. When completed, the constitution contained for the first time a bill of rights. It also granted suffrage to African Americans, defined their citizenship status, prohibited segregated schools, and forbade segregation in public accommodations. Nearly six years had elapsed since the arrival of federal troops and the euphoric expectations that the Civil War was more than an epic conflict to restore the Union and end slavery, that it was in fact a battle to make the principles of democracy and equality a reality for the more than four million black southerners. The suffrage provision in Louisiana's constitution made political empowerment possible and enabled black leaders to alter their strategy. Instead of petitioning and confronting public officials from a position of weakness, black leaders had the political means to influence and shape local and state issues. African American voters did not possess the numerical strength to dominate city and state politics but gained enough political influence to force elected officials to consider and address their demands.[26] They did not, however, desire special considerations for their racial group. National leaders such as Douglass and local ones such as Roudanez expressed the view held by many African Americans that they wanted neither special favors nor special obstacles to their advancement. In an April 1865 speech titled "What the Black Man Wants," Douglass forcefully stated, "What I ask for the Negro is not benevolence, not pity, not sympathy, but simply justice." Along with that plea or insistence, he also called on the white South not to place obstacles in the way of African American advancement. And in language more hopeful of an outcome than certain of it, Douglass continued: "All I ask is, give him a chance to stand on his own legs! Let him alone! If you see him on his way to school, let him alone, don't disturb him! If you see him going to the dinner-table at a hotel, let him go! If you see him going to the ballot-box, let him alone, don't disturb him! If you see him going into a work-shop, just let him alone,—your interference is doing him positive injury."[27]

African Americans in New Orleans hoped that the 1868 constitution would provide Louisiana with a new system of government and a political and social framework that would prevent "positive injury" to their post–

Civil War aspirations and yearnings. They looked, then, to elected legislators to transform the principles embodied in the new constitution into workable laws. Anticipating the eventual adoption and ratification of the constitution and the subsequent call for statewide elections, Republican leaders in early December 1867 expressed a need for a nominating convention to select candidates for state office. The Republicans convened in January 1868 and produced a biracial slate of candidates headed by Henry Clay Warmoth for governor and Oscar J. Dunn for lieutenant governor. The selection of Dunn placated a group of African Americans, headed by Roudanez, who had insisted on the selection of a black candidate, Francis E. Dumas, for governor. Roudanez's support for Dumas reflected the general political thought of African American leaders at the start of congressional Reconstruction. They believed that African Americans with ability should vie for political offices and obtain top political positions.[28]

African American leaders such as Dumas, Dunn, and Roudanez wanted voting and office holding to produce tangible benefits for the black community, especially in the area of education, employment, and race relations. Indeed, efforts to acquire education were well under way by the close of the constitutional convention. Soon after their arrival in April 1862, Union soldiers had taken the first tentative steps to establish formal and universal education for African Americans. Their task was daunting, for before 1862, when New Orleans came under Union control, the institution of slavery precluded any debate or consideration of public education for free blacks and any education at all for slaves. Free blacks enjoyed many privileges in antebellum New Orleans, such as the right to own property, enter contracts, inherit and will property, and legally marry. They could not, however, attend public schools. They managed to amass a certain amount of wealth and supported several private academies. Additionally, some free blacks sent their children to study in France or hired tutors. Many less-prosperous free blacks attended school because of the generosity of Madame Maria Couvent, a free woman of color. Other free blacks received instructions from the Sisters of the Holy Family, a congregation of black nuns, as well as at a school run by Carmelite nuns.[29]

Many slaves in antebellum New Orleans had risked their safety in an attempt to gain an education. Because education remained a dangerous, furtive enterprise, it is difficult to assess accurately how many slaves achieved a degree of education. In New Orleans the limited autonomy that came with city life probably facilitated the black quest for an education. Scholars estimate that at least 5 percent of the South's slave population had learned to read by 1860, although the historian Eugene Genovese suggests that a higher number did. Given the greater freedom of New Orleans slaves and their interaction with the area's free blacks, slave literacy in New Orleans probably did surpass 5 percent. Even so, as another scholar has concluded, "the overwhelming majority of the Negroes in New Orleans during this period were illiterate." Still, literacy was only one way that slaves gained and shared knowledge. Oral instruction was an important feature of knowledge acquisition and transmission in slave communities.[30]

Efforts to educate African Americans lacked consistency and structure until Union officials established black schools. In October 1863 Maj. Gen. Nathaniel P. Banks gave black education a significant boost when he authorized the creation of black schools and later created a board of education to take charge of them. The schools established by the Union army represented the first organized attempt by a public agency to educate southern blacks.[31] The board chairman, B. Rush Plumly, voiced satisfaction with the initial efforts and held that "the aptitude to these Colored children to learn is equal to that of the men of color for the act of war. Neither of them is excelled in their respective places, by any race on record."[32] Plumly was not the last official to comment on the freedmen's determined capacity to learn. A year later another board of education official, Mortimer A. Warren, wrote favorably about an advanced grammar school class. "I wish that this room of the Lincoln School might have a visit from all scoffers of Negro education. I shrink from no comparison with any other school of children, of the same age of any other color, of any other city, of any other clime or time."[33]

During the first year of operation most of the schools were single classrooms in rented houses. They usually bore the name of the teacher who had started them: Miss Strong's School, Miss Buggie's School, Miss Clarkson's School, or Mr. Williams's School. Most of the teachers labored alone as teacher and principal. Enrollment, attendance, and classroom decorum varied tremendously during the first year of operation. Few, if any, of the students had been exposed to the structure of a formal classroom. Nonetheless, the rod, a fixture in nineteenth-century pedagogy, and the threat of dismissal soon produced acceptable classroom behavior. "The children are remarkably attentive in class and making progress," reported J. H. Ford, one of the school site inspectors. Overcrowding remained a concern at some schools, but apparently board of education officials managed to alleviate the worst of it by opening additional schools.[34]

In March 1865 Congress authorized the creation of the Bureau of Refugees, Freedmen, and Abandoned Lands, and the following month the board of education became a part of it. A significant consequence of the absorption of the board of education was a complete reorganization of the schools. The reorganization occurred in September 1865, just before the start of the 1865–66 school year, and included the creation of the office of superintendent, graded classrooms, and the establishment of school districts. Under it New Orleans constituted one of the state's seven divisions and possessed nineteen schools. In these schools the overwhelming majority of students received instruction at the primary and intermediate levels, generally in grades 1 through 5. Three of the schools — Banks, Conway, and Lincoln — offered night classes; students attending at night only accounted for a small percentage of total student enrollment. The bureau also sponsored a Normal School to train teachers and a school for industrial training. Two hundred and sixty students attended the Industrial School. Instructors continued to emphasize reading, writing, arithmetic, and geography. In the main students made satisfactory progress, drawing praise from teachers and school officials. Educational progress occurred because of dedicated Freedmen's Bureau teachers such as Edmonia Highgate and George T. Ruby, who persevered despite white opposition. It was small comfort to them that other Freedmen's Bureau teachers in the state and region experienced similar opposition and violence.[35]

In 1867 black New Orleanians gained additional educational opportunities with the opening of the first public schools for African Americans operated by the city. The local school board established a committee to administer black education and opened nine schools. The school board then took steps to gain control of schools still run by the Freedmen's Bureau. The transfer, completed on 15 November, included teachers, buildings, furniture, and equipment. In all the bureau transferred eleven primary schools, which brought the total number of new black public schools to twenty. Average daily attendance at the schools stood at sixteen hundred. Pleased with the initial venture into black education, superintendent William Rogers pronounced "the results thus far . . . most satisfactory" and requested authority to "expand departments as necessary." Concerned black citizens must have been optimistic when a board member proudly proclaimed that "nothing has been omitted to make them [black schools] as efficient as any of the schools of corresponding grade in the city."[36] That was not the case. In 1868, for example, the projected school budget submitted to the city council totaled $396,900. School officials planned to allocate only $65,000 of that sum to black schools. As a result, the continued inequitable distribution of school funds gave additional impetus to the push for desegregated schools. There were no polls conducted in the 1860s and 1870s to ascertain what African Americans in the city thought about desegregated schools. The city's black leadership, however, made its views very clear. The most successful black newspaper in the 1860s, the *New Orleans Tribune,* voiced the ideology and aspirations of many African Americans and strongly favored integrated schools. A typical editorial supporting mixed schools declared: "Separation is not equality. The very assignment of schools to certain children on the ground of color is a distinct violation of the first principles of equality." Political developments soon demonstrated that many in the black community agreed.[37]

The city's white press consistently opposed all efforts that undermined the dominant position of the majority population. But nothing enraged the shapers of white public opinion more than the thought and prospect of integrated schools. Even the sharing of political power failed to elicit the same degree of editorial virulence. None of the newspapers exercised restraint or adopted a wait-and-see position. "The schools now established in this city have been founded by white people for white children," stated the *New Orleans Times*. A letter to the *Times* from the group Fair Play considered it "unjust to us poor people who cannot afford to send our children to private schools" to face the choice of mixed schools or no schools. By 1867 the white press and citizens such as those in Fair Play stated they did not object to the idea of educating blacks, but they wanted it done in separate schools.[38] The actions of whites opposed to black advancement and the caution of white Republicans delayed the start of desegregated schools in New Orleans. Many of those in favor of a unified system of public education urged caution in pursuing desegregated schools.

Thomas W. Conway, state superintendent of education from 1868 to 1872, was one such individual. Conway gained his position as part of the Republican electoral surge of 1868. A former chaplain in the Union army, the New York native had held various positions related to freedmen between 1863 and 1868. At one time he served as superintendent of the Bureau of Free Labor and assistant commissioner of the Freedmen's Bureau in Louisiana. He had also aided the struggle for black suffrage. Conway believed that support for public education rested on fragile ground and that the entire common school effort could collapse under the weight of too stringent a demand for mixed schools, especially in the rural parishes.

Conway thought the public schools suffered because of "the indifference, amounting to virtual opposition, which, in large sections of the state, has obstructed every endeavor for the establishment of public schools." He predicted that time would lessen the prejudices and passions of men and separate schools would suffer the fate of slavery.[39] But the seductive allure of time itself as an agent of positive change did not appeal to the majority of African American leaders in New Orleans. They consistently and repeatedly demanded mixed schools. Neither the abolition of slavery nor the acquisition of the ballot had resulted from a change of heart among southern whites. Union guns had secured the former and Republican ideology and political pragmatism the latter. Armed with the vote and buoyed by the presence of federal forces, African Americans saw little reason for gradualism. Then, too, little evidence existed in New Orleans to indicate a softening of white attitudes toward the freedmen. The haunting memory of the 30 July 1866 massacre at Mechanics Hall, in which a white mob wounded or killed hundreds of blacks, persisted years after the event. After fighting for six years to gain the vote and an opportunity for a public education, blacks doubted "time" would favor their cause.[40]

African American leaders championed desegregated schools because public schools opened to all races were consistent and evidence of "public rights and privileges." They wanted racial distinctions eliminated from post–Civil War society; political influence and dogged persistence gave them an opportunity, at least for a brief time, to transform their ideals into reality. In January 1871 an experiment in desegregated education began. Just how many schools actually had students of both races is impossible to determine because school officials reported enrollment figures without indicating race. Comments by contemporaries, however, suggest that at least one-third of the public schools experienced some desegregation between 1871 and 1877. "Some of the schools of the city are almost wholly white, others are partially mixed, while some of the best grammar schools are about half and half," reported a Methodist journal. "Colored scholars are in our high schools, and also in our State Normal School." Several months later the *Weekly Louisianian* stated that one-third of the schools were mixed. But African Americans knew, and later events demonstrated, that desegregated schools and the other vestiges of civil equality depended on the retention of suffrage.[41]

Although it is true that "blacks soon ascertained neither state law nor federal guarantees could ensure full equality," it is equally true that between 1865 and 1885 the pattern of race relations in New Orleans underwent some change because African Americans had suffrage. Commenting on southern race relations during this period, C. Vann Woodward observed "it would be a mistaken effort to equate this period in racial relations with either the old regime of slavery or with the future rule of Jim Crow. It was too exceptional."[42] Before Jim Crow began its "strange career," many blacks in New Orleans rode on integrated streetcars, attended integrated schools, and patronized integrated public facilities. The reception they received varied greatly. Some white business owners refused to serve African Americans and often physically removed them from their facilities; other charged them exorbitant prices or served them undesirable goods. It was not unusual for them to be heckled, jeered, or insulted when they tried to use public facilities. The integration laws, however, permitted African Americans to file suits against the discriminatory practices of white businessmen. C. S. Sauvinet, Emily Loke, and William Smith, for example, won monetary compensation after successfully suing local saloonkeepers. Their suits sometimes tempered but failed to eliminate racial discrimination.[43]

As a result, black Creole leaders such as Louis Roudanez and non-Creole leaders such as P.B.S. Pinchback welcomed any sign that indicated a softening of white opinion on matters of suffrage and civil equality in post–Civil War New Orleans. And some of them believed common justice was possible through cooperation with whites in the Unification Movement—an organized attempt at political compromise and racial conciliation. Influential white business leaders believed that continued racial polarization, reflected in disputed elections and sporadic violence, would lead to the state's ruin. Indeed, many thought that Louisiana under Republican Party rule had long since entered a state of decay. Moreover, many white leaders blamed northern opportunists for what they considered rampant political corruption and government mismanagement. White business leaders, acting on the assumption that "the great port metropolis needed political stability to achieve economic prosperity," attempted, albeit briefly, to charter a new course in New Orleans's race relations. Isaac N. Marks, a wealthy New Orleanian with diverse business interests, emerged as one of the leaders of the movement. Other white leaders included Gen. P.G.T. Beauregard, James I. Day, and Judge William M. Randolph.[44] African Americans, of course, also wanted better race relations, so in addition to Roudanez, other black participants who supported the Unification Movement included Lieutenant Governor Caesar C. Antoine, state senator George Y. Kelso, and Aristide Mary, a black landowner who had been active in the struggle for suffrage and civil rights. Yet not all African Americans were enthusiastic about the movement's potential. Editors for the *New Orleans Republican* questioned the wisdom of joining any political movement other than the Republican Party. With all of its alleged faults and political vices, the Republican Party, in the opinion of many African Americans, represented the path to liberation and black suffrage. Many of them remained reluctant to venture into uncharted waters.[45]

Despite some political gains under the banner of the Republican Party, the architects and supporters of the unification plan thought they had developed the perfect means to achieve political peace and economic prosperity in post–Civil War Louisiana. And perhaps the potential did exist for meaningful change. After several months of discussion and planning, a citizen's committee composed of fifty black and fifty white leaders, a racial composition strikingly similar to that of the 1867–68 constitutional convention, presented its list of recommendations to the public. As a citizen committee devoid of legal legitimacy, the Committee of One Hundred sought widespread public support and presented its views as "An Appeal for the Unification of the People of Louisiana."[46] Considering the proposals contained in the "appeal," one scholar noted that "no group of Southerners in the Reconstruction era was willing to go farther in harmonizing race relations than the authors of this document." White leaders in the group of "unifiers" hoped to secure black support for a political alliance dedicated to honest government and devoid of out-of-state influence. In return African Americans would be guaranteed political and civil equality.[47]

The Unification Movement, centered in the city and led primarily by New Orleanians, received little support outside the area. Except for a well-attended mass meeting on 15 July 1873, the movement failed to produce a viable and lasting black-white political coalition. Ushered in during the promise of spring, the movement lost its momentum after the July meeting. Why did it fail? It failed partly because African Americans doubted the ability of white leaders such as General Beauregard and Isaac Marks to make good on their promises. In his careful study of New Orleans for this period, historian John Blassingame noted that "the chief defenders of white supremacy in the city were the white-owned newspapers which continually vilified and ridiculed the Negro." The sheer thought of seeking and accepting political counsel with African Americans was far outside of most white southerners' notion of the proper relationship between the races. The shouts of one white participant at the meeting questioning whether Marks would send his children to mixed schools did not allay their fears. The shouting spectator, more than Marks, reflected the sentiments of most whites in New Orleans. The primary cause of the movement's failure, then, rested with the refusal of whites to accept racial equality.[48]

The disavowal of violence and other extralegal means of popular protest by many conservative white leaders eventually waned as it became clear that Republicans would not willingly surrender the political arena. Failure to reach a quick settlement during the disputed state elections in 1872 had resulted in the establishment of rival governments, both claiming legitimacy. The failure of the brief Unification Movement, however, was but one indication that "white conservatives remained determined to do whatever was necessary to reverse the results of the war to the greatest extent possible short of reinstating slavery."[49] Paramilitary gatherings became an accepted form of political expression. One group, the White League, grew in strength and boldness, and the level of violence increased during the spring and summer of 1874. Indeed, by that year "everyday collective violence" was becoming a key feature of whites' attempts to eliminate Reconstruction gains. The term *massacre* became a familiar one to the black community. In September 1874, at the "Battle of Canal Street," the political momentum turned perceptively and permanently in favor of the White League and the Democrats.[50] The Democrats solidified their gains after the 1876 presidential election and the political compromise that followed. And by 1877 even the most radical Republican realized, given the level of white hostility and violence, that it would take a major commitment by the federal government to sustain effective black political participation. Most of the nation's leaders, however, thought it best to return the "Negro Question" to the region where the problem resided: the South. White northerners as well as southerners turned their attention to what they considered a more important agenda, which was the building of an industrialized North and a New South with an industrial emphasis. The importance of protecting the civil rights of African Americans paled in comparison.[51]

In the mid-1870s efforts to improve race relations declined as city leaders, both black and white, concentrated on the battle for political control of the city. The competing groups camouflaged themselves with party labels, but they fought over whether newly enfranchised African Americans would continue meaningful political participation. The black community, led by such political leaders as P.B.S. Pinchback and C. C. Antoine, eventually lost the fight to retain the significant political influence gained between 1868 and 1877. For more than a decade black leaders had waged a battle for suffrage, civil equality, and acceptance into the larger society. Their struggle had its taproots deep in basic American values — democracy, equal opportunity, and equality before the law. In Louisiana the election of Governor Francis T. Nicholls presented the black community with a major ideological crisis. At what point should principles give way to pragmatism? It would be a continuing dilemma that often found expression in issues related to education, the instrument of America's vision of itself and the vehicle for the attainment of the aspirations of its people.

The resolution of Louisiana's second disputed election of the decade brought Robert M. Lusher back into office as state superintendent of education, replacing William G. Brown, the first and only African American to hold that office. During the period of the Republican ascendancy, Lusher had served as Louisiana's agent for the Peabody Fund and administered the fund to finance a private school system for whites. He returned to public office in 1877 determined to amend "the anomalous provisions of Articles 135 and 136 of the State Constitution." With the Democrats in power, Lusher expressed confidence that the new legislature would not "delay in replacing these articles by more acceptable provisions for the mental instruction and moral training of the two races, in separate schools, with equal facilities and advantages for both."[52] And at a special meeting on 22 June 1877 the school board sought to codify white sentiment for a racially segregated school system. Archibald Mitchell outlined the rationale for it in his committee's report to the board. "Personal observation and universal testimony," he stated, "concur to establish the fact that public education has greatly deteriorated since colored and white children were admitted indiscriminately into the same schools." Detrimental effects of desegregated schools, the committee members contended, included a decline in white enrollment because white parents refused to send their children to desegregated schools. African Americans also suffered because of the "turbulent spirit" of whites, manifested most demonstratively in the school disturbances of December 1874. Mitchell was "not reluctant to recommend separation" because in his view "both races favor[ed] separate schools." To give added weight to their proposal, committee members maintained that they believed northern cities such as Cincinnati, New York, and Philadelphia also had separate schools.[53]

African American leaders responded to the proposal to resegregate the schools by appealing to Governor Nicholls to intervene before the board voted. Aristide Mary led a delegation of African Americans who met with the governor. The group denounced the board's plan, but Nicholls simply replied that his pledge to promote black equality did not include support for desegregation. Frustrated in their attempt to gain the support of Nicholls, black leaders tried a more direct approach. When the board met on 3 July 1877, a large delegation of African Americans attended and presented a lengthy petition protesting separate schools. Again, Mary provided leadership and counsel to the black protesters. The board received the petition, took no action on it, and proceeded with its agenda. Without rancor or rhetoric, the spokesman for the segregationist forces, Archibald Mitchell, offered a motion to resegregate the schools. For the school board members the vote was routine but both psychologically and politically meaningful. The favorable vote demonstrated that whites had regained control of the city's political landscape, and psychologically, it was another advance in healing the psyche wounds caused by the white South's failed attempt at national independence and the subsequent sharing of political power and civic responsibility with a race that most whites considered inferior. Many African Americans and their leaders, on the other hand, understood the vote differently. They thought the vote indicated that the political arena was fast closing as a viable vehicle for social change.[54]

The proposal to resegregate the schools won board approval by a vote of fifteen to three. Three of the black members cast the only dissenting votes—George H. Fayerweather, Louis A. Martinet, and Pascal M. Tourné. The other black member, Joseph A. Craig, voted with the majority. Why did Craig vote to end the experiment with mixed schools? Neither Craig nor any of the other members gave a reason for their vote, so a definitive answer remains elusive. Available evidence suggests one or two plausible reasons. Craig supported the Democratic Party and according to one source was the founder of a "colored conservative club." The term *conservative* in Craig's case probably meant an acceptance of the "Redeemers" pledge of peace between the races based on a policy of racial separation but access to public education and individual economic opportunity. Craig's vote could have reflected the belief that separate schools would lead to improved race relations. On the other hand, his vote may have been merely a gesture to the politicians who had placed him on the board. Craig's vote, of course, had no influence on the final decisions to segregate the schools. Even if African Americans had voted as a "bloc," they were, as Governor Nicholls aptly phrased it, "sandwiched in" without control. The significance of Craig's vote lies outside the school board and its decision to segregate the schools and within the development of the black community.[55]

The struggle for desegregated schools revealed some interesting truths about race relations, politics, and the role of education in post-Reconstruction New Orleans. Efforts by African Americans to promote school desegregation centered on the proposition that the schools should serve as an example of racial harmony for the larger community. "Every discrimination which is maintained against us is a blow upon us," the editor of the *Tribune* had argued as early as April 1867, "and will have an influence to postpone the realization of equality before the law and impartial protection to our people." Separate schools represented the antithesis of a nation of "one people," the Reconstruction goal of the African American community. Whites in the city also interpreted desegregated schools as a harbinger of a nation of "one people," and that is why they fought to eliminate them. Most whites viewed any type of interaction between the races that failed to demonstrate or buttress white supremacy as an attempt by African Americans to gain social equality. And as historian Richard Follett has argued, "Just as enslaved people entered free society with skills and attitudes hewn from bondage, slaveholders approached freedom with their own values, experiences, and ideologies rooted to a history of racial and class exploitation."[56] That assessment, of course, extends beyond Louisiana's sugar parishes, the focus of Follett's essay. Being less than one generation removed from the institution of slavery and white domination, whites throughout the South had little tolerance for the twin evils of mixed schools and social equality. The state elections in 1876 failed to answer all of the political and social questions of the day but did lead to a white consensus on the separation of the races. Although Archibald Mitchell, other school officials, and city leaders expressed a willingness to provide African Americans with educational opportunities, they emphatically rejected desegregated schools.[57]

The State Constitution of 1879, enacted after the Democrats gained power, did not place any specific disabilities on black suffrage, and the delegates passed a resolution "assuring the Negro that his newly acquired rights would not be jeopardized or impaired." The constitution, moreover, addressed the issue of desegregated elementary and secondary schools by making no reference to them at all. Tellingly, however, the new constitution removed the more equalitarian notion of civil, political, and public rights. And the constitution contained a race-specific article (Art. 231) regarding higher education. Rather than use a constitutional measure to exclude African Americans from the existing universities attended by whites, white political leaders authorized the establishment "in the city of New Orleans [of] a university for the education of persons of color." The article also mandated a minimum annual appropriation of five thousand dollars and a maximum of ten thousand dollars.[58] In 1880 lawmakers passed the necessary enabling legislation, and Southern University, nurtured into existence by black politicians P.B.S. Pinchback and T. T. Allain, opened in 1881 as a state university for African Americans.

The establishment of Southern University occurred at a time when many African Americans had abandoned the idea that a racially integrated society could exist in the South. Southern University represented an attempt by some African Americans to live and adjust to conditions in the post-Reconstruction South. Southern University remained a university in name only for the next several decades but did provide black New Orleanians with their only source of public secondary education until 1917. Aristide Mary and other Creole leaders were in the forefront of those who assailed Pinchback for his support of Southern University. Pinchback faced the issue squarely and admitted that establishment and attendance at Southern "will deprive us of a great part of our civil rights." And in words strikingly similar to those of W.E.B. Du Bois over a half-century later, Pinchback attempted to justify his position. "However true this may be," he asserted, "it is not in this state, nay, I venture to say in the whole South a single institution of learning where the colored and white children are educated together. What we want is education, whether it be acquired in a mixed or colored school it must be had."[59] Pinchback's pragmatic pronouncements failed to convince his critics in the 1880s, yet many of their heirs would later make their own bargain with ideology and conscious and would support separate schools. Some opponents believed that the acquiescence of black delegates at the convention gave "the appearance of consenting to their own debasement." Support for Southern University, they charged, "helped to create a system they knew would deprive the black children of the advantage of education available to other children in the state." Criticism against Pinchback and other black supporters of Article 231 increased from the black Creole community. Mary, for instance, argued "that this line of demarcation, once established, chiefly by their consent, would serve as the basis and the pretext for other measures contrary to the interests and rights of our citizens." Both groups, however, had seen the future; the quarrel between them centered on how best to respond.[60]

As Mary, Pinchback, and other leaders struggled with the changing political environment, ordinary African Americans had to contend with the challenges and opportunities of Gilded Age New Orleans. Many new arrivals to the city found the urban life just as challenging as the farms and plantations they had left. Nonetheless, New Orleans's black population continued to increase in the 1880s and 1890s. These new residents came to the city because many of them knew from personal experience "that a reign of terror exists in many parts of the state; that the laws are suspended and the officers of the government, from the governor down, afford no protection to the lives and property of the people against armed bodies of whites, who shed innocent blood and commit deeds of savagery unsurpassed in the dark ages of mankind."[61] The new arrivals entered an environment with less racial violence than where they had come from but one that struggled to provide essential services to all its citizens. New Orleans had its own version of machine politics that at times resembled party machines in northeastern cities such as Boston, New York, and Philadelphia—if not on the same scale, at least similar in its reliance on corruption and self-interest. The Democratic-Conservative Party was the most successful machine party in New Orleans in the 1880s and 1890s, drawing support and members from white supremacy groups such as the White League. Democratic-Conservative Party members often charged their opponents, especially those running on a reform platform, with having Republican Party support and by extension favored by African American voters. It remained a highly effective tactic in most municipal elections.[62]

White politicians in New Orleans expanded their efforts to eliminate African American voters after they helped elect Joseph Shakspeare mayor in 1888. Shakspeare, who had won a previous term in 1880, ran on the reform platform of the Young Men's Democratic Association and defeated Judge Robert C. Davis, the Democratic-Conservative candidate. Shakspeare's second term proved difficult, and he encountered criticism and opposition from many quarters. Perhaps the most damaging opposition came from former supporters, who blamed him for failing to support all their reform measures. Shakspeare, in many ways similar to other reformers who saw themselves as virtuous and committed to acting in the public's best interest, at times appeared dogmatic and unyielding when he would have been better served politically by employing tact and pragmatism.

One issue eroded his support among reformers, and another issue provided a political opportunity for his opponents. Shakspeare unwisely and unsuccessfully opposed, through administrative actions and court challenges, the creation of a police board of commissioners with control of the police department, effectively removing that function from the mayor's control. His actions surprised some reformers and angered others. On the other hand, without apparent irony, he supported the creation of a citizen board to manage a paid fire department. His support pleased reformers but drew the ire of the Fireman's Charitable Association, a volunteer group with a contract to provide firefighting service to the city. The association had influential political supporters, and its members were also adept at the art of Gilded Age urban politics. Shakspeare's success in this effort proved as politically costly as his lack of success proved to be in the police reform issue. But before he lost control of the police department, he appointed fourteen African Americans to the force. His detractors pointed to this move as evidence of a payment to African Americans for their support in the mayoral election. Shakspeare was not alone in suffering politically for that perception.[63]

Throughout the 1870s and 1880s African Americans successfully resisted attempts to remove them entirely from New Orleans politics. The return of Democrats to power in the mid-1870s had marked an important departure but not a sudden end to black political participation. Before the complete ascendancy of reactionary white leaders intent on not just political, social, and economic power but the debasement of the city's black population as well, African Americans continued to vote, though not always freely and not always receiving the desired result. But their limited political participation at least helped to forestall the harsher manifestations of white supremacy that surfaced in the 1890s and reigned, though always challenged indirectly and often opposed directly, until the 1940s. The sometimes genteel paternalism that had influenced politics and race relations at the start of the 1880s had declined perceptively by 1890. The white South began to close ranks on the Negro Question as effectively as it had done on the question of slavery forty years earlier. Moreover, during the process most white northerners were conspicuous by their silence, at least as voices of dissent. Louisiana joined the rush to legal racial segregation in 1890 with the passage of a railroad car bill mandating separate but equal seating for blacks and whites. Other segregation laws followed, separating or excluding African Americans from streetcars, railroad terminals, restaurants, hotels, and places of entertainment. The laws had little to do with altering the existing behavior of most blacks and whites in New Orleans. They represented the ideological statement of a dominant group; in other words, as historian Leon Litwack has suggested, segregation laws were "deeply rooted in the white psyche": "Jim Crow came to the South in an expanded and more rigid form, partly in response to fears of a new generation of blacks unschooled in racial etiquette and to growing doubts that this generation could be trusted to stay in its place without legal force." In response to the growing rigidity of the color line in New Orleans, many African Americans would later leave the South, as thousands had already done, most noticeably in the 1870s. Most African Americans remained in New Orleans, however, and some resisted.[64]

"It was in 1890 that the Citizens' Committee was formed, when a return to exaggerated fanaticism about caste or segregation once again alarmed the black people. We were face to face with a government determined to develop and establish a system by which a portion of the people would have to submit to the rest."[65] So began an account by Rodolphe L. Desdunes, one of the participants who tried to prevent the complete legal subjugation of African Americans in New Orleans. Protest of the railroad segregation law encompassed several elements of the community's black leadership. But black Creoles were the driving force throughout the entire period of litigation, and Louis A. Martinet emerged as the leader of the protest against the railroad car bill. Martinet, a former state representative, school board member, and attorney, had recently started publishing the *Crusader,* a black newspaper. In his editorials Martinet attempted to recapture the militancy of the *New Orleans Tribune,* which had ceased publication in the 1870s. As the "men of Tribune" had done before him, Martinet promised to fight without compromise. Martinet and other black leaders tried to defeat the railroad segregation bill before it became law. Together with a group of non-Creole and black Creole leaders — including James Lewis, P.B.S. Pinchback, and William J. Rudolphe — Martinet helped organize the American Citizens' Equal Rights Association, drew up a petition, and presented it to the legislature. A.E.P. Albert, a Methodist minister and editor of the *Southwestern Christian Advocate,* served as president of the organization.[66]

Martinet was aware of the support throughout the South for segregation laws, so he joined others to "protest against the passage of any class legislation now pending before the General Assembly, or which may hereafter come before the honorable body." They appealed to the legislators to remain true to their professed values of justice and equality and said they found it "difficult to conceive how any caste legislation can maintain the sacredness of these truly American principles." They also offered a biblical argument: "Men should not do unto others what they do not wish should be done unto them." African Americans knew that the proposed laws "would be a free license to the evilly-disposed that they might with impunity insult, humiliate and otherwise maltreat inoffensive persons." For all those reasons and more, they appealed "in the name of God and the constitution . . . that the chalice of political bitterness may be snatched from the grasp of intolerant persons and made to melt into the sacred fires of patriotic mercy."[67] The language, infused as it was with Christian and Revolutionary ideology, still influenced and guided black protest appeals in New Orleans, but it was no match for the stark espousal of speech that stressed white supremacy and white racial domination.

In 1890, however, political expediency rather than an outright rejection of a siren call to justice and morality temporarily halted the march to legal racial segregation. The Louisiana legislature still contained a few black members, and they opposed the railroad bill. After the bill fell three votes short of passage in the Senate, the *New Orleans Times Democrat* chided the Senate "because it placed Louisiana in opposition to the other Southern States, and . . . the failure will be misunderstood by the Negroes and produce unpleasant results." A bill once defeated could of course rise again. This one did. On 10 July 1890, Act 111, "to promote all railway companies carrying passengers on their trains, in the state, to provide equal but separate accommodations for the white and colored races," became law. Martinet and others castigated the black "political men" for their naïveté at best or at worst their crass dishonesty. "They worked," according to Martinet, "with might and main against the bill, no doubt, but after it was too late." Many of the black legislators aligned themselves with the state's infamous lottery interest and voted for the lottery's extension, ostensibly in exchange for white support to defeat the separate railroad car bill. After the lottery bill passed, Act 111 gained approval three days later. Protest and the legislative process having failed, African Americans turned to what they hoped to be the guardians of equality under the law, the courts.[68]

An appeal to African Americans, within the city and throughout the country, and sympathetic whites enabled the Citizens' Committee, a new organization formed after the passage of Act 111, to raise sufficient money to test the constitutionality of the segregation law. Between 1892 and 1896 the case moved slowly through the judicial system before the United States Supreme Court rendered its decision on 18 May 1896. The Supreme Court that heard arguments and decided the case "followed," in the opinion of historian J. Morgan Kousser, "a confusing and contradictory path on its rulings on occupational and voting rights." And that path would not bode well for African Americans, for "in its decisions in cases involving segregation and discrimination in public accommodations and education, the Court's opinions and impact became even more tangled." The legal "tangle" would become for black southerners more like a vise to restrict their pursuits of the fruits of full citizenship enshrined, in their view, in the Fourteenth and Fifteenth Amendments. In *Plessy v. Ferguson* the Supreme Court gave legal sanction to "separate but equal." Judge John M. Harlan's lengthy dissent notwithstanding, race relations in America for the next half-century would be governed by the idea that "legislation is powerless to eradicate racial distinctions based upon physical differences, and the attempt to do so can only result in accentuating the difficulties of the present situation. If the civil and political rights of both races be equal one cannot be inferior to the other socially, the Constitution of the United States cannot put them upon the same plane." But there would be additional efforts to restrict full citizenship for African Americans.[69]

Between the 1896 *Plessy* decision and the start of the new century, white Democrats in Louisiana sought the definitive answer to the Negro Question. Confronted with a brief but potentially worrisome alliance between whites operating under the new National Republican Party and the state's Populist Party, leaders in the Democratic Party took measures to reduce the effectiveness of poor white voters and eliminate black voters entirely. After a harrowing, though successful, reelection campaign in 1896, Governor Murphy J. Foster finally gave his total support to the restrictive suffrage campaign that was gaining momentum in the South. Democrats such as Foster on the state level and machine politicians in New Orleans such as John Fitzgerald believed that the benefits derived from an expansive suffrage were outweighed by the potential pitfalls. Indeed, though Foster won his race by more than 28,000 votes, he trailed in most of the state's parishes that had a majority of white voters. And Fitzpatrick lost the mayoral race to the reform candidate Walter C. Flower. Two legislative measures substantially reduced the state's electorate: an election bill that required voters to use a secret ballot at the polls and a registration bill that mandated the re-registration of all current and potential voters after 1 January 1897. The effects of the changes, in the opinion of historian Michael Perman, were "devastating." By 1 January 1898 the number of black voters in the city had declined to 3,089 and in the state to 12,902.[70] Louisiana Democrats then used the state's third constitutional convention since the end of the Civil War to disfranchise blacks and some poor whites permanently.

The constitutional convention convened in February 1898. "We are all aware that this convention has been called by the people of the State of Louisiana principally to deal with one question," the president of the convention reminded the delegates, "and we know that but for the existence of that one Question this assemblage would not be sitting here today. My fellow delegates, let us not be misunderstood! Let us say to the large class of people of Louisiana who will be disfranchised under any of the proposed limitations of the suffrage, that what we seek to do is undertaken in a spirit, not of hostility to any particular men or set of men." Ernest B. Kruttschnitt went on to add "that the Question which we are trying to solve here is one which imperils the integrity of the future government of the State of Louisiana." The spirit of democracy was greatly injured because of the successful efforts to restrict the electorate, but it was not dead, as leaders of the convention allowed some discussion at the convention, even regarding suffrage. One group hoping to obtain the franchise and another group attempting to retain it made appeals to the convention's suffrage committee. In a perfect world maybe the groups would have made a joint statement in support of universal suffrage to include both women and African Americans. But the political world of Carrie Chapman-Catt, who appeared before the suffrage committee to support women's right to vote, and Booker T. Washington, who had a representative make his appeal for fair voting laws, was anything but perfect in 1898. Faced with a white male majority that rejected both of their group's suffrage aspirations, they made separate appeals.[71]

Washington, in his "Open Letter" to the convention, conceded the need to place restrictions on suffrage but believed that Louisiana had "an opportunity to settle for all time the race question, so far as it concerns politics." Settling the race question, in Washington's view, meant that suffrage restriction laws should "be so clear that no one clothed with State authority will be tempted to perjure and degrade himself, by putting one interpretation upon it for the white man and another for the black man."[72] Democrats had called a constitutional convention to accomplish exactly what Washington asked them to forgo. His plea for an impartial suffrage law was reasonable and democratic but completely at odds with the prevailing commitment to black disfranchisement that gripped the South in the 1890s and early 1900s. Louisiana was not an outlier in southern race relations. And as historian Steven Hahn has reminded us, campaigns to restrict universal suffrage were national issues as well and were linked to "fears that the rapid industrialization of the country and the swelling immigrant working class accompanying it threatened the fate of the republic."[73] As a result, convention delegates and white political leaders were confident of victory when they crafted a document that included literacy, property, and poll tax requirements as a prerequisite for suffrage. The suffrage article also contained a "grandfather clause" that attempted to ensure that most whites excluded from suffrage because they could not meet literacy, property, or poll tax requirements would still retain the franchise. Although those eligible to use the clause only had a few months to do so, approximately forty thousand whites were "grandfathered" in.[74]

By 1900 the number of white registered voters had increased to 125,437, but the number of black voters continued to decline. The removal of African Americans from the political process, however, was not accomplished by legislative and judicial decree alone. Acts of violence directed at African Americans rose steadily during the last two decades of the nineteenth century. Between 1882 and 1903 mob violence was responsible for the lynching of at least 232 African Americans in the state. During the first year of the new century, a race riot in New Orleans left many African Americans dead, injured, jailed, or homeless. The editor of a white newspaper recommended the extermination of all African Americans. In 1900 public school officials reduced black education to grades 1 through 5. The frequency and cruelty of lynching and other acts of violence dampened the resolve of many African American leaders, including the city's black Creole leadership, to push for full equality. Perhaps most African Americans in New

Orleans had grown tired of the trauma associated with the political process and the struggle for full citizenship; some of them, indeed, may have been "left [only] to brood over the message imparted by the Jim Crow laws and the spirit in which they were enforced." The collective dreams and aspirations of African Americans had been transformed into a nightmare of death, intimidation, and violence. Booker T. Washington probably spoke for some African Americans in New Orleans when he stood before the Atlanta Cotton Exposition in 1895 and articulated with force and conviction his "Atlanta Compromise," a speech considered by some of his contemporaries as a virtual surrender of full citizenship for African Americans.[75]

In the ensuing twenty-five years Louisiana enacted segregation laws to give legal sanction to what often had been accomplished through illegal and extralegal techniques. The various laws maintained that the two races must drink in separate saloons, live in separate neighborhoods, and attend separate schools. The laws also segregated the races in jails and streetcars. The effect of the Jim Crow laws, historian C. Vann Woodward concluded, "gave free rein and majesty of the law to mass aggressions that might otherwise have been curbed, blunted, or deflected." For African Americans who had labored tirelessly for enfranchisement and equality after the end of the Civil War, the loss of suffrage and the onset of Jim Crow perhaps did produce feelings of resignation and surrender. One contemporary noted that some African Americans, "seeing that the tyranny of their oppressors was limitless, that they were using all their genius to multiply degrading laws against blacks . . . believed it was better to suffer in silence than to attract attention to their misfortune and weakness."[76] Through law and custom white leaders and citizens in New Orleans had defined what they considered the proper place for African Americans in southern society. But many African Americans rejected that view of their future, and with their leaders they began the slow process of personal advancement, community development, and liberation. And how they tenaciously held onto the capacity to love, live, dream, and aspire and also to maintain faith and hope in the South during the Jim Crow era was a testament to their character as a group. The wonder is not that some of them experienced fear, hopelessness, and despair; the wonder is that the great majority of them did not.

2

Higher Education and Individual Initiative

"How does it feel to be a problem?" That is one of the major questions W.E.B. Du Bois asked at the start of the twentieth century in an essay in his now classic book *The Souls of Black Folk*. To some African Americans being a "problem" was too big a burden to bear. Many others, however, transformed the question into a quest for personal advancement and social justice. In his writings and throughout his career as a scholar and social activist, Du Bois insisted that African Americans needed well-trained college graduates to wage the struggle for full equality for African Americans effectively. In his scholarship Du Bois documented the contributions that black college graduates made to black community development and liberation as teachers, ministers, physicians, and lawyers. His early opposition to the leadership of Booker T. Washington stemmed in part from Washington's tepid support for black higher education. Du Bois maintained that "all men cannot go to college but some men must," and he forcefully contended that "it is the trained, living human soul, cultivated and strengthened by long study and thought, that breathes the real breath of life into boys and girls and makes them human," an argument that African Americans in New Orleans supported. Du Bois held expansive thoughts on black higher education that saw college graduates not just as teachers, ministers, and physicians but as educated mothers and fathers as well.[1]

Washington, on the other hand, conceded that a small number of African Americans needed access to liberal arts colleges but thought that "for years to come the education of the people of my race should be so directed that the greatest proportion of the mental strength of the masses will be brought to bear upon the every-day practical things of life, upon something that is needed to be done, and something which they will be permitted to do in the community in which they reside." He argued that the "pushing of mere abstract knowledge into the head means little" and considered it "discouraging to find a girl who can tell you the geographical location of any country on the globe . . . [yet] does not know where to place the dishes upon a common dinner table." Washington believed that African Americans had to progress through a series of stages that started with agricultural and industrial education, and he was convinced that achievement in industry and agriculture would reduce white prejudice and racial violence. And by May 1900 Booker T. Washington's ability to influence race relations and black education was ascendant. He was already meeting with wealthy industrialists, the type of individuals able and willing to use their new and substantial affluence to fund social, civic, and educational projects at schools such as Washington's beloved Tuskegee Institute. In a few years he would dine with a president of the United States. Although he had not yet fully earned the name the "Wizard of Tuskegee," his deft ability to pursue sometimes contradictory policies evidenced a certain degree of political mastery. Yet this son of the New South, often publicly conciliatory to white southerners' notions of white supremacy and black inferiority, was not invited to participate in the first conference of the twentieth century held to discuss southern race relations. Washington and other African Americans did attend but as spectators in the gallery.[2]

The Southern Society for the Promotion of the Study of Race Conditions and Problems in the South organized and hosted the conference that convened in Montgomery, Alabama, in May 1900. In an earlier letter to Washington the conference's most ardent supporter and chief organizer, Edgar Gardner Murphy, assured Washington that white leaders of the conference "realize that the welfare of each is involved in the welfare of the other; that whatever is a difficulty for one, is a difficulty for both; and that the true removal of difficulties must open the way of development for all classes of our population."[3] Perhaps it was in the context of that spirit that convinced Washington to give the conference organizers his support and advice. For three days white leaders discussed what they viewed as the "Negro Problem" or "Negro Question," and at the conference there was scant evidence of a genuine concern for the welfare of African Americans. Indeed, in the opinion of historian Robert J. Norrell, Murphy "loaded the program with some of the most vociferous anti-black voices in the South."⁴ And although Washington may not have participated in the public program, his ideas, especially regarding black education, were ever-present in the thoughts and statements of many of the participants. Speakers frequently evoked his name and ideas. Hollis Burke Frissell, head of Hampton Institute, noted that "the sort of education that produced a Booker Washington . . . is capable of producing a class of hard-working, docile Negroes, which will place the South in the foreground among the industrial countries of the world." Frissell may have preferred that another speaker who shared his views would have used Hampton as a model to emphasize his points but would not have disagreed with the speaker's general ideas. W. Bourke Cockran from New York saw schools such as Tuskegee as the solution to the race problem. "Let the Negro be prepared for life as Booker Washington prepares him," he maintained. "Let there be a Tuskegee in every community." All the speakers who supported some educational opportunities for African Americans believed that industrial education would cure many of the South's perceived ills. The mayor of Wilmington, North Carolina, Alfred M. Waddell, supported that view and saw it as the only kind of education African Americans should receive. J.L.M. Curry, an agent for the Slater Fund, supported industrial education as well because he considered "the Negro a valuable laborer" and wanted to "make his labor more intelligent, more skilled, more productive."⁵

Becoming a more intelligent and valuable laborer, in the opinions of the various speakers, did not represent a path to full citizenship in southern society. Indeed, some African American leaders were reaching the plausible conclusion that educational and economic success strengthened white efforts to oppress and restrict them. The black writer Charles W. Chesnutt, for one, believed it. "Heavily handicapped," he observed, "they have made such rapid progress that the suspicion is justified that their advancement, rather than any stagnation or retrogression, is the true secret of the virulent Southern hostility to their rights." More alarming to Chesnutt and African Americans in New Orleans, white southern opinion leaders had "so influenced Northern opinion that it stands mute, and leaves the colored people, upon whom the North conferred liberty, to the tender mercies of those who have always denied their fitness for it."⁶ African Americans would remain a race apart, subjected to the economic, social, and political decisions of white southerners. A participant from Georgia, John Temple Graves, rendered an emphatic no to the rhetorical question

"Will the white man permit the Negro to have an equal part in the industrial, social, and civic advantage of the United States?" Graves reduced the question to race and race alone. "When will we learn that this is, from first to last, a race question," Graves insisted. The question was "an issue of race and not politics, an issue of color and not section; a thing of skin and not of achievement or condition." Graves was so emphatic in his support for rigid racial segregation because he believed African Americans desired equality and would unceasingly work to achieve it. The best and ultimate solution for Graves was removal of African Americans from the United States. Waddell, a supporter of industrial education, strongly opposed black suffrage at the conference as well. "Unrestricted Negro suffrage in the Southern States," he maintained, would produce "the most ignorant, corrupt, and evil government ever known in a free country"; he thus favored repeal of the Fifteenth Amendment. In the absence of repeal, in 1898 Waddell had made his response to black political participation clear as one of the leaders of the reign of political terror directed against African Americans in Wilmington, Delaware, which resulted in numerous African American deaths, property loss, political erasure, and migration. Curry, too, lamented the passage of the Fifteenth Amendment and, after stating that he was one of the founders of the Confederate States of America, noted that passage of the Fourteenth and Fifteenth Amendments was not a "necessary consequence of emancipation."[7]

Not all participants and speakers at the conference understood race relations and the place of African Americans in southern society in the same manner as individuals such as Frissell, Waddell, and Curry. Those who expressed more moderate views were in the minority, and their comments fell well short of a vigorous defense of full racial equality. Still, those African Americans in the gallery, in rural areas, and in southern cities such as New Orleans saw some hope for improved race relations and increased opportunities from the comments of speakers such as Father John R. Slattery of St. Joseph's Seminary and William A. MacCorkle, a former governor of West Virginia. Slattery gave examples of fraud directed against African Americans and wanted white southerners to exercise fairness and honesty in their relations with them, especially in the area of employment. "Indeed the impressions left from slavery, the many dishonest transactions upon them; unpaid wages, 'store pay,' bad titles to land, unjust mortgages upon their crops, these and similar wrongs make the Negro suspicious of the whites," Slattery courageously stated. MacCorkle condemned specific efforts to disfranchise African Americans because such efforts weakened democracy and hindered economic and social improvements in the South. He favored, instead, a restricted franchise with property and education requirements that were fairly enforced for all voters.[8] Yet he knew that the South was moving in a different political direction and later confided to Washington "that the determination seems to be to disfranchise the Negro. This is a crying wrong and I hope such will not be the case. There is nothing to do, however, but to stand up and give them a hard fight for what is right and just."[9]

Washington in his own way gave white southern leaders a sustained fight to maintain black suffrage, and having a restrictive franchise linked to property ownership and educational attainment impartially administered was a policy that some African American leaders in New Orleans had supported and continued to support at the start of the twentieth century. What concerned them were the effective campaigns to close avenues of advancement in the workplace and in education. They were also concerned about the limited view of black citizenship and the support of legal racial segregation held by most white southerners, as evidenced by statements made at the race relations conference in Montgomery. Group and individual progress, they believed, depended on effective and appropriate types of education, including higher education to produce and maintain a leadership class. Most white leaders in New Orleans, however, supported limited higher education opportunities for African Americans. The "practical industrial arts," rather than higher education, represented the best type of education, one of the city's leading newspapers editorialized in 1910, and it claimed that Booker T. Washington was "doing a great work for his race and for the country."[10] Unfortunately for African Americans in early-twentieth-century New Orleans, some whites considered even that level of education to be too much, sharing a view expressed by Tulane University professor and author William Benjamin Smith: "Nearly forty years of devoted and enthusiastic effort to elevate and educate the Southern Negro lie stretched out behind in a dead level of failure."[11]

Du Bois understood probably sooner than most Americans that rigid racial segregation produced a greater, not a lesser, need for black college graduates. Unlike poor and working-class whites, whose "guidance and training in the higher matter of social evolution can be safely left to the result of their contact with the best of their fellow citizens, racial segregation denied African Americans such opportunities. As a result, Du Bois maintained, "what the Negro needs . . . of the world and civilization, he must largely teach himself; what he learns of social organization and efficiency, he must learn from his own people." He conceded that it placed "upon a people just emerged from slavery, with neither time, traditions, nor experience, a tremendous task." Throughout the Jim Crow period African American leaders in New Orleans held fast to the ideas that Du Bois expressed at the start of the twentieth century: "Education and work are the levers to uplift a people. Work alone will not do it unless inspired by the right ideals and guided by intelligence. The Talented Tenth of the Negro race must be made leaders of thought and missionaries of culture among their people. No others can do this work and Negro colleges must train men for it."[12] Through individual initiative, focused leadership, the black self-help tradition, and assistance from white Americans still committed to black higher education, African Americans throughout the nation worked to expand higher education opportunities. The New Orleans black community also participated in this effort.

At the beginning of the Jim Crow period the city had four black colleges — Leland, New Orleans, Southern, and Straight. All the schools with the exception of Southern were private institutions and affiliated with a religious denomination. The American Missionary Association (AMA) founded and supported Straight, which received its charter in June 1869. Organized during the optimistic phase of Congressional Reconstruction, Straight's supporters pursued an ambitious educational mission. Straight's goal, according to some supporters, was to become the future "Harvard of the South." It also attempted to foster improved race relations. These were worthy goals and were certainly needed and desired by a group of Americans newly freed from slavery. Nonetheless, they were ambitious and difficult to achieve because of the high level of white opposition and the steep financial resources needed to achieve them. By its charter and the policy of early administrators, Straight admitted black and white students. During its early years of existence the college received a twenty thousand–dollar grant from the United States government. Through the Freedmen's Bureau the trustees used the money to build a school at Esplanade and Derbigny Streets on property owned by the American Missionary Association. Straight also benefited from the support of influential white and black politicians and civic leaders. Seymour Straight, a wealthy white Baptist merchant, for example, donated money and land to the school. In 1880 Valaria G. Stone provided twenty-five thousand dollars to build a dormitory for females. And during Reconstruction the support of politicians and government officials matched that of the private sector. School officials could depend on the assistance of politicians such as C. C. Antoine, Edward Heath, P.B.S. Pinchback, and Henry Clay Warmoth.[13]

Affiliation with the AMA and support from politicians eliminated some problems, but many others remained. Two fires of questionable origins destroyed the first school in February 1877 and the school that replaced it in November 1891. School officials decided to rebuild on the same site as the second school, at Canal and Tonti Streets. Developing and expanding the curriculum proved just as challenging as erecting and maintaining buildings. By 1900 Straight had experienced the ebbs and flows common to many of the black colleges established during or immediately following Reconstruction. Hampton Institute in Virginia, for example, prospered despite its founder's limited vision for black education. Samuel Armstrong, who served as president from the school's origins in 1868 until 1893, believed that a wide educational and social chasm existed between the races. Indeed, Armstrong believed African American students were docile and impressionable and sought to train them for teaching careers that would perpetuate racial inequality rather than challenge it. Hampton's curriculum prepared its students for teaching careers to accommodate the educational needs of African American students in what today are called elementary and middle school grades.[14]

Straight's curriculum, however, reflected both the limitations implicit in Armstrong's approach at Hampton and the more optimistic and expansive view of education held by other Reconstruction and post-Reconstruction education leaders. Four years into its existence Straight maintained ten departments, though only three of them offered college or professional training. Six students received instruction in the college department, five in medical training, and nine in theology. Nearly 69 percent of the 429 students enrolled at Straight were in the elementary department. Enrollment during the next year reflected the same trend. The number of college and professional students grew in the 1870s and 1880s but was followed by two decades of decline beginning in the 1890s. Straight was not alone, for other black colleges experienced a drop in enrollment as well. Educational aspirations most often competed with scarce economic resources, which prevented African Americans from pursuing higher education. In addition, public support of black secondary education, where it existed, declined throughout the South in the 1880s, eliminating a crucial educational bridge to college enrollment. In the 1880s New Orleans was not an exception, and high school education for African Americans ended. The educational door, however, remained partially open even during the ascendancy and triumph of racial segregation and exclusion in the 1890s, as black colleges enrolled more secondary and college preparatory students.[15]

The city's second private school, New Orleans University, developed from Union Normal School. Located in the uptown section of the city on Camp and Race Streets and operated by the Methodist Episcopal Church, Union made teacher training available to blacks and whites. In 1873 church officials expanded the school's mission and changed its name to New Orleans University. Five departments operated that first year, and students paid a one-dollar monthly fee. According to an account in a Methodist newspaper, New Orleans University did not admit anyone "under the fourth reader." Despite the efforts to create minimum standards, the educational needs of the black community forced New Orleans University to offer instruction at the elementary school level. Methodist leaders, black and white, realized "that whoever educates and aids the people in their ignorance and suffering, will have their hearty co-operation in the future. If the Protestant church educates this race, it anchors it to Protestantism."[16]

The number of African Americans "anchored" to Protestantism because of attendance at New Orleans University is unclear. Available records indicate, however, that the school had an average enrollment of approximately four hundred students between 1873 and 1900. To increase enrollment, Methodist leaders encouraged ministers to "talk about the University from the pulpit and urge young men and women to attend." During some school years insufficient classroom space, rather than apathy, produced low enrollment figures. In the 1881–82 academic year, for example, the school rejected one hundred students because of overcrowding. Rev. A.E.P. Albert, pastor of Wesley Methodist Church, realized that schools such as New Orleans University would continue to experience overcrowding until state and city leaders provided adequate revenues to support public education. Until that time, Albert conceded, New Orleans University was "obliged to take students from the primary grades."[17] The decision by school officials to offer elementary and high school instruction compromised but did not eliminate their commitment to higher education. Another door of educational opportunity remained slightly ajar in New Orleans at the start of the Jim Crow era.

Leland University's origin and growth followed the general outlines of Straight and New Orleans Universities: Reconstruction origin, denominational affiliation, and small enrollment in the college department. In 1870 officials of the American Baptist Free Mission Society, the American Baptist Home Mission Society, and the Consolidated American Baptist Missionary Convention established Leland. Holbrook Chamberlain, a northerner interested in black education, donated $65,000, and the Freedmen's Bureau supported Leland with a grant of $17,500 to construct a classroom building. Society officials purchased land on St. Charles Avenue and constructed the school at the site. It opened in January 1871 as a liberal arts college with a mission that focused on teacher and clergy education. Reflecting the egalitarian beliefs held by some of Leland founders and supporters, it was open to blacks and whites, males and females. The egalitarian sentiment extended to governance; four African Americans were members of the first group of trustees. Chamberlain continued to donate money to the school, greatly augmenting the financial support that Leland received from the various Baptist denominations. In 1886 university officials removed the school from direct denominational control and maintained that system of organization until 1923. By that time the school had been moved to Baker, Louisiana. Leland University, like many buildings in the city, suffered extensive damage when a severe hurricane hit the city in September 1915.[18]

Before its relocation, Leland helped to nurture black New Orleans's initial efforts in higher education. Indeed, between 1890 and 1910 Leland was one of only several black colleges that offered a college-level curriculum. Students who pursued the college curriculum studied Latin, Greek, English, modern languages, history, social sciences, natural sciences, mathematics, philosophy, and pedagogy. By 1910, however, Leland also offered classes in manual and industrial education. The school's trustees and administrators viewed the addition of manual and industrial education as evidence of growth and not as a capitulation to a narrow view of African American education. "It would be difficult to overestimate the service which these institutions of higher learning, inadequate in certain respects, and certainly not 'universities' at the outset, rendered to the people," observed a black New Orleans educator. Still, progress was at times slow and decidedly uneven at Leland and at all the city's black colleges.[19]

In 1895 Straight University had 2 college students out of a total enrollment of 563. This figure represented a marked departure from its idealistic origins in 1869 and the euphoric expectations of its earlier supporters. From 1892 to 1918 the percentage of college students rarely constituted more than 10 percent of Straight's total enrollment. But proponents of college education knew opportunities should be available to those who could take advantage of it. And in 1892 Alice Ruth Moore, who would later marry the writer and poet Paul Laurence Dunbar, took advantage of the opportunity and graduated from Straight. She eventually achieved acclaim as a writer, educator, and activist and later remembered her time at Straight as "halcyon days." She left New Orleans after graduation, but her love for the city and the school never dimmed. In a diary entry for 25 May 1927, for instance, she wrote: "Graduated from Straight on this date in 1892—just 35 years ago today! And it's just as clear and vivid as if it were five years."[20] Opportunities for others to harvest fond memories of college life such as those held by Alice Moore declined for several reasons. First, the economic depression of the 1890s affected donations to the school and put the cost of a college education further beyond the reach of most African Americans. Second, the missionary idealists and philanthropists who had played a prominent role in Straight's infancy were no longer around in significant numbers. Finally, and most important, the triumph at the turn of the century of the Tuskegee-Hampton idea of industrial education hindered the development of schools such as Straight. To its credit, Straight University supporters remained committed to a liberal arts curriculum. Similar to most black colleges around the turn of the century, Straight officials added several classes in "manual" training and accepted students below the college level.[21]

Few African Americans in New Orleans had illusions regarding the difficulties they faced in their struggle for better lives for themselves and a better community. Education, they knew, was becoming the American-tested solution to many of the problems that they encountered. Their community-building efforts depended on access to quality higher education. If churches, primary and secondary schools, civic and social organizations, and businesses and professions were to improve, college graduates had to lead the way. To do so, New Orleans's black colleges had to overcome challenges. Indeed, early in the twentieth century it appeared that they were failing at one of their most important goals: training teachers to meet the needs of a growing black elementary school enrollment. Between 1899 and 1901, for instance, only twelve of ninety-five African Americans passed the local school board's certification examination. School board members and school administrators looked beyond their own role in the high failure rate and placed the blame on the black colleges. They considered the results "discouraging" and noted that "candidates presented themselves for examinations bearing credentials from higher institutions that inspired the hope that this year the results would be more satisfactory than last year." Improvements "must be found in the institutions which prepared these candidates for their chosen work," school officials charged. "The fault must exist there, and it must be the duty of these institutions to correct it." To assist in correcting it, school board members instructed the superintendent to send copies of the examination results to the presidents of the four black colleges. School officials were just as disappointed with the examination results the following year but were more restrained in their public comments. They were content with the statement: "We can only hope that the future will bring about improvement in results, and that those in charge of the higher training of these young people will be effective in producing better material from which we may draw teachers for the colored youth of this city."[22]

When black Reconstruction leaders Henry Demas and P.B.S. Pinchback headed the effort to establish Southern University, they hoped the institution would eventually assume a central role in black higher education in New Orleans and the entire state. And when the state legislature designated Southern as a land-grant college for African Americans, it appeared a leading role was possible. But Southern University's emergence as an institution of higher education developed slowly and was limited by inadequate funding and a poor elementary and secondary school system in New Orleans. The state seldom appropriated more than ten thousand dollars annually to the institution between 1880 and 1912, and student fees were always an extremely small share of yearly revenues. The institution's slow growth was also linked to the limited vision for black higher education held by white leaders and politicians. Because Southern University was directly controlled and financed by the state legislature and governor, its mission and goals often, at least until the 1920s, reflected the vision of white leaders more so than the educational aspirations of African Americans. In the 1912–13 school year, for instance, Southern University still did not have a four-year college department.[23] The limited vision by white leaders for black public colleges helped to produce an educational environment in which "as late as World War I virtually all of the black college students were enrolled in privately owned colleges." In other words, only two years before President Woodrow Wilson asked all Americans to support and fight a war to save democracy, black land-grant and state colleges in the southern states enrolled twelve college students. Indeed, at that time Southern University operated mainly as an elementary and secondary institution.[24]

In 1914 Southern University moved from New Orleans to Scotlandville, a small community northwest of Baton Rouge, Louisiana. The move to a much larger site and the appointment of Joseph Samuel Clark as president raised hopes that the institution would finally develop as a college. Clark, a native of Louisiana and graduate of Leland University, worked tirelessly to expand the school's academic program and relevance to the African American community.[25] Between the move from New Orleans and the publication of a survey of black higher education in 1928, some positive changes occurred at Southern University, and not all of them emanated from the vision of state policy leaders. Several seemingly contradictory impulses may have contributed to a change in black public higher education policy. By the summer of 1919 it was clear that World War I had not made democracy either safe or probable for black southerners. Nonetheless, their military participation, indirect and direct support for the war effort, and the inclusive focus of the informational campaign waged by the national government all contributed to a wider acceptance by African Americans of the belief that the promise of America was theirs as well. Writings and statements by elite African Americans echoed this changed attitude more than shaped it. Ideas expressed in an editorial in the NAACP's *Crisis* magazine in May 1919 represented the thinking of many "ordinary" African Americans: "Make way for Democracy! We saved it in France, and by the Great Jehovah, we will save it in the United States of America, or know the reason why."[26] White leaders in New Orleans and across the state did not respond with fear to ideas such as those articulated in the *Crisis*. But they realized that they had to become more responsive to African Americans' aspirations and demands for greater equity in educational funding.

How the rising educational expectations of African Americans affected Louisiana's support for black higher education is suggested by the increase in state funding for Southern University from 1919 to 1927. "The growth of the appropriations . . . shows that the State of Louisiana is deeply interested in the development of the university and willing to give it more and more adequate support," concluded a survey released in 1928. What did greater funding from the state produce at Southern University? The survey documented a substantial increase in facilities, including academic buildings, dormitories, dining hall, hospital, auditorium, and housing for teachers. Other areas of operations that garnered praise in the survey were budgeting and financial management. And "the home economics department in particular was notable for its attractiveness and neatness."[27] The special attention given to the "attractiveness and neatness" of the home economics department would have been cause for concern by black leaders who championed Southern University's growth if the overall curriculum and academic work had not improved as well. By 1928 the energetic and committed leadership of President Clark had enabled Southern University to move beyond the program of industrial and agriculture training, its main focus after the move from New Orleans. The school offered four college degree programs: a bachelor of arts, a bachelor of arts in education, a bachelor of science and mathematics, and a bachelor of science in agriculture. Attempts to raise admission requirements continued, and by 1928 students needed a high school diploma and sixteen academic units of credit to gain admission. President Clark and school officials also attempted to determine the quality of high school work entering students had completed. This task was difficult, as evidenced by the practice of admitting students conditionally. Students who were admitted conditionally were assigned courses designed to remedy any academic deficiencies. That practice had two apparent results, only one of them clearly positive. The number of students enrolled in the college program rose steadily during the 1920s. Higher college enrollment, however, did not produce a proportional increase in the number of college graduates at the school.[28]

Between 1920 and 1930 New Orleans University and Straight College also enrolled more college students and moved closer to their original mission of providing higher education. For several years, from 1904 to 1907, no college students enrolled at Straight, but in 1925, 124 students attended the college department. New Orleans University experienced a similar change; the school enrolled 213 college students in 1925. What accounted for this change? A researcher writing during the last years of the Jim Crow period offered one explanation. "As the public school system for Negroes developed in Louisiana," he argued, "and tax-supported elementary and secondary schools multiplied throughout the state, such institutions of Negro higher education as Straight University were gradually relieved of the responsibility of furnishing instruction on lower levels and were consequently able to devote themselves more properly to Negro higher education."[29] Four interrelated factors also contributed to the change. The normal departments at both schools produced graduates that through their teaching helped to strengthen the black community's faith in education as a means of achieving progress, and many of these normal graduates eventually earned undergraduate degrees. Another factor involved the development of black institutions and in the growth of the black middle class; the institutions contributed to the growth of the black middle class, producing more students who wanted higher education. The third factor was the sustained work of black leaders and officials with the American Missionary Association and the Methodist Episcopal Church's Board of Education to transform the schools into centers of higher education. When Rev. Otto E. Kreige became president of New Orleans University, for example, he required all of his college instructors to possess at least a master's degree and encouraged the faculty to pursue graduate training. Finally, black higher education reflected and benefited from changes in the American economy that produced a more specialized labor force, which increasingly needed additional educated workers.[30]

When the *Survey of Negro Colleges and Universities* was published in 1928, New Orleans University still occupied its prominent and accessible campus on St. Charles Avenue. And it still maintained a strong relationship with the Methodist Episcopal Church's Board of Education. That relationship and the governance structure that was a part of it appeared, in the opinion of the survey authors, outdated. According to the survey, too many vital and daily operational activities required the approval of the board of education central staff, located in Chicago. The appointment of faculty members, the survey pointed out, needed approval from the central office. One result was a greatly diminished role for the school's board of trustees. It is not at all clear, however, that local school supporters and school officials saw the relationship as negatively as the survey asserted. Affiliation with the Methodist Episcopal Church provided access to funding, friends, and administrative assistance that many supporters considered invaluable, benefits that were not readily available elsewhere. The organizational and administrative structure, at times cumbersome and inefficient, represented a small price to pay for the benefits associated with the relationship. While it was true that support by white southerners for black higher education had increased, few African Americans believed the support was sufficient enough to supplant the contributions of the various missionary organizations. And even fewer accepted the notion that the "missionary era [in black higher education] had largely passed away."[31]

Still, concerns about Straight College's development had been growing for several years among African Americans leaders in New Orleans, Straight College administrators, and board of trustees members. Several issues dominated their thinking in the late 1920s: maintaining academic quality, the lack of adequate secondary education opportunities for African Americans in the New Orleans area, the physical plant, and the school's location. Straight College attempted to maintain a college program comparable to or better than the leading black colleges and chose administrators and faculty carefully, resulting in a faculty that, in the opinion of college administrators, compared favorably with that of other black colleges. In 1927 Straight College president James P. O'Brien assured board members that the faculty remained committed to steady improvement. By 1927 in the college division all but one faculty member had a master's degree, and most of them continued to pursue additional graduate work in the summer. The African American faculty members who attended graduate school during the summer months did so outside the South because none of the black colleges offered the kinds of graduate training they needed. White universities such as Tulane and Loyola in New Orleans and the state's public university, Louisiana State, did not admit African American students.

African Americans and black college administrators recognized the difficulties associated with pursuing graduate training outside the South. In the 1920s O'Brien supported the start of graduate work at Straight College. In one report to board members he acknowledged that "there have been and there are students who are not in a position to go to the northern schools, for whom I believe we ought to do this work, if we can." Opportunities for graduate work would improve the quality of classroom instruction and academic research. In addition, obtaining advanced and terminal degrees would enable African Americans to assume greater leadership at black colleges. Straight College, like the majority of private black colleges, had a white president but an interracial faculty. Increasingly, however, and this was true for Straight, African Americans occupied other senior-level positions such as dean. That position was considered the chief academic position, and for most of the 1920s Ludwig T. Larsen served as dean at Straight. Before assuming his position there, Larsen held successful positions at LeMoyne Institute in Memphis, Tennessee, and at Talladega

College in Talladega, Alabama. Taking an opportunity to assess Larsen's work, O'Brien noted, "He has done a strong piece of work here in readjusting the classes, readjusting the students, and in maintaining standards."[32]

What did maintaining standards mean for Straight College supporters and those individuals interested in the school's success? One measurement, as already noted, was a strong faculty. In the closing years of the 1920s O'Brien believed Straight College had improved throughout the decade. He also believed that his faculty possessed good character and considered that quality to be as important as intelligence and academic achievement. Maintaining standards, of course, also pertained to the students. Admission standards and graduation requirements were two types of measurements. Straight required fifteen units for regular admission but admitted students lacking the fifteen units conditionally. This policy was comparable to that used by other colleges in the area. The policy also acknowledged and reflected the overall condition of black secondary education in the city and state. New Orleans's only black public high school, for example, was not accredited, thus making its graduates ineligible for regular admission to Straight College. So, despite the efforts to "keep our entrance requirements somewhere within reach," Straight only enrolled 124 college students in the fall of 1927. That number would have been lower still if, as President O'Brien explained, "we should administer the requirements for entrance to the freshman class much more strictly, and require a higher degree of work in the freshman class than we are now doing, we would be a good deal like a perfectly good engine, with steam up, and engineer aboard, but half a mile down the track, while the train is standing up at the station. If the engine is going to pull anything, it will have to back up and hook on."[33] How much to "back up" in order to provide the kind of higher education the black community and individuals needed to progress was the dilemma and delicate balance that institutions such as Straight College faced. Another challenge involved efforts to maintain some control of the purpose and quality of higher education. As historians of black education have pointed out: "Although black educational objectives were often frustrated by powerful whites, the black community was not powerless. Their hopes played an important part in shaping southern black educational institutions."[34] African American opinion leaders, educators, churches, and parents in New Orleans attempted, in myriad ways, to influence decisions that affected the type of higher education available to the black community.

In the 1920s an increase in the quality of instruction and the quantity of students contributed to optimism over the future of black higher education in the city but also raised concerns at two of the three African American colleges operating in the city—Straight College and New Orleans University. The schools occupied sites in two of the best sections in the city, New Orleans University in a residential area on St. Charles Avenue and Straight College in a residential and commercial area on Canal Street. Both locations were accessible by public transportation but lacked adequate land needed for possible expansion. Enrollment trends in the 1920s suggested that the future effectiveness of the schools would depend on improvements to their physical plants. In addition to concerns related to the size of their campuses, Straight and New Orleans officials faced escalating operating costs. They sought greater support from several agencies, including the General Education Board and the Julius Rosenwald Fund. By the late 1920s some educators and fund officials had started to question the wisdom and rationale of financing two Protestant-supported schools with similar missions located in the same city. This idea led to the closing of Straight College and New Orleans University and the founding of Dillard University.

Merger plans gained the endorsement of influential blacks and whites in the city. Supporters from the white community included A. D. Danizer, the president of the Association of Commerce, and Edgar B. Stern. Stern, a wealthy local businessman, served on the Straight trustee board and had become a steady supporter of black education. The local black newspaper and Methodist bishop Robert Elijah Jones favored the merger. The success or failure of the proposal, however, rested with the schools' governing boards and with Rosenwald Fund and General Education Board officials. Straight College and New Orleans University had maintained a presence in the city for more than fifty years with limited cooperation between them, and their different religious affiliation did not bode well for the plan's success. In January 1929, however, the board of education of the Methodist Episcopal Church declared its support and appointed a committee to discuss merger plans with Straight. By that time Straight officials and the American Missionary Association had given tentative approval.[35]

Throughout 1929 representatives from the various schools, governing boards, and foundations met, usually in New Orleans or New York, to reach a merger plan acceptable to all parties. The task was not easy. In the opinion of historians Joe Richardson and Maxine Jones, the conferees reached an agreement on the scope of the merger, finances, governance, and mission only "after considerable infighting, consultation, and temporary stalemates."[36] Straight College and New Orleans University would cease to exist, and a new university, Dillard, would replace them. Dillard would also absorb Flint-Goodridge Hospital, then a part of New Orleans University. A minimum of $2 million would be spent for construction of the school and hospital. Each church board pledged $500,000, and the General Education Board and Rosenwald Fund promised $750,000 if citizens in New Orleans raised $250,000. Activities to raise New Orleans share of the $2 million pledge occurred almost simultaneously with the beginning of the Great Depression. Stern led the fund-raising efforts for New Orleans. Donations from black citizens and the larger community fell below expectations during the first two years of the campaign and threatened to derail the project. Contributions by African Americans eventually increased, and with the financial support of the white community, New Orleans raised a substantial part of its quota. The new university would have its own seventeen-member board of trustees, six each appointed by the church boards, which in turn appointed the remaining five members. The school derived its name from James H. Dillard, a native of Virginia, former president of Tulane University and agent for the Slater and Jeanes Fund.[37]

Finding an adequate location for the school soon surpassed fund-raising as a potential obstacle to the creation of Dillard. A black newspaper editor asked the Dillard trustees "to give us a suitable site, not less than twenty-five acres because less than that will place us in the same predicament that we are in now." Schools such as Hampton, Howard, and Tuskegee were offered as examples of institutions "with acreage to expand for several years to come." Individuals involved in planning the new university agreed that the school needed sufficient land to accommodate future growth and a campus accessible by public transportation. Securing a suitable site for even a black elementary school in New Orleans often entailed risk, so finding one to create a liberal arts college with at least twenty-five acres was a difficult task. Stern was selected to serve as the first president of Dillard's board and used skill, tact, and his influence within the white community to secure a suitable site with sufficient space to expand. The trustees purchased a seventy-acre tract of land in the Gentilly area of the city for $379,750 and made the sale contingent on gaining city council approval to build the school at that site.[38]

Choosing his words carefully at a 19 June 1930 city council meeting, Stern outlined the plans for the school. He opened his remarks with references to known facts, tracing the origins and progress of the merger plan that had resulted in Dillard's existence and pointing out that the council had "already passed an ordinance granting permission to locate the hospital on Louisiana Avenue." He then shifted his focus to the issue that had brought him to the council chambers. The Gentilly site, Stern pointed out, "was decidedly the most available and the only one which seemed entirely adequate to the requirements, it being obvious that such an institution must build not only for the present but must look towards its requirements for at least one or two generations." If interest in the educational needs of the white community had brought him to the council, Stern would likely have at that point thanked the council members and returned to his seat. As a representative for black higher education, he knew he had to counter white opposition. "In making this decision the trustees had in mind not only the physical requirements of the institution," he continued, "but had uppermost in their thoughts the importance of a selection which would conform with the sentiments of the community, and which would now, and in the near future, tend to promote and maintain a friendly relationship between the races without undue friction." The council accepted an ordinance to build the school and scheduled a hearing for the following week for comments from the public.[39]

When the council met again, several whites attended the meeting to register their opposition. One of the opponents, James Dunn, raised objections identical to those usually made to the Orleans Parish School Board whenever that agency attempted to locate or maintain a black school in an area deemed by some a "white section." Dunn believed that property values would decline, African Americans would move to the area, and friction would increase between the races. Mrs. J. Hildebrand also argued for a different location and noted that "virtually every piece of property in the vicinity of the Rosehill tract had been offered for sale since the property ordinance was offered." Stern again spoke in favor of the city ordinance, and several "prominent" white citizens joined him, including Warren Kearny, a member of Dillard's board of trustees, and John Legier, president of American Bank and Trust Company. In the end the council approved the ordinance, removing one of the last major obstacles to the construction of the school.[40]

Dillard University began operations in September 1935 and, like the two schools it replaced, selected a white president, Will W. Alexander, at the time of his appointment the director of the Commission on Interracial Cooperation. Yet Alexander remained president for only a year after the school opened. And during his official one-year stay as president he was often away from the campus. As a result, board president Edgar B. Stern often assumed the duties of president, sharing academic responsibilities with Dean Horace Mann Bond and budget and finance responsibilities with Albert W. Dent. The trustees conducted a national search to fill faculty positions in hopes of obtaining outstanding scholars, and several joined the faculty, including Bond, Charles W. Buggs, Allison Davis, S. Randolph Edmonds, Frederick Hall, Clarence T. Mason, and Lawrence Reddick. That effort was also influenced by concerns with southern racial etiquette. Board members discussed whether the search for the best faculty should include black and white candidates. In 1935 Stern, who would continue to work tirelessly for more than two decades to make Dillard a first-rate university, adhered to southern racial norms and supported a black faculty. Thus, in the end northern philanthropy could not overcome white southern objections to interracial relationships that brought blacks and whites together as equals. But over the years Stern "softened his earlier stance on segregation" and "learned, grew, and changed."[41]

During the first year 281 students enrolled, and 29 graduated at the first commencement exercise held in May 1936. The following year 36 graduates heard W.E.B. Du Bois deliver that year's commencement speech. Du Bois shared the platform with William Stuart Nelson, the first African American to serve as president of Dillard. In fact, neither Straight College nor New Orleans University had employed an African American president during their existence. For several years Nelson provided leadership, and during his time there composed "Fair Dillard," which became the school song. He resigned at the end of the 1939–40 school year and accepted a position at Howard University. Nelson's inability to raise sufficient money to meet a three million–dollar endowment goal probably hastened his departure. Whatever the reason for his resignation, members of the board of trustees faced an important decision. The board had several African American members, including Straight College graduate Fannie C. Williams. Williams participated in all phases of the search for a new president, and members of the board often sought her advice on potential candidates. In addition, the opinions of board members Phillips Bradley of Queens College in New York, Fred Brownlee, secretary of the American Missionary

Association, Warren Kearny, and Edgar Stern also carried considerable weight.[42]

By September 1940 the short list of possible candidates consisted of Horace Mann Bond, Albert Dent, Charles Johnson, and Robert Weaver. All four men had the support of one or more trustee members. Brownlee made it clear that Johnson was his first choice but thought Dent would make an excellent president as well. Brownlee wanted to know the extent of support Dent enjoyed within the black community and the possible reaction of black leaders if the trustees selected him to head Dillard. He sought a "frank" opinion from Williams. Described by a former student as the "great lady," Williams gave Brownlee her candid assessment. "For the President of an institution like Dillard, I would like to have a man thoroughly trained and prepared in the administration of a college, who knew young people as well as elders, [and] who had a way of life in human relations." Williams did not think Dent was that individual, despite her high regard for his work. "I agree with you in the fact that Mr. Dent has done a good job at the hospital," she conceded to Brownlee. "He has been able to get the hearty support of the local Southern white man as well as men from all over the country. He has many friends among the people of his race." But his lack of a background in higher education was a concern to Williams. Still, Williams assured Brownlee that "if the forward march of Dillard in the right direction depended upon the election of Mr. Dent, I would reluctantly give my assent." If the trustees chose Dent, however, Williams hoped that a "Dean of vision and education would be found to do the type of work which is so essential in a college where leaders and intelligent followers are being prepared."[43] Her comments reflected the then nearly universal acceptance of the idea, long championed by Du Bois and others, that black universities had to train students not just to earn a living but to lead the community as well.

Williams, like Brownlee and members of the black community, recognized that Dent possessed exceptional administrative and leadership abilities. Nevertheless, his lack of an educational background, in the opinion of many of his supporters, made it difficult to select him as president. Dent, at the time of the search, was superintendent of Flint-Goodridge Hospital and Dillard's business manager. His education, training, and work experience had been in business. In a letter to Stern, Brownlee expressed the same level of candor that Williams had expressed to him. Brownlee maintained that "only two of the men possess the qualities and abilities most needed at Dillard." Unlike the opinion held by Williams, Dent was one of Brownlee's two choices. Charles S. Johnson, an educator, researcher, writer, and administrator, was the other. Brownlee considered Johnson "prepared by training, experience, and in his comprehensive, practical outlook on life in all its ramifications to produce a college set-up . . . second to none in America." Dent, on the other hand, had "remarkable possibilities" and could become "an excellent president." If Dent and Johnson were the final two candidates, Brownlee stated that he favored Johnson. If not Johnson, Brownlee indicated his intent to vote for Dent.[44] Stern was so high on Dent and impressed with his abilities, however, that Dent received his unwavering support for the position despite his background. Stern's view became the dominant opinion; the trustees selected Dent to become Dillard's president. It proved to be a very good choice. Under Dent's leadership and the continued commitment of white leaders such as Stern and black leaders such as Fannie C. Williams, Dillard University became an important institution of higher education that trained many students who participated in the community development and liberation struggles of black New Orleans during the Jim Crow era.

By the time of the proposed merger of Straight College and New Orleans University, another institution of higher education for African Americans had opened in the city. Responding to a request from the archbishop of New Orleans, Rev. James H. Blenk, the Sisters of the Blessed Sacrament arrived in the city to start a school for black students. The Sisters of the Blessed Sacrament purchased and renovated the former site of Southern University at 5100 Magazine Street. The new school opened in September 1915 and enrolled black Catholics and non-Catholic students. Katherine Drexel, the founder and leader of the Sisters of the Blessed Sacrament, had a more ambitious plan for the school, and her order possessed the financial resources and commitment to implement it. From the beginning Drexel and her religious order intended to operate a four-year college in the city. Indeed, when the school opened in 1915 it opened as Xavier University, and school officials embarked on an ambitious educational program that within twenty years of its founding in 1915 enabled it to offer undergraduate and graduate programs. High school enrollment continued to increase, and in 1917 the school began a normal department to train elementary teachers. Even though the New Orleans public school system operated a normal department to train white students to become teachers, it did not afford African Americans in the city similar opportunities. African American leaders and educational activists eventually influenced the local school board to change its policy and operate a normal school for blacks. And beginning in 1922, it did, providing Xavier officials the opportunity to expand the university's postsecondary program. Displaying the type of orderly growth that would characterize Xavier's educational work in New Orleans, school administrators first expanded the normal course to a two-year program of teacher education.[45]

The year 1925 was a pivotal one for Xavier; school officials expanded the academic program to include a college of liberal arts, sciences, and education. Xavier's 1918 charter from the state legislature gave it the right and authority "to graduate students and to confer such literary honors and degrees, and to grant such diplomas as are conferred and granted by any colleges, universities or seminaries of learning in the United States and Europe." Xavier officials were rapidly realizing the school's mission statement: "The object of the college is to offer young men and women of the colored race an opportunity of receiving a thorough liberal education." Xavier's curriculum featured a mix of required and elective courses. And students needed a minimum of sixteen high school units for admission, in addition to being at least sixteen years of age and in good health, with good moral character. Thirteen of the sixteen units consisted of courses in English, Greek or modern languages, Latin, mathematics, history, and science. Xavier's academic standards were consistent with many liberal arts colleges of the era, including the requirement of the completion of 128 credit hours for graduation. Tuition and fees for the inaugural year ranged from approximately forty-five to fifty-five dollars per semester.[46]

In 1927 the school started a college of pharmacy "to afford young men and women desirous of entering upon the pharmaceutical profession an opportunity of securing the special training necessary for the successful practice of that profession." Before Xavier started its pharmacy department, African Americans had had to leave the state to receive such training. During the next decade the school continued its progress and added master's degrees in education, English, history, and science. School officials also established a school of social service and maintained evening and Saturday classes for students who could not attend the regular day school. Xavier's growth increased throughout the 1930s, mirroring the overall rise in enrollments experienced by many American colleges and universities during the Great Depression. Pre–World War II enrollment peaked at nearly one thousand students before declining as African Americans, like white Americans, joined the military as volunteers or draftees.[47]

The importance of black higher education to community development, individual initiative, and liberation can be understood not just by looking at black colleges but also by examining the private and public lives of college graduates. For in the end the graduates of these colleges had to make contributions to the larger struggles of the black community before the colleges' relevance to African American advancement during the era of Jim Crow could truly be assessed. While a majority of the black graduates—like most graduates, black and white—did not, or only rarely, participate in activities designed to benefit the community, some did much more, including Lucille Hutton, George Longe, Ferdinand Rousseve, A. P. Tureaud, and Fannie C. Williams. Williams moved to New Orleans in 1898 from Biloxi, Mississippi, to enroll in the high school program at Straight University. She remained at Straight for several years and graduated in 1904 from the normal division. At the time of her graduation, public school officials only funded elementary grades 1 through 5 for black children, which limited educational opportunities and reduced the demand for black teachers. In addition, white teachers still staffed several black schools. With prospects for employment dim, Williams decided to seek a teaching position in her native state of Mississippi. She taught in Gulfport and Pass Christian for four years before returning to New Orleans in 1908. She passed the Orleans Parish Teachers' Exam and accepted an appointment at Fisk Elementary School. Fisk was typical of most of the black schools at that time; it was overcrowded and in need of major repairs.[48]

Williams embarked on her new position with the same degree of commitment and determination that she had observed her mother exhibit as a missionary and educator for the Methodist Episcopal Church. And Williams, for nearly a half-century, worked to advance black education in New Orleans on a scale similar to the accomplishments of Mary McLeod Bethune in Florida, Charlotte Hawkins Brown in North Carolina, Nannie Burroughs in Washington, D.C., and Lucy Laney in Georgia. Unlike these women, she was not a school founder but nonetheless left her mark on black education in the segregated South. During her stay at Fisk Elementary School she assisted African American leaders, parents, and the Colored Educational Alliance in the campaign to improve black education. She contributed in several ways, most immediately and effectively as a classroom teacher. African American children had few sources available to them to gauge their worth to society and to develop self-esteem. She attempted to do this at a period in southern history and of race relations when the white South had perfected and accepted the etiquette of whiteness designed to support and sustain white supremacy and privilege. Williams's demeanor and behavior in the classroom challenged the prevailing ideas of black inferiority. She presented in her dress, speech, and instruction an oppositional framework to her students. She realized she had them for too brief a time, but she was determined to use that time well.

In 1912 Williams accepted a transfer to Miro Elementary School, located in the city's Seventh Ward. Miro existed because of the persistent efforts of the Seventh Ward Civic League to expand school facilities and educational opportunities for African American students. Members of the league had purchased several lots and a double house and donated them to the Orleans Parish School Board for use as a school. After her transfer to Miro, Williams continued her work with the Colored Educational Alliance and also aligned herself with the Seventh Ward Civic League. In 1913 the school board changed the school's name to Valena C. Jones to honor a deceased black educator and civic activist. Williams remained at Jones for forty years and led the campaign that resulted in the building of a modern school plant in 1928. Civic engagement to advance the black community, however, did not diminish Williams's desire for individual growth and advancement. Indeed, she saw the two goals and activities as complementary, one reinforcing the other. Personnel changes at Jones school during World War I illustrate this point. In 1917 school officials selected Williams to serve as acting principal when the regular principal, Hattie Feger, took a leave of absence to pursue graduate study. Before the 1917–18 school year ended, school officials granted Williams a sabbatical to attend Michigan State Normal College, where she earned two undergraduate degrees before returning to New Orleans in 1921. She later received a master's degree from the University of Michigan in 1938 and completed additional graduate studies at Ohio State and Columbia Universities. Forced to travel outside the South for graduate training because she could not obtain it in her adopted city and state made Williams keenly aware of the costs of racial segregation and racial exclusion. She was committed to protest and group struggle even as she advanced as an individual.[49]

"I trust that as the years have passed you have been able to observe the effects of your influence upon my life in general as well as in the area which you and I have such mutual interest and concern," Dr. Mack Spears, who later became the first African American in the twentieth century to serve on the Orleans Parish School Board, wrote Williams.[50] Their "mutual interest and concern" involved teacher training. Williams's efforts to promote and expand black educational opportunity at Jones and throughout New Orleans produced favorable results. School enrollment increased steadily after World War I, and escalating enrollment and the removal of white teachers from black schools created additional employment opportunities for black teachers. In 1931 school officials transferred the normal program from McDonogh No. 35, the city's only black public high school, to Jones and placed Williams in charge. For eight years she simultaneously served as principal of Valena C. Jones Normal and Valena C. Jones Elementary. One former student, Andrew J. Young, who later left New Orleans and became a civil rights leader, ambassador to the United Nations, and mayor of Atlanta, recalled that "Miss Williams went about the task of uplifting the race with great gusto and an almost legendary determination, pacing the halls with her thick ruler ever at the ready."[51] A state law requiring new teachers to possess a bachelor's degree ended the normal school at Jones in 1939. Nonetheless, Williams continued to influence generations of black teachers through summer assignments at Alcorn State College, Southern University, Tuskegee Institute, and West Virginia State College. She also conducted teacher workshops in Alabama, Louisiana, and Mississippi.

Williams maintained an interest in Straight College and served on the school's board of trustees. She was one of the key black leaders (the other was Bishop Robert E. Jones, a 1901 graduate of New Orleans University) who participated in the merger of Straight College and New Orleans University to form Dillard University. She participated in many Straight activities and frequently attended commencement ceremonies. Quite possibly, she was present on the evening of 30 May 1917 when George Longe, the Straight Preparatory School class president, gave his speech, "The Possibilities of the Negro." Four years later Longe graduated from Straight College magna cum laude with a bachelor of science degree. During that commencement program he spoke on "The New Negro Leader." Shortly after graduation he joined a growing list of Straight graduates contributing to community development, individual initiative, and black liberation.[52]

In the following years Longe served as a teacher in several schools, an elementary school principal (Fisk, McDonogh No. 36, Alfred Lawless, and

Macarty), and a secondary school principal (Albert Wicker Junior High). At all of the schools Longe headed, he brought dedication, enthusiasm, and professionalism. He also brought to his task a keen appreciation for the duties and responsibilities of an education leader. For Longe this role entailed more than ensuring that his students had adequate facilities and sufficient playground space. Longe wanted them to acquire the kind of knowledge that would elevate the individual and liberate the race. The black historian Carter G. Woodson also emphasized the benefits of education and maintained that "the education of the Negroes . . . is almost entirely in the hands of those who have enslaved them and now segregate them." And in 1933 Woodson was not very optimistic about the prospects for an immediate change. "With mis-educated Negroes in control themselves," he argued, "it is doubtful that the system would be very much different."[53] The careers of Longe, Williams, and other African American college graduates, however, suggest that it did make a difference. Several activities during Longe's career support this view.

From 1934 to 1936 Longe served as chairman of a public school committee to devise a curriculum that included the teaching of African American history with American history. Several black principals and teachers worked with Longe. The committee's first set of instructional materials and guidelines covered grades 1 through 4. Longe and the other members encouraged teachers to supplement the committee's instructional materials but in bold print warned their colleagues "what to look for and what is not wanted." They suggested that teachers expose the students to contemporary black achievers and cited Langston Hughes and Robert Moton as examples, also recommending the inclusion of deceased leaders such as Paul Laurence Dunbar, Booker T. Washington, and Phillis Wheatley. The committee urged teachers to use "poems and stories that are beautiful in feeling and arrangement." Committee members wanted students to read and appreciate stories and poems that had a "cultural, refined, and exalted spirit." They made clear what teachers should omit as well: material that emphasized black oppression or dialect.[54]

Committee members were well aware of black oppression, white hatred, racial injustice, lynch law, inferior schools, slum neighborhoods, rigid racial segregation, white-on-black violence, crop lien laws, peonage, white primaries, grandfather clauses, residential segregation laws, white-only ads, colored-only signs, back doors, back alleys, and white men–only government. Focusing solely on black oppression, they reasoned, only invested power and control in the hands of whites; it did not empower African Americans. Longe thought that programs that stressed achievement would inspire students to want to achieve. As a result, during the Jim Crow period black principals and teachers placed additional emphasis on African American history during "Negro History Week." As principal of Albert Wicker, for example, Longe had his teachers highlight a particular theme in black history each day.[55] Woodson's belief that "if you teach the Negro that he has accomplished as much good as any other race he will aspire to equality and justice" found expression in black New Orleans because of the efforts of the city's version of a "Talented Tenth."[56]

In 1916 nineteen-year-old Lucille Hutton graduated from the normal department at Straight College. She would later recall that she had "never thought of being anything else" but a teacher. Two factors shaped her career choice: teaching was the profession most accessible to women, and several of her family members were teachers. She spent the 1916–17 school year at McDonogh No. 32 School and the next eight years at Valena C. Jones. Trained as an elementary school teacher, her true love was music. She later rendered her most important contribution to the black community as a music teacher. She prepared herself well for the task with periods of study at Mills College in Oakland, California; Columbia University in New York City; Oberlin Conservatory of Music in Oberlin, Ohio; and Northwestern University in Evanston, Illinois. She earned a master of music degree from Northwestern.

Unlike Longe and Williams and many other black education leaders in the city, including John Hoffman, Hutton never became a principal but influenced the black teaching corps as a music consultant in the public schools. Appointed to the position in 1939, Hutton worked primarily with teachers to strengthen the music curriculum. Many students, because of poverty or isolation, had few opportunities for musical training. This was true even though New Orleans had produced renowned jazz musicians such as Louis Armstrong and Jelly Roll Morton and acclaimed gospel vocalists such as Mahalia Jackson. To expand students' interest in music, Hutton helped sponsor annual music programs at various schools. Eventually, students had the opportunity to participate in annual citywide music and dance festivals. One such program featured "America's Music." The program contained music that expressed the Pilgrims' experience as well as that of Native Americans. Two songs, however, revealed something about the black education experience and the role of black educators in fostering and sustaining community development and liberation in New Orleans. The students performed "God Bless Africa" and "Nobody Knows the Trouble I've Seen." The songs indicated both identification with Africa and an awareness of struggle and resistance by African Americans in the United States.[57]

Obtaining an education, entering a profession, and raising living standards did not separate those like Hutton and Longe from the masses of the city's black population. In fact, the difficulties and challenges faced by many members of the African American community while attempting to advance their education served to deepen their appreciation for struggle and resistance and their commitment to serve their community. Hutton's decision to earn an undergraduate and graduate degree had entailed considerable expense. Unable to secure the type of training she desired at the black colleges because they did not offer it or at the white colleges because segregation laws prevented her enrollment, Hutton had to leave the state for extended periods of time, forcing her to take unpaid leaves from her job. In addition, of course, she had to spend money for travel, housing, and tuition. Sometimes she managed to secure small scholarships and grants but often used her savings or acquired a loan through the school she attended. To complete her studies at Oberlin, for example, she had to borrow $250. Teacher salaries remained notoriously low during this period and for black teachers much worse, so the repayment schedule of $5 for twelve months and then $10 until the loan was paid, though deferred until after graduation, must have appeared burdensome at times.[58]

When Ferdinand Rousseve graduated from Xavier Preparatory High School in 1922, he decided to chart an educational course different from that of other members of his family, deciding to pursue higher education outside the city. The decision was costly and affected his undergraduate academic performance. Lacking adequate finances, Rousseve worked to support himself, taking valuable time away from his studies. Nonetheless, he earned a bachelor's degree in architecture from MIT, a master's degree in art history from the University of Chicago, and a doctorate in architecture and art history from Harvard University. He taught for three years at Howard University during the administration of Mordecai W. Johnson, before joining the faculty at Xavier University in 1934 to start a fine arts department. Rousseve's pioneering work in the fine arts department established a foundation that produced excellent graduates and attracted a stellar faculty. He remained at Xavier until 1948. During his stay in New

Orleans he opened an architectural firm, served on the New Orleans Urban League Board of Directors, and worked for improved race relations.[59]

A contemporary of Rousseve, Alexander P. Tureaud, took an even more indirect route to a professional degree. Born to a Catholic family in 1899, Tureaud lived in the racially mixed Seventh Ward neighborhood. And reflecting the still somewhat fluid state of race relations in turn-of-the-century New Orleans, he had white teachers at both elementary schools that he attended. Still, his home and neighborhood life, along with his church experience, enabled him to gain exposure not only to African American history and culture but to aspects of his black Creole culture as well. As important for Tureaud, however, was the stress placed on education by his parents, especially by his mother. He was a very good student, and, after completing the seventh grade at Bayou Road Elementary School, he looked forward to attending Thomy Lafon to continue his education. The enthusiasm he had for learning and the emphasis his parents placed on it was tempered and soon nullified by the limitations that white southern leaders placed on black education and the meagerness of financial resources of black New Orleanians, even those with middle-class aspirations such as the Tureauds. When Tureaud finished the seventh grade at Bayou Road, the public school system still did not have a high school for African Americans and offered eighth grade at only a few schools such as Thomy Lafon. Unfortunately for students such as Tureaud, who lived in the downtown section of the city, none of the nearby schools offered eighth grade. As a result, Tureaud had to take public transportation to attend Lafon, at times a daunting trip because of neighborhood rivalries and lack of money for transportation. Nonetheless, he persevered for part of the school year, before leaving Lafon in the spring. In April 1914 Tureaud found himself in the same situation as many African American teenagers in New Orleans: out of school and with limited employment opportunities.[60]

A life of self-inflicted limitations, however, would not be his fate. Tureaud worked with his father, a carpenter and contractor, for a few years, until 1916, when he became part of the Great Migration. He left the South like tens of thousands of other African Americans on the Illinois Central Railroad bound for Chicago. And like many of them, he secured employment with the same railroad as a strikebreaker. For his unskilled labor he earned one dollar an hour and free housing. But his role as a strikebreaker caused a certain degree of personal anguish. With assistance from family friends in Chicago, Tureaud soon left the railroad yards and secured employment at a steel plant, a job he held for several months before leaving Chicago to join a brother in New York. Living with his brother and exploring parts of New York brought Tureaud more satisfaction than his job as a dishwasher. His employment fortunes changed considerably when he was offered and accepted a civil service position as a clerk in the law library of the United States Justice Department in Washington, D.C. At last he had found a work environment suited to his contemplative temperament and natural intelligence. Tureaud realized, however, that he needed more than intelligence alone to achieve his growing ambitions. The first thing that he needed to do was earn a high school diploma. He did so and after three years graduated from Washington's famed Dunbar High School. The following year, in 1921, Tureaud enrolled in Howard University's night school law program; he was twenty-two years old.[61] He completed the four-year program in 1925 and returned to New Orleans the next year. "I always had an interest in returning home," Tureaud later recalled, "even though I had opportunities elsewhere. I felt that I might be able to make a contribution." Much had changed in Tureaud's life by the time he returned to the city, and much was changing in parts of the city's black higher education landscape.[62]

3

The Religious Dimensions of Community Development

The early-twentieth-century emphasis on black self-help produced economic activities and an emerging professional class relatively free from white control. The absence of direct economic ties to the white community enabled some leaders to pursue a black freedom agenda without fear of economic retaliation from whites. In an early study on black professionals and the community, the historian Carter G. Woodson documented and analyzed the level of community involvement of black professionals. Although Woodson criticized segments of the black professional class, he conceded that "the Negro professional man because of his outstanding position in the community has been forced to the front in making the appeal for those things which his people deserve."[1] Leadership within New Orleans's black community during most of the first half of the century confirmed Woodson's assessment, and without the contributions of professionals, the community-building efforts of black New Orleans would have been hampered.

At the dawn of the twentieth century the building of modern black America involved the conscious efforts of tens of thousands of African Americans; many of them approached the task confident of ultimate success. In southern communities, both urban and rural, black leaders organized and worked to strengthen their churches, schools, and self-help organizations. African Americans in New Orleans also participated in the community-building campaign. The black church, as it had throughout slavery and the advent of freedom in the 1860s, emerged as one of the most important components of community building. And black Christians continued to believe in an activist God that emphasized human equality and thought of themselves as children of God. They viewed Christianity as a religion of salvation, uplift, and liberation. In their beliefs, practices, and relation to their churches and church leaders, they attempted to live the creative tension that religious scholars C. Eric Lincoln and Lawrence Mamiya termed "other-worldly v. this-worldly." The churches not only were the spiritual vehicles for their religious beliefs and practices but provided meaning to their lives as well. African Americans were active in their churches, participating fully in Sunday services and church governance. Their participation provided leadership opportunities and gave many of them enhanced status within their immediate communities. And religious leaders remained, as they had during slavery and the postslavery period, influential members of the African American community. They maintained positions of leadership by possessing and exhibiting a strong sense of religious faith, knowledge of the Bible, expressive and engaging preaching skills and styles, a commitment to church growth, and engagement with the daily lives of their members. These traits and behaviors were shared by church leaders in all of the denominations populated by African Americans.[2]

"Religion derives from specific human needs and experiences," according to C. Eric Lincoln, and "functions in the interest of helping man to cope with the more traumatic aspects of human existence."[3] To help "cope" with life in general and life in the South in particular, African Americans in New Orleans found religious sanctuary in a variety of denominations. Before the end of the Jim Crow period, all of the major African American denominations had affiliated churches in New Orleans. In addition, major white church organizations, in particular the Methodist, Catholic, and Congregational denominations, also had affiliated African American congregations. Four of the major denominations attracted the most members: Baptist, Catholic, Congregational, and Methodist. Black church life in New Orleans, however, was not a monolithic experience: the religious life of the city's black Catholics, for example, differed in significant ways from that of black Protestants. The establishment and development by Protestants of separate black congregations and religious leadership, a process that had started before the Civil War and found fertile ground after Reconstruction, had no parallel among New Orleans's black Catholic community. The drawing of the color line that began in the 1890s initially strengthened rather than weakened the resolve of black Catholics to remain in integrated churches, in their minds one of the last remaining edifices of Christian brotherhood. It is not surprising that black Catholic leaders in New Orleans opposed efforts to force them from the church, for many of them had led the dogged fight against legal segregation that produced the *Plessy v. Ferguson* suit.[4] At times, however, black Catholics maintained their optimism on faith rather than works, for they often faced discrimination during church attendance and had at best a circumscribed role in church services and affairs. Still, as James B. Bennett shows in *Religion and the Rise of Jim Crow in New Orleans*, "Catholic parishes in New Orleans remained mixed because the city's Catholics of color were loyal to the church and continued to attend Catholic services." They resisted and avoided segregation longer than most black Christians in the city.[5]

The start and development of institutions by African Americans have reflected, to a large degree, one of three trends: exclusion, expulsion, or voluntary withdrawal. Efforts to dislodge black Catholics from white-majority churches in New Orleans failed in the 1890s and early twentieth century despite the actions of church members and officials. Their more complicated route to segregated churches demonstrates the complexity of race relations, tradition, and social change. Beginning in 1888, with the arrival of Archbishop Francis Janssens to head the New Orleans diocese, Catholic leaders promoted the creation of separate parishes for black Catholics with increasing resolve. By the time Janssens arrived in New Orleans, black Catholic parishes existed in northern and southern cities. Janssens's ideas and actions to promote segregated parishes represented a national trend that was linked to an official policy of the Catholic Church. Janssens attempted to convince black Catholics that they would benefit from segregation by insisting that it would provide African Americans with leadership opportunities and the chance to develop their institutions free from white control or influence. Many black Catholics, including black Creole leaders in the city, rejected his arguments and remained opposed to separate congregations.[6] Nonetheless, Janssens pursued the creation of separate black Catholic churches with sincerity and vigor, occasionally voicing dismay with the opposition he faced.

More than the vocal protest of black Catholics initially frustrated Janssens's agenda. The black Catholic community had influential allies within the church hierarchy and could appeal to tradition in the battle with Janssens. In addition, despite the nineteenth-century Americanization of New Orleans, aspects of French culture and influence remained. French influence was particularly evident in the Catholic Church. Janssens, a native of Holland, was the only archbishop between 1865 and 1906 who was not a French native. Some church leaders and black Catholics were bound by their shared French culture and language, and for some church officials this bond was more powerful than race. As a result, local Catholic leaders such as Louis A. Chasse, a native of France who served as chancellor of the New Orleans archdiocese in the 1880s and 1890s, opposed Janssens's plan, just as he had opposed similar attempts before Janssens's arrival.[7] Janssens, however, possessed three substantial weapons of his own: the power inherent in the office of archbishop, the official position of the Catholic Church in 1884 sanctioning separate churches for blacks and whites, and the support of most white Catholics. His first success occurred when he converted an abandoned church, St. Joseph's, to St. Katherine's and organized it as a "national" church, ostensibly open to all Catholics.[8] During dedication ceremonies on Sunday, 19 May 1895, however, Archbishop Janssens made it clear that the designation *national* was but another "thin disguise" for establishment of another all-black institution. Janssens, according to a local reporter for the *New Orleans Times-Democrat,* "was glad that the colored people had a church of their own, where they could come and take any seat in the house that they chose; where they could have a choir of their own, composed of their own people; where altar boys and acolytes could be of their own color; in fact a church for the colored people."[9] Fourteen years passed before another Catholic Church official had an opportunity to express similar sentiments.

Starting and sustaining institutions of any type, including churches, were difficult, problem-filled activities. And the vagaries and challenges related to southern race relations quite often made such efforts exceedingly daunting. This was especially true when African American institutions resided within larger hierarchies such as the Catholic Church. A case in point involved the chronic shortage of priests needed to serve all Catholic parishes. The dearth of priests complicated efforts to create separate black Catholic parishes. Even if Janssens had not met resistance from most black Catholics in the city to remove them from their churches, a shortage of priests would have frustrated his efforts. Reassigning priests to black parishes, he knew, would retard a more important church goal: building the community of white Catholics. Using African American priests to service black Catholic parishes was not an option; through the entire nineteenth century the Catholic Church only ordained five African American priests. Also, in addition to a shortage of priests, the New Orleans diocese "suffered from a lack of money."[10]

Janssens died only two years after the opening of St. Katherine's; his successor, Placide Chapelle, the last of the city's French-born archbishops, maintained St. Katherine's but dropped efforts to expand the creation of separate black Catholic churches. Despite the temporary failure of Janssens's plan, his motives deserve scrutiny. It would be far too simplistic to label Janssens a racial segregationist for his attempts to establish separate churches for African Americans. His comments at the first mass at St. Katherine's may provide a better explanation. By outlining what he hoped St. Katherine's would provide for black Catholics, he also chronicled what the other Catholic churches in the city systematically denied them. Janssens's comments suggest that he realized that African Americans who attended predominately white Catholic churches often faced discrimination within the church or exclusion from church organizations. Indeed, Janssens knew that many African Americans had left the Catholic Church and joined Protestant churches because of ill treatment and discrimination. In August 1893, for instance, he wrote, "There is nothing in my administration of the Diocese that worries me more than our colored people; to see what is done by the Protestants to capture them, & how often they succeed."[11] He wanted to stem the tide of black flight and possibly induce some black Catholics who had left the Catholic Church to return. By his stance, and probably unwittingly, Janssens contributed to the African American community-building process embraced by black Protestants.[12]

The nudge in establishing separate churches for black Catholics provided by Janssens became a firm push when, in 1909, the parishioners at Mater Dolorosa built a new church and voted to exclude black members. Now churchless, the expelled black members, many of them recent arrivals to the city from neighboring St. John and St. Charles Parishes, supported the efforts of Father Pierre LeBeau, a Josephite priest, to organize a new church at the old site of Mater Dolorosa. Refurbished and renamed St. Dominic Church, it opened in March 1909, becoming the second black Catholic parish in the city. This initiative had the endorsement and financial assistance of Archbishop James H. Blenk. Archbishop Blenk had headed the New Orleans archdiocese since 1906 and favored the establishment of separate black churches. Indeed, "it was during Blenk's tenure as Archbishop of New Orleans that systematic segregation was given official sanction and became the established practice within the Catholic

Church of South Louisiana."[13] Janssens had predicted the eventual rise in the development of black churches with the opening of St. Katherine's. "If one succeeds," he had written to Mother Katherine, who in the 1890s was already making financial commitments to African American schools and churches, "we will have far less difficulty with the following."[14] Within the next two decades Catholic officials and the black Catholic community completed the transition to black churches. The change occurred, however, amid continued resistance from some members of "old Creole stock." That opposition, one student of the subject argues, would have been more intense if Catholic officials had not deliberately linked additional school facilities with the maintenance of black parishes. All of the churches had an affiliated school. Many black Catholics and their leaders accepted separation as the price they were willing to pay for increased educational opportunities for their children.[15]

The establishment of black Catholic churches, a move seen by some as surrendering to the proponents of Jim Crow, nonetheless provided black Catholics with an opportunity to maintain institutions vital to their individual development and that of the African American community. After the opening of St. Dominic's, Catholic officials next opened Blessed Sacrament in October 1915. Located on Magazine Street in the Uptown section of the city, Blessed Sacrament shared its site with the newly created Xavier High School. Between 1915 and 1950 nine additional black Catholic churches opened. Corpus Christi opened in 1916 and was an important new addition. As they had since the colonial period, most black Catholics, and those with the most influence, lived in downtown New Orleans in the Sixth and Seventh Wards; Corpus Christi served that area of the city. Because opposition to the establishment of black Catholic churches had been most intense among residents in those wards, the support Corpus Christi received from black Catholics in those areas signaled a shift in attitudes. Again, however, the educational needs of segments of the black community hastened the acceptance of a separate church. Prior to the opening of Corpus Christi, in September 1915 a hurricane hit the city and left extensive property damage in its wake, including Couvent School. Many black Catholics had attended Couvent; it was one of the few institutions maintained by black Catholics in downtown New Orleans. The destruction of the school left an educational void that black Catholic leaders could not fill. The New Orleans archdiocese could and did. The result was another black church and school.[16]

By 1916 New Orleans church leaders had unofficially placed the black Catholic community under the direction of the St. Joseph Society of the Sacred Heart (Josephites). An idealistic English priest named Herbert Vaughn had formed the order in 1866 in hopes of conducting missionary work in Africa and Asia. Father Vaughn remained committed to those two regions but agreed, in response to requests from Archbishop Martin J. Spalding of Baltimore, to conduct mission work among black southerners. The first group of Josephite priests, including Vaughn, arrived in the United States in 1871. Josephites made their first appearance in Louisiana in 1897 in the small rural community of Palmetto and began work in New Orleans twelve years later. The Josephites made an important contribution to black community development in New Orleans. Still, some African Americans wanted national and local leaders of the society to train more African Americans for the priesthood. Indeed, between 1891 and 1954 the society admitted only four African Americans into the order. And during the entire Jim Crow period it refused to assign any of them to one of New Orleans's black Catholic parishes. The Josephite order, of course, was not the only Catholic order with few or no African American priests. But because the Josephites worked exclusively with the black community, many black leaders considered the policy offensive as well as counterproductive to their religious mission.[17]

The social dynamics of race — or, more accurately, Catholic Church leaders' perception of African Americans at the turn of the century — influenced the development of black Catholic parishes and the efforts to recruit and train black priests. Many church leaders, including those fervently committed to black Catholic growth, held negative opinions of African Americans. One church report, for example, claimed that African Americans had low morals and a "proclivity to material pleasures," reaching the conclusion that "they cannot but find a serious difficulty in the sanctity of Catholic morality." The report's author opposed the ordination of African Americans and, despite widespread evidence to the contrary, believed black Catholics, unlike their Protestant brethren, preferred white religious leaders. The report also claimed that black Catholics accepted the view that whites were "from a superior race and hence had greater trust placed in them."[18] Nonetheless, some Catholic Church leaders who shared many of the unenlightened ideas on racial differences expressed in the report supported admitting African Americans into the priesthood. Their reasoning was simple: they believed additional black priests would assist in their goal to increase the number of black Catholics and enable the Catholic Church to administer more effectively to the religious needs of existing and new black Catholics. One church leader, Father John E. Burke, believed black priests would have a better understanding of African Americans and, as a result, structure their evangelizing accordingly. In Burke's view whites "live next door to the negro and yet he is like a sealed book. His lips are closed to the white man. It is only a colored priest who could know all about him." Wanting Catholic leaders to understand his position clearly, Burke forcefully stated, "The Catholic Church will never gain the colored race until she has a colored priesthood." Burke was more than a casual observer of aspects of African American culture; he had worked in African American communities for thirty years. Indeed, one scholar of black Catholicism considered Burke judicious in his assessment and believed that he possessed a "sincere respect for the people whom he served."[19]

Sincere respect by Burke and other Catholic leaders and priests such as Father John Albert, a Josephite priest who also supported the admission of African Americans into the priesthood, did little to alter the restrictive policies on black ordination. The restrictive policies pursued by the various Catholic religious orders affected not only the black community but also the lives of individuals, as the case of John J. Plantevigne illustrates. Plantevigne, a native of Chenel, Louisiana, in Pointe Coupe Parish near Baton Rouge, attended Straight University in the 1890s. John and his brother, Albert, fervently wanted to make a contribution to black community development. The brothers chose religion. But unlike most young blacks who opted for a religious vocation, John Plantevigne wanted to become a priest. He attended Epiphany Apostolic College from 1898 to 1901. By the time he completed his last year at Epiphany, he had successfully negotiated the difficult admission standards and gained admission to St. Joseph's Seminary in 1901. In 1907 he completed his training and received ordination into the society in Baltimore, Maryland.[20]

Plantevigne's career started successfully. In October 1907 he returned to Louisiana for a brief visit and served mass in New Orleans and Chenel. Between 1907 and 1909 he received instruction in missionary work and later worked in several states, including the Lower South states of Florida and Mississippi. He worked with John Albert, a white priest who had been his classmate at St. Joseph's Seminary. Plantevigne and Albert became friends at St. Joseph's, and their friendship blossomed into a deep mutual respect that sustained the two young priests in their early work. The pair encountered stares of disbelief when they traveled together or exhibited expressions of friendship, for they presented an unusual sight in the increasingly racially segregated South. They offered no grand plan for improved race relations and were not part of any network of reformers such as those working in the emerging northern social gospel movement. Some social gospel believers, historian Ralph Luker has argued, insisted that improved race relations would occur through blacks and whites sharing a "common culture of education and religious values."[21] Although they experienced some success in their work, traveling on Jim Crow trains and hearing insults that were commonplace for black southerners tore at the fabric of Plantevigne's soul. His frustration and desire for social justice occasionally found expression in his sermons, much to the consternation of his fellow parish priests.[22]

Plantevigne had much to be angry and frustrated about. The memory of the brutal murder of his brother, Albert, by two whites in Point Coupee Parish still haunted him. After graduating from Straight University, Albert had returned to their home in Point Coupee Parish to start a high school for African Americans. Albert's relatives, friends, and neighbors considered him courageous and thought of him as a humanitarian; whites in the parish saw him as a threat to white supremacy. They subsequently killed him. For the surviving brother Jim Crow was never just a legal issue. Even so, neither the discrimination John Plantevigne encountered nor the violence that threatened his existence prevented him from wanting to work among black southerners. His first choice was to open a school in Chenel. The opposition of the local white parish priest in Chenel and the timidity of his Josephite superiors forced him to abandon the idea.[23]

Archbishop Blenk of New Orleans played a role in John Plantevigne's next disappointment. As part of a mission tour in early 1909, Father Pierre LeBeau of St. Dominic Church agreed to allow Plantevigne to preach at his church. Blenk nixed the idea to avoid opposition from white Catholics. Plantevigne made an unsuccessful effort, including an appeal to the Vatican's apostolic delegate in America, to reverse Blenk's decision. Blenk also opposed efforts to assign Plantevigne to a parish in Palmetto, Louisiana. And requests by black parishioners at St. Katherine Church to have Plantevigne assigned to their church had no chance of success. Blenk was not directing a crusade against Plantevigne specifically; his crusade was to prevent any African American priest from serving in his diocese. After attempts to assign him to other Lower South parishes failed, Josephite officials placed him where they thought he would encounter the least resistance: the first black Catholic parish in the United States, St. Francis Xavier in Baltimore, Maryland. His stay there was all too brief. Tuberculosis and mental exhaustion overcame him, and he died on 27 January 1913. But even in death his beloved Louisiana and South would not hold him. After the death of his brother, the Plantevigne family had moved to Baton Rouge from Chenel. His family's concern about the possibility of renewed violence led to their decision to bury him outside the state. He was buried in Baltimore.[24]

Black Catholics in New Orleans and the rest of the nation had supported Plantevigne in his work and his call for additional black priests. In the end, however, the Josephites abandoned the idea of developing a black clergy, fearing that white opposition would undermine efforts to increase the number of black Catholics more than the use of black priests would help realize that goal. After Plantevigne the Josephites did not ordain another black priest until 1941. Other religious orders had slightly better success. And the opening of St. Augustine Seminary in Bay St. Louis, Mississippi, was an important development for the New Orleans black Catholic community. In St. Augustine Seminary's first graduating class in 1934, one of the four black graduates was a native of New Orleans, Maurice Rousseve, the brother of the architect Ferdinand Rousseve. By 1961 the Society of the Divine Word, which operated St. Augustine Seminary, had added thirty-seven black priests to its order. Despite what some black leaders saw as a dismal record in admitting black priests, the Josephites and the Society of the Divine Word, with the assistance and advocacy by black Catholic leaders, helped to develop and sustain a growing and vibrant black Catholic community in New Orleans. But just as important to the development of the Catholic Church in the lives of blacks in New Orleans was the assistance and advocacy of black Catholic leaders.[25]

One example of the community- and institution-building ethos that influenced and shaped the behavior of black Catholics, and which had parallels among Protestants as well, was their work with the Knights of St. Peter Claver. The Knights first developed in Mobile, Alabama, as a mutual aid and benevolence society for black Catholics patterned after similar organizations for white Catholics, most notably the Knights of Columbus. The tolerance that allowed white Catholics in New Orleans to attend church with their coreligionists did not extend to auxiliary and affinity organizations that serviced both the spiritual and social needs of white members. Excluded from joining those organizations when most black Catholics in New Orleans still attended majority-white churches, once they were secure in their separate churches, black Catholics organized and developed the Knights of St. Peter Claver into a dynamic organization that provided services and benefits to the New Orleans Catholic community. Eventually, New Orleans became the headquarters of the Knights of Peter Claver. That organization became a vital part of the black community through service and leadership development. In addition, its official publication, the *Claverite,* was published in New Orleans and provided news and a forum to discuss religious, social, and political issues.[26]

Protestant clergy and church members also needed the type of commitment to denominational and church growth exhibited by black Catholics. And they also needed committed and unselfish leadership like that of Father John Plantevigne. Robert Elijah Jones, who moved to New Orleans in 1897 to become assistant manager of the *Southwestern Christian Advocate,* the regional newspaper of the Methodist Episcopal Church, was such an individual. The son of a Greensboro, North Carolina, shoemaker, Jones made a commitment to Methodism and the ministry early in his life and became a licensed preacher in June 1891. He remained the assistant manager of the *Advocate* until he resigned in June 1901 to become field secretary of the southwestern region of the Sunday School Union of the Methodist Episcopal Church. For the next several years Jones traveled extensively and worked tirelessly to organize Sunday schools and distribute religious literature. His trips outside New Orleans exposed him to the economic misery and racial oppression of African Americans living in rural areas and helped to shape his religious ideology, which centered on service and community development.[27] He learned and experienced on a much deeper level the accuracy of an observation Du Bois had published in the late 1890s: "The Negro church is not simply an organism for the propagation of religion; it is the centre of the social, intellectual, and religious life of an organized group of individuals."[28]

Unlike most southern blacks who found religious and church sanctuary in the Methodist faith, Jones did not join one of the two major black Methodist denominations—the African Methodist Episcopal Church or the African Methodist Episcopal Church Zion. He affiliated with the northern-based, predominantly white Methodist Episcopal Church. It is not clear if Jones decided to remain a part of the Methodist Episcopal Church because he identified with the denomination's efforts to promote religious interracialism, though that is a plausible explanation. Historian James B. Bennett has argued that religious interracialism influenced the denominational affiliations of many blacks and whites, contending that members of both groups "shared a confidence in the transformative power of their church in American society." But we do well to remember, as Bennett has acknowledged, that interracialism functioned most often at the administrative level within state and national conferences. In essence, then, most African Americans in New Orleans who affiliated with the Methodist Episcopal Church experienced their Methodism in all-black church congregations. Although they were part of what some scholars refer to as the "Greater Black Church," they were only a partially divided denomination and thus still shared aspects of religious rituals and practices with whites.[29]

Jones traveled to many Louisiana communities to promote Sunday schools and Methodism. On 7 October 1901, for example, he visited Gary and the next day Houma, where he encountered heavy rain but a community receptive to his work. He spent 9 October in another small town speaking to a small group in a "plantation church" surrounded on three sides by sugarcane fields. Before returning to New Orleans on 12 October, Jones made stops in Thibodaux and Napoleonville. He arose early the following morning, a Sunday, to help reorganize the Sunday school at Mount Zion Church. He ended the day "in a section of this city where there is a great need of a Sunday school." Jones visited over twenty homes in the area, where he read Scriptures and prayed. The month of October was typical and established the pattern and performance Jones would follow as field secretary for the next three years. That pattern was a familiar one to many members of the black clergy. Historian William Montgomery has noted that ministers such as Jones "were the only group of leaders who crossed the lines between the political, religious, and social realms and who represented the status and economic elites on one hand and the masses of poor and illiterate freedmen on the other."[30]

Jones's work as field secretary was personally rewarding and brought thousands of African Americans into the Methodist fold, many of whom were, indeed, "poor and illiterate" but receptive to the Christian brotherhood and hope that Jones posited as a feature of Methodism. But the days and weeks of travel, often by buggy, proved taxing to Jones and his family. When the editorship of the *Southwestern Christian Advocate* became vacant in 1904, the General Conference offered the position to Jones. He accepted but only partly because it would allow him to spend more time with his wife, Valena, and his two daughters, Grace and Mary. Irrespective of family obligations, the editorship of the *Advocate* was a prestigious and important position within the Methodist Church, a position once held by Methodist leader and founding editor of the *Advocate* Joseph Hartzell. Jones also realized that the *Advocate,* though a religious-oriented newspaper, provided news and editorials that were of interest to black communities in Louisiana, Mississippi, and Texas. Most communities, including New Orleans in 1904, did not have a black-owned newspaper. The *Advocate,* published in New Orleans since the 1870s, became a vital part of Jones's church and community-building efforts. The new assignment brought Jones and his wife closer together, for Valena often worked as a proofreader and literary editor.[31]

Despite Jones's civic and community-building work, he was first and foremost a religious leader concerned with questions of morality, spirituality, and salvation. And from 1904 to 1920 he used the pages of the *Advocate* to implore his readers to live God-centered lives that included a commitment to individual initiative, community development, and black liberation. A key component of that effort, as revealed in his editorials, was the conduct and training of black ministers. Jones knew that church building and individual uplift entailed more than bricks and mortar. He often assumed the mantle of teacher, not just to the congregation but also to his fellow clergy. Those occupying the pulpit, he argued in one typical column, should be dignified, with "no loose swagger of the body [and] no jerking around of the pulpit furniture."[32] According to Jones, the pastoral needs of New Orleans's black community had changed: "In the early days of freedom our fathers who preached without learning to an unlearned pew — and all honor to the pioneer ministers of our race — had only one point of appeal, that was the appeal to the emotions. But to-day when the light of intelligence has dispensed the gloom of ignorance, it is clearly a reflection on the people for the preacher to make his appeal altogether through emotions and not through the channels of thought."[33]

Jones's critique of emotionalism in the pulpit did not reflect the scorn of a disapproving educated elite, but rather, it revealed his understanding of the connection between theology and liberation. A dependence only on style at the expense of substance deprived church members of the chance to hear, and ultimately to ponder and act upon, clear and specific sermons that focused on this-worldly as well as other-worldly concerns. Religious scholars C. Eric Lincoln and Lawrence H. Mamiya's dialectical model of the black church, which regards African American churches as "institutions that are involved in a constant series of dialectical tensions," can be observed in the thinking and work of Robert E. Jones. For worship services, in the opinion of content-oriented ministers such as Jones, should be transformative and speak to the needs of the present and the afterlife. His rejection of emotional preachers reflected another view as well: that progress was measured by change. In this connection, then, standards and accepted practices of preaching used in the nineteenth century had to yield to newer methods that kept pace with black educational aspiration and attainment.[34]

Jones was not alone in his critique of the African American clergy. In the early twentieth century and in later decades, commentary regarding black religious leadership and practices was constant and came from both clergy and lay leaders, both males and females. Concern with the quality of the clergy and the black church reflected, of course, the importance of the church in the lives of African Americans. Few black leaders at the time stressed this point more than W.E.B. Du Bois. In a 1912 issue of the *Crisis* magazine, for instance, Du Bois noted the many positive features and contributions of the black church. Nonetheless, he concluded that "all is not well with the colored church." Several tendencies concerned him. He believed the black church was "still blaming educated people for objecting to silly and empty sermons, boasting and noise, still building churches when people need homes and schools, and persisting in crucifying critics rather than realizing the handwriting on the wall." Because the black church played such an important role, the debates, disagreements, and critiques of church leaders were no mere theoretical exercises. The socioeconomic and political position of African Americans in the first decades of the twentieth century depended on effective group action and leadership, including church leadership.[35]

Like many effective teachers, Jones stressed the positive and provided members of the clergy with specific modes of behavior to which they should aspire. It took a special individual to accept the call to preach, Jones believed, one "secure in his position to declare the whole truth and not to feel . . . afraid." On one occasion he listed the qualities of a good minister: sincerity, frankness, loyalty, reliability, stamina, alertness, mental vigor, moral rectitude, and courage. The emphasis on courage formed a central part of his list of attributes, which perhaps developed during his travels in rural Louisiana, where he saw firsthand evidence of white hostility to black progress. "A preacher must have the courage of a crusader," he often stated "and the endurance and persistency of a saint." Ministers needed courage because the "task of the Negro preacher is to take the slavery attitude out of the Negro. Slavery and Christianity are incompatible," Jones argued. The minister must "have Christian courage to suffer . . . [if he] is to awaken in his race an ethical conscience, a fine sense of moral action and a steadiness of purpose in all things that concern individual and social righteousness."[36]

Jones did not place the burden of spiritual salvation and the achievement of a "steadiness of purpose" solely in the hands of the clergy. Indeed, such a view would have conflicted with his unwavering belief in personal responsibility. Firmly rooted in the black self-help tradition espoused by Booker T. Washington and scores of other African American leaders of that era, many of Jones's sermons and editorials stressed Christian and moral themes related to individual responsibility. Many leaders believed that group advancement depended on the spiritual, educational, and economic elevation of individuals. In that sense the individualistic ethos articulated forcefully by nineteenth-century leaders such as Frederick Douglass remained a vital and successful component of African American thought. It usually, however, operated in the private sphere of African American life, thus existing beneath another type of veil than the racial identity one so often analyzed and referenced by Du Bois. Individual church leaders such as Jones provided black New Orleans with a theology and ideology that stressed individual initiative, community development, and black liberation. The development of black churches and church communities in New Orleans reflected, as it did for black higher education, a working synthesis of the uplift ideology of Washington and the liberation ideology of Du Bois. Realizing that goal, both leaders knew, would require the efforts of thousands of African Americans participating in hundreds of churches.[37]

The origin and early growth of Beecher Memorial Congregational Church offers some insight into the church-building process within the New Orleans black community and demonstrates the diversity of the black church experience. While it is true, as religious scholars contend, that "African Americans have invested more authority in the charismatic personality of the preacher than in any organizational forms of bureaucratic hierarchy," the New Orleans experience also suggests that group-centered leadership was as important as charismatic ministers in the development of black churches.[38] The origin of Beecher is an example of church development that relied on the work of many individuals. In 1901 African Americans started moving to a developing residential area in the vicinity of Elysian Field and St. Bernard Avenues, located in the city's Seventh Ward. By 1904 several members of the Morris Brown Congregational Church had also moved into the area but continued to attend services at Morris Brown. Inadequate public transportation and poor streets, chronic problems in much of New Orleans and pervasive in majority-black neighborhoods, made the more than one-mile journey to Morris Brown difficult in good weather and virtually impossible in bad. On 4 September 1904 several African Americans, under the energetic leadership of Alfred Lawless Jr., Edward H. Phillips, and Frank Simmons, all former members of Morris Brown, organized a new congregation: London Avenue Congregational Church, with Reverend Lawless serving as the first pastor. On that first Sunday, with great solemnity and equally great expectations for their new church, they "enter[ed] in a covenant with one another as a church." A year later the members voted to change the name to Beecher Memorial in honor of Henry Ward Beecher.[39]

Lawless, Phillips, and the other founders realized the difficulties of sustaining a new church. But theirs was an optimistic generation, often willing to endure hardships if they thought progress would result. Concerns for family and community influenced and shaped this attitude. Membership at the church grew slowly, but the members established the normal church procedures and policies, including a nine-member board of trustees. They put in place procedures for accepting members from other churches and held Sunday school services. They also organized a Women's Missionary Society, which, among other activities, assisted the sick and the needy. Women members such as Harriette Lawless and Eliza Phillips helped to build the spiritual life of the church. They also worked to solve the most important challenge encountered by Beecher during the early years: the construction of a church. Real estate prices in the largely undeveloped area were low, allowing Beecher's trustees to purchase two lots on Miro Street for five hundred dollars. After purchasing the lots, the trustees received a five hundred–dollar loan and a five hundred–dollar grant from the Congregational Church Building Society to erect a church. In the best community and self-help tradition, Beecher members, their friends, and their families provided most of the labor during construction. On 14 October 1907 church members heard Rev. Henderson H. Dunn preach the first sermon in their new building. It was a good beginning. During the Jim Crow period Beecher organized and sponsored a Boy Scout troop, childcare center, and other community service programs. The new church structure "was funded and raised as a community effort, and the church building became the community forum, the public school, the conservatory of music, the place where the elocutionary arts, the graphic arts, the literary arts, and the domestic arts were put on proud display."[40] And it was theirs to manage and to grow. It was a place to give witness to love and marriage, to welcome new members into the Christian fold, and to grieve and eulogize the death of current members. And often it was a place to mend one's soul.

An examination of the growth of Central Congregational Church offers additional insight into the church-building process and the role of the church and religion in New Orleans's black community. Central traced its origins to June 1872, when under the leadership of Rev. Charles Thompson thirty-two individuals met for the first time at a newly purchased building at South Liberty and Gasquet Streets. Reverend Thompson, a white theology teacher at Straight University, led the effort, which resulted in the American Missionary Association (AMA) acquiring the building for use by Central for twenty thousand dollars. Few black churches in New Orleans enjoyed such an auspicious start. Eventually, the members did pay the AMA five thousand dollars to defray part of the cost, but the AMA retained ownership of the church until Central relocated in the 1930s. Financial assistance from the AMA remained an integral part of Central's growth well into the twentieth century. Nevertheless, without the vision and commitment of church leaders and members, financial assistance from the AMA, no matter how substantial, would have been insufficient to sustain the church.[41] And in many ways the triumphs and travails of Central between 1900 and 1920 mirrored those of the larger black community. During this period Central members failed to find permanent solutions for many of the church's problems, but they managed to lay the foundation, which made more sustained progress possible beginning in the 1920s.

By the time Reverend Dunn accepted the call to head Central in 1906, the active membership had declined to thirty-five, the trustee board had difficulties reaching a quorum for its monthly meetings, the church building needed repairs, and the church remained dependent on the AMA for

THE RELIGIOUS DIMENSIONS OF COMMUNITY DEVELOPMENT

part of its operating expenses. Dunn, the trustee board members, and the congregation spent the next fourteen years of Dunn's pastorate attempting to solve those problems, which at times appeared daunting.[42] On 5 August 1912, for instance, only Reverend Dunn, David Holland, and Robert E. L. Hutton attended the monthly trustee board meeting, too few for a quorum. Holland, who served as president of the board at the time, shared with Dunn and Hutton the church's grim financial picture. Despite efforts to increase monthly revenues, receipts for July totaled a mere $71, which forced Holland again to authorize only partial salary payments to the pastor and organist. Four members attended the next month's meeting, the minimum needed for a quorum, and money collected during July rose slightly, to $122. Over the next several months collected revenues averaged $93, and consistency in obtaining a quorum remained elusive. The lack of a quorum often prevented the trustee board from making decisions vital to Central's operation. In the spring of 1913 Holland welcomed the decision of the church members to reduce the number of trustee board members needed for a quorum to three. Efforts to boost monthly revenues, however, did not yield such a quick solution.[43]

Dunn, Holland, and other Central leaders understood that improving the church's finances depended on substantially increasing membership and raising per capita contributions. Despite the efforts to increase the number of members, Central remained a relatively small church before the 1930s. On the other hand, efforts to increase church revenues proved more successful. From its inception in 1872, Central's close identification with Straight College shaped its place in the black community and defined, though did not limit, its membership. Thus, by 1900 Central was one of the Protestant churches that attracted members of the city's small but growing black middle class. Teachers, physicians, and business owners made up a significant percentage of Central's membership. As the number of black professionals in New Orleans rose in the first half of the twentieth century, so, too, did the pool of potential Central members. And if Central's reputation for having a black middle class membership kept many blacks from joining, the educational attainment and material wealth of its members enabled Central to assume a greater share of the financial operation of the church.

Central's members never wavered in their efforts to develop their church. It is difficult to identify the specific factors that inspired, and at times seemed to compel, them to continuously strive to build the church.

The addition of nonpracticing Christians, of course, represented a gain to the Christian fold, and that was reason enough for many to work to attract new members. Still others, perhaps, needed a growing membership to validate their own association with Central. Then, too, identification with a "big" and prestigious church inspired some members. It is possible, however, that many of the faithful Central members worked to build their church because they recognized the importance of Central in meeting their religious needs and in developing the black community. The church was not just their spiritual and religious home. The historical secular role of the black church also existed at Central. It provided a place to socialize after services and at church-sponsored events. Members aided black education through need and merit scholarships to members attending college. And Central members and nonmembers received financial help during times of individual or family need.[44] It is possible that some central members believed, as did the black theologian and educator Howard Thurman, that "there is something inherent in the religious experience that always pulls back toward the personal center out of which the individual operates and the religious context that gives existential meaning to the experience itself."[45]

In March 1919 Constant C. Dejoie Sr. became secretary of the newly reorganized trustee board. Other officers included William Jones, president, and Dr. L. T. Burbridge, vice president. The election of new officers and the reorganization of the board reflected dissatisfaction with the state of church affairs. And Dejoie emerged as one of the new church leaders who insisted on immediate and specific changes. Dejoie apparently thought that part of the problem rested with the current pastor, Reverend Dunn, for several of the measures he supported either reduced the responsibility of the pastor or required an enhanced performance. At the April meeting the trustees voted to recommend that the church adopt several new proposals.[46] The eight recommendations encompassed four areas: finances, membership, condition of the church, and church service. To improve the church's finances, the trustee board wanted the finance committee to assume responsibility for the collection of members' dues and assessments. To improve the physical condition of the church, they recommended purchasing new furniture, paying greater attention to cleanliness, and installing better lighting and heating. Although Central was not known for having emotional services, Dejoie and the other members also hoped creation of a committee on church music would improve singing, choir membership, and church attendance. Their concerns were consistent with elements identified as important in creating and sustaining "a dynamic black worship program."[47] The success of the new program depended in part on Reverend Dunn's reaction to the two recommendations that involved him: the trustees wanted him to conduct an orderly service and to preach better sermons. At the church meeting that followed the April meeting, the members approved the list of recommendations. They also recognized, at least implicitly, the importance of Reverend Dunn to the success of the new church initiative when they voted to increase his salary to one hundred dollars a month.[48]

When church members approved the changes, only 90 of the 189 members on the church roll financially supported the church. They would gauge the success of their work by their ability to attract new members. For the next several months church leaders focused on finances and strategies to boost the number of active members. The finance committee, with assistance from a ladies' auxiliary, visited most of the 189 members to explain the new efforts being undertaken to build Central and to convince them to support the church financially. The personal visits had an unexpected result: inactive and active members candidly discussed what they perceived as the problems at Central. Many members criticized the financial practices of the church and wanted church leaders to implement more efficient accounting methods and procedures. Reflecting the new and energetic leadership, the trustee board acted quickly and stipulated that "all monies of the church be deposited in the Commercial Trust and Savings Bank and all disbursements be made by checks bearing the signature of the President and Secretary of the Board of Trustees and Church Treasurer."[49] In addition, several board members received a commitment from church treasurer Mollie Smith that she would discontinue her "loose" accounting practices and comply with the new procedures.[50]

In the fall and winter of 1919 Central members decided to become self-supporting by the following January. They would not, in other words, accept any subsidies for recurring expenses from the American Missionary Association, although they did continue the practice of soliciting and accepting loans and grants for capital improvements. Such institutional decisions, of course, reflected the prevailing ideology of individuals. And the decision to decrease Central's dependency on the AMA indicated that Dejoie, president of the trustee board William Jones, and other members had confidence in their abilities to sustain black institutions. Moreover, the rising tide of optimism that prevailed among many African Americans throughout the country following the end of World War I also found expression in the behavior of black New Orleanians. The end of the war, the approach of a new decade, and the passage of time all pointed to the need for greater black self-sufficiency. The actions and decisions of the leaders at Central were consistent with the new mood in black America.[51] And Central, unlike most black churches in New Orleans, utilized an annual pledge system rather than the vagaries of weekly church collections for most of its operating expenses. This method allowed Central to adopt, each December, a proposed budget for the following year. In December 1919, for instance, the finance committee finalized plans for an "Every Member Canvass" and proposed a 1920 operating budget of $2,000. That figure reflected both growth and caution. Money collected in 1919 totaled $2,038, and in constructing the 1920 budget, the finance committee cautiously anticipated that collections would at least equal the amount received in 1919. A degree of optimism also prevailed because money collected in 1919 exceeded the amount for 1918 by approximately 75 percent. And even a 50 percent increase in 1920 would probably satisfy the most ardent proponents of church growth.[52]

Central's eventual importance as a religious institution in New Orleans owed as much to its organizational structure, its dynamic church membership and leadership, and its affiliation with the Congregational Church as it did to its reliance on charismatic ministers. But in most black Protestant churches charismatic ministers were often necessary for success and growth. And even Central needed an able minister, if not for growth, then at least to retain the members that church leaders gathered into the fold. During the 1920s Central struggled to find the right person for the church and had to issue a pastoral call on three occasions. Choosing a minister, as church leaders all too frequently learned, represented at times a leap of faith. Central's task was more difficult because church members wanted a trained minister with a degree from an accredited divinity school. But many promising candidates were reluctant to consider a position at Central because of its location in the Lower South. Then, too, by the 1920s educated African American ministers had greater career options due to the migration of black southerners to northern cities.[53]

Many black southerners had their mind on a better life outside the South and, realizing that Africa and Central America were not viable options, went North. According to one observer, 50 percent of the positive stories about opportunities for African Americans in northern cities were not true. But it was the other half that helped sustain out-migration from the South. From 1870 to 1910 approximately 470,000 African Americans left the South. In the following decade, 1910–20, more than 450,000 migrated. Three quarters of a million migrated in the 1920s, going to select cities, significantly increasing the black population in Cleveland, Detroit, Indianapolis, Philadelphia, and Pittsburgh. Two cities, however, received the largest number of black southerners and became for some the symbol of both hope and opportunity in America: Chicago and New York. Still, as late as 1940, 77 percent of African Americans lived in the southern states. And New Orleans's urban appeal attracted many of those that remained in the South. During the 1920s, for example, New Orleans experienced a 30 percent increase in its African American population.[54]

The pastoral instability Central endured began in December 1920, when Reverend Dunn resigned to accept the position of secretary of the AMA League of Southern Schools. Dunn, a former schoolteacher, had remained active in education policy and activities through his affiliation with the Colored Educational Alliance and a day nursery operated by Central. Quite possibly, however, Dunn's acceptance of the AMA position was related to the growing tension between him and members of the board of trustees. Dejoie, whose influence in church business continued to grow, often voted against proposals offered by Reverend Dunn. Several of the changes that had been implemented within the past two years transferred responsibilities from Dunn to the trustee board or to various committees. And the sentiment expressed in an entry in the board of trustee minutes book for 5 January 1920 did not bode well for Reverend Dunn. In rejecting Dunn's request for higher pay, the trustees "suggested that when he had by his own efforts so materially increased our membership that we could pay him more we would gladly do so."[55] Two months later they voted against another requested raise. The board's refusal to grant the raise was not based on financial considerations but on its members' evaluation of Dunn's potential to lead the church to its next stage of development. Dunn apparently viewed the salary request not simply as a bid for more money but as a vote of confidence in his ministry. By December 1920 a vote of confidence in the form of a raise had not occurred, and Dunn thought it best to sever his pastoral relationship with Central. Nevertheless, he and his family remained active and influential members of Central. And a close examination of Dunn's work at Central reveals some positive accomplishments. During his ministry the number of active members increased fivefold, church revenues rose, and the church underwent renovations and expansion.[56]

Before starting the search to replace Reverend Dunn, Central's members approved another major reorganization plan. They reduced the number of trustees to nine with staggered terms and requested the resignation of the current board. Members hoped that a smaller group would function more efficiently and would enhance the quality of the board. Although Dejoie and Robert E. L. Hutton voted for the reduction, they both expressed reservations about it because they feared women might be omitted from the smaller board. Their fears were well-founded, for the new board contained an impressive list of individuals—Constant Dejoie, W. W. Hadnolt, William Jones, Robert Hutton, J. A. Palfrey, Arnold Moss, Joseph W. Nelson, James Thompson, and Dr. E. C. Thornhill—but had no female members.[57] The new board took office in January 1921 and began the search for a minister. To attract a "good" and "satisfactory" minister, church leaders knew they had to pay him more than the $100 a month Dunn had received. With a commitment to increase the amount "as soon as the financial conditions of the church would warrant," they agreed on a salary of $125 a month.[58] Central conducted a national search and enlisted the aid of Rev. Alfred Lawless and the Pastoral Supply Office of the Congregational Church. Because none of the black colleges in the city or state offered a divinity degree, Central leaders had to seek candidates from outside the state if they wanted the next minister to possess a college degree. The challenge of finding such a candidate was not unique to Central, for other black communities throughout the Jim Crow period faced similarly difficulties in their attempts to secure educated and progressive ministers. Those individuals were in short supply, especially in the segregated and still educationally impoverished South.[59]

Finding the first satisfactory minister took Central approximately nine months. In the interim Arthur Simmons served as acting pastor and made it known that he wanted the job permanently. In the end church members did consider Simmons but by a greater than three-to-one margin voted to offer the position to A. Angold Brown of Washington, D.C. Despite the overwhelming support for Brown, Central proceeded cautiously and only offered Brown a six-month probationary contract. Brown accepted and began his duties in September 1921. The relationship between Brown and Central started positively and optimistically. Church leaders helped to defray his moving expenses, purchased equipment for his study, including a telephone, and gave him an advance on his November salary.[60] They also made several needed improvements at the church; they painted the interior and installed six gas heaters to replace the coal-burning heaters. But the most significant manifestation of their optimism was the decision to purchase a $2,150 church organ. To finance the purchase, they resorted to a practice that would gain in popularity in the 1920s, payments by installments. Church leaders paid one-third of the price and agreed to pay the balance in twelve monthly installments at 6 percent interest. To meet the monthly payments, they established an organ fund and took "steps . . . to ascertain if assistance could be gotten from the Carnegie Fund."[61] In February 1922 workers installed the organ. Assistance from the Carnegie Fund never materialized, and church members spent the next year finding creative ways to meet the new financial obligation, a practice that one contemporary writer saw as one of the two evils of black church life in New Orleans: the need for constant fund-raising because of indebtedness.[62]

A far more serious problem than meeting the monthly payment for the organ developed during that year. Reverend Brown's six-month contract ended in March 1922, and he then received the standard one-year appointment. Almost immediately, a rift developed between Brown and members of the trustee board and congregation. Initially, tensions arose over financial matters. In April the board members instructed Brown "not to make any bills unless authorized by the board."[63] Brown also encountered the wrath of several board members when he held more than one offering during service. Clearly, Brown sought a degree of independence and autonomy that Central's leadership and members refused to grant him. Soon the power struggle that had started over financial issues escalated into intense hostility. By August 1922 Brown was in open revolt against church leaders and temporarily stopped attending board meetings. He continued to conduct the Sunday school service but restricted his formal conduct with the church to written statements and reports. Reverend Brown's continued association with Central remained problematic for the next several months. A ministry that had started with such promise was quickly unraveling.[64]

In a September 1922 meeting the trustee board failed to reach a decision on Brown; his status remained unresolved for the rest of the year. Terminating the services of a pastor was a task few congregations wanted to undertake, but with the majority of the active members dissatisfied and with recurring financial woes, the congregation knew decisive action, though unpleasant, was necessary. In January 1923 church members voted not to renew Brown's contract and attempted to dismiss him before his current contract expired. Brown, knowing he had some support within the church, refused to accept his immediate dismissal. The controversy divided the church, and some members considered forming a rival trustee board, and others discussed a possible lawsuit. The congregation avoided a complete schism when Emile LaBranche orchestrated a compromise that allowed Brown to remain until 31 March 1923. But Brown's termination was not definitively settled until church members took the unusual step of requesting an ecclesiastical council to rule on the merits of their actions. Several congregational churches participated in the council, including Central, with two delegates—Victoria Pierson and Elouise Thornhill. To the relief of the congregation, the council sustained the action of Central's leadership. Reverend Brown remained in New Orleans and became pastor of another church located only two blocks from Central.[65]

Church members assigned the task of selecting a new minister to an ad hoc pulpit supply committee. The only viable candidate to emerge was W. L. Cash of Chattanooga, Tennessee, and the members invited him to preach a sermon in late May 1923. Cash's visit to the city went well, as did his trial sermon. During his stay in New Orleans and in subsequent communications to church leaders, Cash indicated that he would accept the position only under certain conditions. He wanted the offer to be made by a unanimous vote, a minimum salary of $125 a month, free housing or $25 to $30 a month for rent, a month's paid vacation, money for moving expenses, and a starting date of 1 August 1923. Although some members wondered if the church could afford to meet Cash's terms, the members voted unanimously to accept them and offered him the position. Cash spent July preparing for his move to New Orleans, and church members used the time before his arrival to secure pledges to meet the current and future expenses of the new pastor.[66]

Reverend Cash remained at Central for the next five years, and his tenure was as harmonious as Brown's had been contentious. Cash brought with him clear-cut ideas on the direction he wanted to take Central. One of his major objectives, as he outlined them to church members, was to expand community service. He thought Central should become a leader in that area and serve as a model for other churches. For Reverend Cash no insurmountable dialectical priestly or prophetic tension existed. He was interested in both the spiritual life of his members and the social and political affairs of the community. He also stressed the need for long-term planning and led the push for the eventual creation of a committee responsible for devising a ten-year plan for the church. Cash managed to infuse the members with a new sense of commitment and optimism, qualities that alone did not eliminate the recurring problems facing Central but which gave members greater resolve to remedy them.[67] Indeed, throughout Cash's ministry Central continued to experience inadequate revenues, escalating expenses, and a deteriorating physical plant. The congregation's decision to purchase a house to meet Reverend Cash's demand created additional financial problems that stretched the church's resources. Central members encountered problems not only in meeting the five thousand–dollar purchase price but in covering maintenance costs as well. On several occasions they had to extend the payments and all too often relied on special collections from the members to retain ownership of the building.[68] At one point several members of the trustee board believed Central's poor financial condition necessitated "an awakening in the spiritual life of the church." Other members agreed and believed a "revival would bring about the needed change in the life of Central Church."[69]

Yet part of Central's financial problems stemmed not from a lack of religious fervor but from a more mundane source, its church building. From the beginning it had been both a blessing and a curse, for while its size indicated grandeur and promise, it also consumed maintenance dollars at a prodigious rate. In addition, the concern with membership growth was to a degree related to the size of the church building. The congregation often appeared small to the members when they looked at the vastness of the church on Sundays. Church leaders eventually acknowledged that the building was too large for the congregation. And in the mid-1920s events beyond their control led them to question the wisdom of remaining at the present location. By 1925 the church needed extensive repairs, and the area around the church was becoming a commercial district. Faced with those hard truths, several church leaders, including Dejoie and Emile Meine, thought it best to sell the church. But getting other members to see beyond the church building as "a testament not only to the religious faith of the . . . [members] but to their material progress" took time.[70] Eventually, however, the thinking of Dejoie and Meine became the consensus opinion, and church leaders started accepting offers for the building.[71]

Many of the leaders of Central were professionals and business owners. They considered themselves knowledgeable about business management and real estate values and sought the highest possible price for the building. When to sell and at what price became a delicate exercise made more uncertain because it occurred in the mid-1920s, a period of rising real estate prices and economic optimism. Even a cursory awareness of regional and national trends in escalating real estate values and stock prices would have influenced Dejoie and others to secure the highest price possible for the building. The effect of that economic trend and the thinking of Central's members can be seen in the changing value they assigned to the building. Initially, they thought the church building would sell for a minimum of forty thousand dollars.[72] One year later, in May 1926, the trustee board rejected an offer of thirty-five thousand dollars, which was considerably lower than the new asking price of fifty thousand dollars. In June 1926 the trustees rejected an offer of forty-five thousand dollars and set the minimum price at seventy-five thousand dollars. By late 1928 a softening in the real estate market forced church leaders to lower the price of the building to sixty-five thousand dollars. By then the window of opportunity had closed. The onset of the Great Depression soon made a sale at any price virtually impossible. Filled with thoughts of lost possibilities regarding sale of the church building, Central left the building in 1934. By then it had deteriorated to such an extent that without extensive and costly renovations it was barely habitable.[73]

During the prolonged ordeal of attempting to sell the church building, Central experienced another change in leadership, the third such change of the decade. Reverend Cash resigned for the opportunity to pursue "larger service" at Plymouth Congregational Church in Dallas, Texas. His resignation became effective on 30 November 1928, forcing Central to begin another pastoral search. A seven-member Pulpit Supply Committee chaired by Albert Broussard immediately contacted the Congregational Church for possible candidates. The national search eventually produced several good candidates. But influential members Broussard, Dejoie, and Victoria Pierson opposed filling the vacancy at that time because they believed "the indebtedness of the church was too heavy at present to justify the calling of a pastor under the present conditions." Dejoie, seldom a pessimist or naysayer, argued that retrenchment represented the most prudent strategy. Charles Thornhill and Emile LaBranche disagreed and persuaded other members to accept the view that despite Central's financial problems, the church "needed a spiritual leader and if the right man could be found we could pull through the existing financial difficulty with his guidance and help."⁷⁴ Several months later, in April 1929, church leaders believed they had found the "right man" in the person of Norman Holmes. Reverend Holmes accepted the position and began his ministry at Central on 1 July 1929. At a church meeting two days later Holmes received a warm welcome from the congregation. During the meeting he outlined some of his beliefs and plans for Central. A top priority was greater involvement by children and young adults. Holmes also "favored the establishment of a question box" and discussion among members after Sunday services. Nonetheless, Holmes, like his predecessors, would have to devote considerable time to the task of increasing church revenues and membership.⁷⁵

At the start of Holmes's ministry active membership totaled 178, and the budget was less than forty-five hundred dollars. Holmes and the congregation adopted an ambitious membership goal but a realistic budget for 1930: 100 new members and a fifty-one hundred–dollar budget. In addition to membership campaigns and budget goals, Holmes had to assist in solving the major policy question that confronted Central during his twenty-year stay as head of the church. The decision to sell the old church at Liberty Street and the eventual abandonment of the building made it necessary to find a new home. The search for a new church spanned three decades. When Holmes became involved with the process of finding a new church, Central members were still confident that the old church would sell and that part of the proceeds would help meet the cost of buying a new one. Indeed, AMA secretary Fred Brownlee had assured the group that money from the sale could be used with the only limitation being that fifteen thousand dollars, the amount of AMA's initial investment in the property, had to be repaid.⁷⁶ The failure to sell the old church forced church leaders to alter their original plans. They faced a limited number of options. As the building became more difficult to maintain and the opportunity to acquire a new site more remote, church leaders reluctantly decided to move to a temporary location. They continued efforts to purchase or build a new church. In June 1934 the members voted to relocate to the chapel on the campus of Straight College. At an emotional Sunday service on 2 September 1934, Holmes presided over the last services held at the old church. An anticipated stay at Straight of two to three years grew into ten. And even then, church members had to endure a move to another temporary home before they acquired a new and permanent church structure in 1945.⁷⁷

Central Church had a resource enjoyed by few other black institutions in the city: an affiliation with the Congregational Church's Building Society (CCBS) gave it access to money needed for building repairs, renovations, and, eventually, a new church. Reliance on external funding, though in the main beneficial, occasionally produced tensions between Central and Congregational Church officials. In December 1932, for example, AMA officials nixed a potential agreement that would have enabled Central to build an office building on the site with a maximum value of twenty-five thousand dollars. That provision, in the opinion of AMA officials, made the deal financially risky. Nonetheless, Central members favored the offer and expressed dismay and disappointment when they failed to get AMA approval. Several years later their frustration rose again as they encountered difficulties negotiating loans and grants to erect a church. "We have been disappointed," Dejoie recorded, "so often by the New York office failure to assist us that it is our purpose to build our church as we desire it without their assistance feeling that our independent stand will be a splendid example of Christian brotherhood and community responsibility."[78] Despite such pronouncements, cooperation more than conflict characterized the relationship between Central and the AMA.

In 1941, after years of on-again, off-again negotiations with CCBS officials, Central received a firm commitment of eight thousand dollars in loans and grants toward the building of a new church. It finally appeared that after more than a decade of involvement, the long ordeal was finally approaching a satisfactory conclusion. But events unrelated to Central or the CCBS produced another long delay. The war in Europe and President Franklin D. Roosevelt's decision to make the United States the arsenal of democracy led to the diversion of building materials to the growing war and defense industry. As a result, in October 1941 Central members voted "that the building of the new church be postponed pending more favorable conditions."[79] The "more favorable conditions" came before the war's end and from an unexpected source. The AMA sold the Straight College building in 1943, and the new owners decided to demolish it a year later. Central managed to reach an agreement to purchase the used building material, enabling workers to begin construction of the church. The church clerk, Elouise R. Thornhill, recorded the optimism that prevailed: "Unlike the previous meeting we adjourned in high spirits feeling that God had showered his blessings upon us."[80] On 18 November 1945 Central members held a dedication ceremony for their new church. At the annual meeting on 24 January 1946, Reverend Holmes reported a membership of 447. Many of the longtime Central members — including Constant Dejoie, Lillian Dunn, Lucille Hutton, Emile LaBranche, and Fannie C. Williams — had participated in an important institution-building process in black New Orleans during the turmoil of Jim Crow. At the same time, of course, other African Americans had played similar roles.

What, then, can we learn about black life during the Jim Crow period from the religious and church experience of select churches and congregations in New Orleans? Historians and religious scholars have contended that black churches have been at the center of the religious, social, political, and economic life of African Americans. That was indeed true for African Americans in New Orleans during the Jim Crow era. Turn-of-the-century religious leaders such as the Methodist bishop Robert E. Jones to midcentury leaders such as Rev. Norman Holmes understood the value and importance of Christianity and the church in the lives of African Americans in New Orleans. That level of understanding was evident in the political articles and editorials that appeared in the *Southwestern Christian Advocate* while Bishop Jones served as editor. It was also evident in the work of Reverend Holmes, for example, in providing early childhood education and social welfare programs to Central members and the larger community. Nonetheless, the social, political, and economic role of New Orleans's black churches should not obscure their important religious and spiritual functions. For many black Christians church membership and attendance gave their lives a higher purpose and helped dampen the often sharp manifestations of Jim Crow that existed in New Orleans. In their churches they greeted one another as brothers and sisters, thus reaffirming their belief in the biblical notion of a common humanity. In the eyes of the God they worshipped each Sunday and praised on the days in between, they were all God's children. Their churches were indeed, as they read in their Bibles, "a rock in a weary land."

4

The Secular Dimensions of Community Development

The efforts of African Americans in New Orleans to improve their lives, develop their community, and end racial oppression led them to start and support various secular organizations. The secular organizations they formed and sustained served multiple functions; some were branches or chapters of national organizations. Affiliation with national organizations provided important benefits to African American leaders and the black community. First in importance was the larger perspective leaders gained through participation and contact with black leaders across the nation, especially those who lived in northern and southern cities. This ever-widening web of relations included travel outside the city to attend meetings, conferences, and conventions. African American communities such as those in Chicago, Detroit, and Harlem, New York, for example, served as models and demonstrated the benefits of community unity in the struggle for personal and group advancement and liberation. The concentration of African Americans in urban areas strengthened churches, schools, businesses, and social and civic organizations. It fostered a heightened emphasis on race solidarity, self-help, and race pride. Affiliation with national organizations also enabled local leaders to share in the administrative and financial resources of groups such as the National Association for the Advancement of Colored People (NAACP) and the National Urban League.

The NAACP was founded in New York in 1909 by a group of liberal whites and African Americans concerned with worsening race relations and escalating white violence against African Americans, not just in the South but also in the North. The escalating violence was vividly demonstrated by a race riot in Springfield, Illinois, in August 1908, in which at least eight African Americans died. The NAACP sought to improve the plight of African Americans by employing several strategies. Leaders of the new organization such as W.E.B. Du Bois, Mary White Ovington, and Oswald Garrison Villard believed information, communication, and protest were crucial to the NAACP's success. These leaders operated within the Progressive era ethos that Americans were basically good, and if they were made aware of social problems, they would work to eradicate them. In 1910 the organization began publishing its official magazine, the *Crisis*, in hopes of placing the issue of race relations and black inequality before the nation. Du Bois, the only black officer, served as editor of the magazine and shaped its tone and substance for the next quarter-century. Circulation of the *Crisis* rose throughout the decade and provided Americans with a clear picture of the concerns of African Americans and the state of race relations. NAACP leaders realized, of course, that they needed more than propaganda and turned to the federal courts and Congress for rulings and legislation beneficial to African Americans. For the next half-century the federal courts proved more of an ally than Congress, and even in the federal courts progress was painfully slow.[1]

Headquartered in New York, the NAACP immediately organized and sanctioned branches throughout the nation. Chicago became the first city with a branch in 1910, and a year later branches opened in Boston and Philadelphia. By 1912 the national office had established nine branches. The establishment of branches in the South started slowly. Their slow growth there reflected how entrenched racial segregation and exclusion had become in the South. Nonetheless, according to Paul A. Landix, one of the charter members of the New Orleans Branch NAACP, he and two other black New Orleanians—Emmanuel M. Dunn and James E. Gayle—sought information from the national office about starting a branch in New Orleans as early as 1912. In January 1913 black leaders held a mass meeting to gain local support for the NAACP. Individuals, churches, and other organizations donated money to the organizing effort. Although it is possible that members of the black community operated a branch prior to gaining official sanction from the national office, NAACP records indicate that the branch received its charter on 15 July 1915.[2]

From its inception the New Orleans Branch NAACP was the most active and continuous protest organization in the state during the Jim Crow era. Charter members included males and females: Thomas Bailey, Walter

Cohen, Constant C. Dejoie, Rev. and Mrs. Henderson Dunn, Dr. Rivers Frederick, Mrs. Ida Johnson, Paul Landix, and Dr. George Lucas. Most black leaders during the Jim Crow period belonged to the branch at least some of the time, and eventually most issues involving community development and race relations came through the branch office. The presence of an NAACP branch served as a real and symbolic indication that African Americans in the city remained determined to contest the racial status quo. In addition, the NAACP branch often served as an umbrella organization for the city's various black civic and protest groups, a role that was especially important for a black community with religious, class, and color diversity. This is not to suggest, of course, that dissension did not occur, only that the branch and its focus and activities provided an opportunity for participation and cooperation that appealed to the entire black community. It is well to remember, as one scholar has maintained, that "whatever the nature of disharmony among elements of the black community, the major concern of all classes was their collective subordination as a group to whites, not the internal rivalries that often marked their relations with each other."[3] Indeed, what viable alternatives did they have? "As the diversity of freedom erased the old easy unity," historian Grace Elizabeth Hale has argued, "African Americans constructed new conceptions of their connectedness to counter white control and the increasingly segregated racial order. If whites would see racial identity as the coin of African American exclusion, African Americans would view their racial identities as the source of their communion and strength."[4]

Beginning in the 1920s, the local branch attracted dedicated and talented activists in the struggle against racial subordination, mirroring developments at the national level and in branches throughout the North and South. Nevertheless, the New Orleans NAACP, like many new organizations, experienced its share of problems during its early stages. Attracting and maintaining members remained a challenge, for membership entailed yearly dues, and active membership involved attending monthly branch meetings. More committed individuals or those with more time served as officers or members of the executive committee. Membership in the NAACP also entailed danger, both physical and economic. If a national field secretary such as Ella Baker faced dangers as she "traveled into the bowels of the American South, suffering the insults of Jim Crow segregation and often putting her own life in danger in order to support local antidiscrimination campaigns," local leaders such as those in New Orleans lived that danger daily.[5] The spirit of the aggressively racist Henry J. Hearsey lived on in New Orleans decades after his death in 1900. The historian William I. Hair did not exaggerate when he maintained that "Major Hearsey's detrimental influence upon the racial and political history of Louisiana cannot be precisely measured, but it was significant."[6] Most whites shunned or openly opposed the local branch, depriving the organization of the type of white financial support and legitimacy enjoyed by northern branches, especially those in Chicago and New York. Racial identity became "the paramount spatial mediation of modernity . . . [and] the crucial means of ordering the newly enlarged meaning of America."[7] For the great majority of white New Orleanians, African Americans had a limited and inferior place in the expansive and prospering United States. NAACP leaders, both locally and nationally, worked to build a grassroots organization with a large membership base to improve the political, economic, and social position of African Americans. Then, too, "a sound branch system was important if for no other reason than local members, almost all of them blacks, contributed the bulk of the association's funds."[8]

Recruiting and retaining members were always formidable tasks, but local NAACP leaders embraced these duties and responsibilities with enthusiasm and buoyant confidence. Whether a monthly membership report contained several names or one hundred, local leaders remained positive regarding the branch's growth. "The prospect of the work for the N.O. Branch is very hopeful," the branch secretary, Emmanuel Dunn, maintained in the summer of 1917. The monthly report that he submitted contained eight names, five of them new members and three renewing members. That membership report and the one for the following month suggested that the local branch had had some success in its efforts to recruit members from across the city. Ensuring that the branch was "represented in every meeting that is put forth by the race in the city," as Dunn stated in one report, contributed to the local branch's appeal. NAACP leaders in New Orleans worked hard to extend the appeal of the branch for practical reasons. "Locally," Dunn candidly admitted in one communication to the national office, "we are suffering with many discriminations in our City and State laws," and branch leaders believed that a substantial NAACP membership would better enable them "to bring these conditions before the public."[9]

Throughout 1917 the branch president, B. N. Petty, and the others officers and leaders worked to build support for the local organization. They dutifully held the required monthly meetings featuring guest speakers and music. In October, for example, the branch held the monthly meeting at the spacious Pythian Temple. Speakers included Rev. E. W. White, the pastor of Tulane Avenue Baptist Church, and Mrs. B. A. Perkins, an educator who had recently moved to New Orleans. In December the branch held what it considered an annual mass meeting that also included the installation of officers. The mass meeting served several purposes. In addition to the goal of increasing awareness of the philosophy and program of the NAACP, branch leaders used the mass meetings as fund-raising events. They solicited ads for the souvenir program from black-owned businesses. In 1917, anticipating a large crowd, NAACP leaders again used the Pythian Temple and held the mass meeting on a Sunday afternoon. Those in attendance had the opportunity to meet the new officers slated to assume their duties the following January. The new officers were Rev. E. W. White, president; L. B. Vigne, vice president; E. M. Dunn, secretary; and N. B. Flott, treasurer. B. N. Petty, the current president, retained a leadership position as a member of the executive committee, which consisted of thirteen members, including the officers. Miss Charlotte Richards was the only female member of the executive committee, although females constituted nearly half (three) of the seven-member membership committee. The fourth female to have a committee assignment was Mrs. A. M. Henly, who served on the meeting committee. And it must have been encouraging that the main address at the mass meeting was given by a white man, Rabbi Max Heller.[10]

In late December 1917 Dunn sent the latest membership report to the NAACP's national office in New York. Reflecting membership activities for much of November and December, the report showed the branch had added thirty-three new members and renewed the memberships of twenty-two current members. It also indicated there was support for the local branch throughout the city, but that support was not evenly distributed; most of the members listed in the report lived in the Uptown sections (below Canal Street) of the city, including nine of the fifteen females listed in the report. Fifty-six new or renewing members provided some justification, as the year closed, to believe that the New Orleans Branch NAACP, a relatively new organization in the city, could successfully join the parent organization in pursuing a strategy "to safeguard the full political, civil, and legal rights of colored citizens and secure for them equality of opportunity."[11]

THE SECULAR DIMENSIONS OF COMMUNITY DEVELOPMENT

Many African Americans in New Orleans could support that goal even if they did not hold leadership positions within the NAACP. Rev. E. W. Kinchen, the pastor at Grace Methodist Episcopal Church, was one such individual. A visit by Oswald Garrison Villard to New Orleans in March 1918 prompted Kinchen to write an impassioned appeal to Villard imploring him to visit his church. Noting Villard's "unselfish labor in behalf of my lowly race," Kinchen asked, "Would it be possible for you to come to my church . . . and meet our people of New Orleans and give us just a frank word?" According to Kinchen, "No place is so much in need of a word, such as you will give us, as is this city." More than Villard's presence in the city made Kinchen "bold in praying this request." He was also animated by the conviction that African Americans were embarking on a "new emancipation." In April, Villard spoke at Kinchen's church, helping to cement the reverend's dedication to the work of the NAACP. He wrote the national office, pledging his support, and the response from the national office was immediate and direct: "We will be grateful to you if you will exert as much influence as possible in New Orleans in making the branch of the Association in that city as large and powerful organization as possible." In a subsequent letter to Walter White, assistant secretary of the national office, Kinchen wrote, "I assure you that I will do all in my power to help in the membership drive now going on in the city."[12]

The membership campaign that Reverend Kinchen pledged to join in 1918 had a goal of reaching one thousand members. It was an ambitious campaign and was linked to the national office's "Moorfield Storey Membership Drive." Each branch had a membership quota, and staff at the national office attempted to foster competition among the branches. The New Orleans branch sponsored meetings and hosted events such as "Ladies' Day," all designed to gain new members. Many of the male leaders who were involved in the membership campaign were also active in their churches and understood well the importance of female leadership and participation in the development of community organizations. The presence of women on the membership committee and as leaders in the membership campaign attested to that awareness. Nonetheless, the organizational leadership the local branch presented to the public was usually male. The NAACP was not unique in that regard and likely had more females in leadership positions than most civic organizations that drew both male and female members. But few if any African American male leaders in New Orleans at that time associated the success of membership campaigns with visible female leadership. Nevertheless, male leaders in the local NAACP sought "to get our fair sex behind such a great cause." The desire to expand female participation and leadership in all NAACP branches contributed to the eventual formation of women's auxiliaries. The "great cause" appealed to an increasing number of women, and they remained a vital part of the NAACP's work in New Orleans throughout the Jim Crow period. In the 1920s and 1930s two women especially exemplified the trend: Alberta Dunn and Deborah Guidry.[13]

At different times in the 1920s, when Dr. George Lucas served as the local NAACP's president, both Dunn and Guidry held the position of branch secretary. Dunn, Guidry, Lucas, and other branch leaders built on the earlier organizing work of Reverend White, who retained a leadership position after his term as president ended, as had been the case when White replaced B. N. Petty in 1918. Throughout the 1920s the local branch enjoyed a productive relationship with the staff at the NAACP National Office, even as the leadership in New York changed and evolved. In the main local branches had the most contact with the assistant secretary, field secretary, and director of branches. During most of the 1920s Walter White, William Pickens, and Robert Bagnall held those positions. Lucas, Dunn, and Guidry had the respect and cooperation of the national staff because of their dedication, hard work, and professionalism. In turn they recognized and appreciated the same qualities in White, Pickens, and Bagnall. The result of this mutual admiration and cooperation contributed to the growth of the branch in the 1920s.[14]

Lucas served as branch president in the 1920s and devoted his talent and time to black community development. A native of Lee, Texas, and a 1907 graduate of Flint Medical College, Lucas had built a good medical practice in New Orleans. He was an active member of several organizations, including the Dryades Street YMCA, the Knights of Pythians, and the Elks. He not only joined; he also led. For several years he sat on the NAACP's National Board. His leadership of the local branch in the 1920s encouraged greater African American political and social activism. During his tenure as president, for example, African Americans in New Orleans successfully challenged the city's residential segregation ordinance. Lucas was also active in the Republican Party but did not seek or obtain state or national leadership in the party.[15] His career as physician-activist could have served as a model for the succinct observation that "unless the Negro can exercise the same rights of citizens in voting and holding office, he cannot transfer the will of the race to the government. In organizing the people toward this end and in stimulating their effort to battle for their rights, the Negro physician has contributed more than any other class, with the possible exception of the Negro lawyer." As historian Thomas Ward has demonstrated, activist physicians also were present in Upper South cities such as Baltimore, Louisville, and Washington, D.C., and Lower South cities such as Columbus, Georgia, and Mobile, Alabama. When New Orleans's African American physicians met their colleagues from other cities at national conventions by groups such as the National Medical Association, they discussed not only topics related to their profession but southern race relations and ways to improve their communities as well.[16]

Achieving increased memberships and funding to support the program goals of the NAACP entailed work, persistence, and cooperation between the New Orleans NAACP branch and the NAACP's national office. It also included creativity and the use of advertising and marketing strategies similar to those used by the makers of consumer products. If, for example, vanity could be used to sell cosmetics and body lotions, then it could be used to sell memberships for a civil rights organization. National and local NAACP leaders clearly believed that it could and entertained a range of ideas that would draw attention to the organization. In 1925 and 1926 they considered the feasibility of sponsoring a baby contest to raise money for the local branch and national office. Field secretary William Pickens was especially keen on the idea. In July 1925 he wrote Lucas "to ask if you don't think we could conduct one of our Popular Baby Contests there?" Pickens insisted that a "Baby Contest would not interfere with other efforts to raise money and would serve the purpose of paying you up in full at the National Office."[17]

The New Orleans NAACP branch, like many other branches of the organization, sometimes experienced difficulties raising money to pay its annual appropriation to the national office. Pickens understood this and hoped to secure Lucas's support by linking the baby contest to a financial obligation that the branch was expected and needed to meet. Full participation at the annual convention was one benefit that branches received for paying their appropriation. Pickens expressed confidence that the baby contest "would go big" in New Orleans and pushed for a contest in the fall that would conclude before the start of the Christmas holiday season. He acknowledged the need for female leadership for the event and believed that if the local branch received the commitment of a minimum of "three really interested women," the baby contest would be a success. Lucas, however, was less optimistic regarding the likelihood of success, even with dependable female leadership. The baby contest failed to gain traction in 1925. But Pickens's support for the project and his confidence in its success did not waiver. In early 1926 he again approached Lucas on the subject. Lucas remained unconvinced and explained his position. Lucas maintained that African Americans, like most Americans, were more likely to donate for a specific cause rather than to support the general operations of an organization. Lucas expressed his concern that a "baby contest would likely break into this line of teaching." His own thinking on the baby contest idea did not prevent him from presenting the idea to the executive committee.[18]

The communication between Lucas and Pickens regarding the branch's sponsorship of a baby contest is instructive for a few reasons. It suggests that the NAACP was not just a hierarchical and bureaucratic organization in which decisions only flowed from the national office. The national organization and the staff understood the importance of local branches to the struggle for racial equality and that the struggle was being, and would be, waged in thousands of local communities. Local branch leaders such as Lucas appreciated the organizational expertise provided by the national office. The staff at the national office assisted the New Orleans branch and other local branches in fund-raising and branch development activities. The communication between Lucas and Pickens also raised the always-present goal of expanding support for the NAACP among all classes of African Americans. Pickens's continued push for the baby contest had as much to do with reaching more of New Orleans's black working class as raising funds. "The Baby Contest gives the smallest givers a chance," Pickens believed, and "would call on the great untouched resources of the common masses and even the poorest people."[19]

Attempting to reach the "common masses and even the poorest people," a goal that Pickens continued to stress, kept local NAACP leaders such as Lucas, Dunn, and Guidry busy with NAACP activities. The lofty goal also kept national leaders such as Pickens on the road working with local branches. Appeals for members were a constant theme for Lucas and branch leaders. A typical annual membership campaign consisted of the formation of an expanded membership committee, newspaper advertisements, distribution of informational literature, mass meetings, monthly updates, and assistance from the national staff. Lucas, who possessed excellent leadership skills, used a variety of messages to win support for the branch. His messages were usually positive but occasionally revealed the frustrations that he sometimes experienced as branch president. Lucas expected opposition from whites in New Orleans to the NAACP program. And he could probably accept that the majority of African Americans in the city would not become active NAACP members. At times he bristled at criticism of branch leadership and activities from individuals who, in his opinion, only criticized but were unwilling to "come out and help fight the good cause." Lucas maintained that local NAACP leaders wanted "honest criticism," preferably from those who were willing to "come out and help run things right." Lucas made those comments at the start of an annual membership campaign, words designed to appeal to the conscious of the entire African American community. It is difficult to ascertain how the community responded. Two months into the campaign, however, Lucas wrote to the national office to report that the annual membership drive would continue because the goal had not been achieved. "In the face of the many recent achievements of the NAACP," Lucas reflected, "I am at a loss to find a reason for the indifference of our people towards the Organization."[20]

Lucas realized that more than indifference contributed to membership campaigns that fell short of their goals. The NAACP often competed with other community projects and causes for the financial support of the African American community. To overcome indifference and competition for scarce resources, NAACP leaders were not averse to using contests to gain funds and friends. This was true despite the earlier tepid response to the baby contest proposal. A contest in 1928 and another one in 1929 were typical. Local branch leaders linked both contests to the NAACP's annual conferences in Los Angeles in 1928 and Cleveland in 1929. In a letter to director of branches Robert Bagnall, Lucas offered a rationale for his support of the contests: "I have discovered that the lack of interest in National work is due to the fact that none of our workers have attended the National Conference, and believing that if some of them could attend at least one Conference their interest in the National work would be stimulated."[21] And to "stimulate" their interest the branch sponsored an "On to California or Get an Education Contest." As for many branch activities, females played a prominent role on the contest committee; indeed, five of the six members were women: Miss Viola Conerly, Mrs. T. W. Gottschalk, Miss V. D. Holt, Mrs. M. Landix, and Miss Zenobia Lockett. The contest featured five prizes. The first place winner received a free airline ticket and lodging or a college scholarship. To claim each prize contestants had to raise a minimum amount. The contest and membership drive were successful and raised eighteen hundred dollars. Lucas's enthusiasm and satisfaction were evident when he shared the results of the campaign with James Weldon Johnson, the NAACP national secretary. "We now have the largest membership in our local branch we have ever had," he noted. Given the difficulty that the local branch had experienced paying its appropriation to the national office in past years, Lucas probably took special pride in reporting that the branch had exceeded its appropriation. Lucas did well to bask in the glow produced by the success of the contest held in 1928, for a similar effort the following year unfortunately produced different results.[22]

The 1929 membership campaign started slowly and eventually fell short of the goal. The slow start was due in part to competition from other fundraising projects. Nonetheless, Lucas promised the national office a successful membership campaign, or as he termed it, the branch would "put it over at any cost." That cost in 1929 would be exceedingly high. Even the formation of a membership committee presented a challenge. Securing commitments to serve on the committee was usually an easy task, so the lack of volunteers was a clear indication to branch leaders that another contest would be needed. Instead of Los Angeles, the destination for that year's winner was Cleveland. All the other prizes remained the same as the ones offered in 1928. Robert Bagnall pledged the support of the national office and promised to come to New Orleans whenever branch leaders determined that it would assist the campaign and confessed that "it is always a pleasure for me to visit New Orleans." By mid-April the contest was fully operational, and Lucas started to make arrangements for Bagnall's visit in May. Competition from another fund-raising project again forced Lucas and branch leaders to alter their plans. Lucas suggested that Bagnall postpone his trip until June. "On account of the other activities here," Lucas admitted to Bagnall, "we find it very difficult to put over our drive successfully." But, he insisted, "we will do the best we can."[23]

Doing their best would not be sufficient to complete a successful membership campaign, not only in 1929 but for most of the 1930s as well. In December 1929 Lucas gave Bagnall and the national office a bleak assessment of that year's events and activities. "Unfortunately everything has gone wrong with our NAACP work in New Orleans this year. Our regular membership drive in the spring had to be postponed on account of the

YMCA drive. In the summer the street car strike plus the general financial depression put New Orleans in the worse fix ever witnessed." The financial "fix" for African Americans worsened before it eventually improved and continued to affect the local branch's fund-raising and membership campaigns in the 1930s. Writing in June 1930, a statement by Lucas could have been made by any branch leader in the 1930s. "Everything that could possibly happen to hinder our drive has happened," Lucas lamented. But Lucas indicated that he was "making a strenuous effort to make another and larger report" by July. He was optimistic that financial conditions would improve later in the year, which would enable the branch to complete a successful membership campaign. His midyear optimism that financial conditions would improve, a view shared by millions of Americans, was not realized. Leaders of the New Orleans NAACP continued to experience difficulties in reaching annual membership and fund-raising goals. African Americans in New Orleans were not alone in their struggle to maintain financial support for the NAACP. Indeed, national membership totals would not exceed levels reached before 1929 until after World War II. Failure to reach fund-raising goals during the 1930s, and in previous and subsequent decades for that matter, did not prevent the branch from addressing issues of racial injustice.[24]

The lack of support for fund-raising and membership campaigns was not the only obstacle to building an effective NAACP branch in New Orleans. Another problem that at times hindered membership recruitment and growth involved internal dissension within the branch; the dissension, however, was usually minor and involved clashes of personalities more than ideology. Strong and effective local leadership was often sufficient to reconcile differences and proved crucial to the branch's growth. The importance of effective leadership of the New Orleans Branch NAACP, irrespective of profession, was evident during the 1930s. During that decade both George Labat and Dr. Aaron Brazier served as president for several years. They served during a period of acute financial distress for many African Americans in the city, which presented immense challenges to achieving effective branch leadership. Their leadership styles—or, as some charged, their lack of leadership—helped to erode support for the branch. As a result, the African American community lost confidence in their leadership and the branch's effectiveness.[25] In early January 1932, for instance, a local black news editor wrote NAACP national secretary Walter White complaining that "the selfish influences which now control the dormant local branch are so intolerable that I prefer not working with them," but he nevertheless promised to conduct a fund-raising activity to benefit the national office. White was understandably pleased with the pledge of financial support and quickly acknowledged it.[26] The content of the letter also underscored the steady need to cultivate and expand an effective black leadership base in New Orleans.

Although not all African Americans professionals in New Orleans embraced active civic leadership, many of them did. And whether they led reluctantly because they "often had a difficult time avoiding leadership in their community," in the end many accepted the challenge.[27] One of the many professionals involved in community development and liberation activities in New Orleans was Dr. Joseph Hardin. A native of Scooba, Mississippi, Hardin had come to New Orleans in 1890 and attended Flint Medical College, where he received a degree in 1904. He decided to remain in the city and started a medical practice that he maintained for several decades. During the 1890s he developed an interest in politics and remained an active Republican throughout his life. His foray into politics soon led to involvement in other civic activities. In 1912, for example, he helped organize the Fourth Ward Poll Tax Association as part of an effort to increase the number of black voters. Concern about conditions in his Seventh Ward neighborhood led Hardin to assist Alex Mollay in forming the Seventh Ward Civic League. Soon Hardin assisted other black leaders in organizing similar groups in various wards. From these neighborhood groups developed, again with Hardin's leadership, the New Orleans Federation of Civic Leagues. The federation and the ward-based civic leagues attempted to solve community problems, especially those related to education, race relations, and politics. It is important to note, however, that the efforts of Hardin and other Federation of Civic Leagues leaders built on the work and momentum of earlier organizations such as the Colored Civic League of New Orleans. And all of these community-building and uplift efforts had parallels in other cities.[28]

The Federation of Civic Leagues emerged as one of the most important black organizations in the city and aided the community development effort in several ways. One of the many consequences of African Americans' second-class citizenship was the neglect of their neighborhoods by city officials. The neglect took many forms, including poor sewerage and drainage service, irregular garbage collection, inadequate street improvement, and insufficient police protection. Members of the federation worked with residents to make city officials more responsive to their neighborhoods and, because of the uneven success of that effort, impressed on black citizens the need to solve problems themselves. The federation participated in neighborhood beautification campaigns and residential rehabilitation efforts. Sustaining support for neighborhood improvement was a constant challenge, for some African Americans exhibited apathy that mirrored city officials' indifference. Federation members often found themselves trying to convince black residents to take positive measures to improve the physical environment, only to have the residents point to the inaction of city officials as justification for their own lax behavior. On the other hand, city officials pointed to the behavior of residents to justify their neglect. Despite resistance within and outside the black community, the federation helped to improve the quality of life for African Americans.[29]

Efforts by leaders and members of the federation to improve black education usually involved cooperation with other organizations, especially the Colored Educational Alliance. Founded in 1913 by a group of African Americans led by Rev. Henderson Dunn, the alliance became one of the city's leading advocacy groups for improving black education during the Jim Crow era. Composed of professionals and nonprofessionals, the group directed its efforts at the guardians of public education: the Orleans Parish School Board. Alliance members never attempted to mount a challenge against Jim Crow; they did attempt, however, to wring as much from the separate-but-unequal public education system as possible. One of the biggest challenges they faced was convincing white citizens and leaders that African Americans needed educational opportunities comparable to those of whites. At various times they informed school officials that African Americans needed additional schools, extensive repairs to existing schools, high school facilities, commercial and industrial training, and a better curriculum. And to get their message across, alliance leaders frequently used the tactics and strategies employed by white progressive leaders in the city. The first generation of black leaders in New Orleans during the Jim Crow era believed that race relations and conditions in the black community would improve if whites and African Americans possessed "facts" and "truths" gained through scientific studies. Reverend Dunn and other alliance leaders gathered statistics, photographed school facilities, interviewed parents and teachers, and visited schools as part of their scientific study of black education. They often used the information in petitions presented to school officials that detailed the inadequate resources directed to black education. This strategy remained a favorite tactic throughout the first half of the century.[30]

The Colored Educational Alliance, like the Federation of Civic Leagues, received assistance from other groups. Between 1900 and 1960 black New Orleanians formed numerous organizations dedicated to improved education. Several organizations such as the Third Ward Educational Association, the Seventh Ward Educational League, and the Ninth Ward Civic and Improvement League attempted to address the needs of an entire ward. Many of them were small and focused on the needs of a particular school or neighborhood. All of the public schools had "Mothers' Clubs" or "Patrons' Clubs." Judging from communication received by public school officials, the school-centered organizations were active and to a degree effective. Members of these clubs could be counted on for school-based fund-raising, supporting petition drives for improved education, and attending school board meetings. Their effectiveness, however, went beyond gaining specific improvements and programs at their neighborhood schools. Their school-related activities and advocacy underscored and reinforced their message to their children of the importance of education. Most of the participants in the school support clubs were members of the working class or lower middle class and demonstrated to their children and the African American community that educational aspiration was not the sole domain of the established middle class.[31]

The various civic and protest organizations provided a communication network for black leaders and active members but not necessarily the entire community. On 19 September 1925 the *New Orleans Herald,* which soon after became the *Louisiana Weekly,* began publication under the leadership of Constant C. Dejoie Sr. For at least two decades prior to its inception, African Americans, either because of financial inability or unwillingness, had not continuously supported a race-specific newspaper. After the demise of the *Louisianan,* in 1882, no other black newspaper, except for a promising but short run of the *Crusader,* edited by Louis A. Martinet, had attained the number of subscribers and revenues needed to survive. The New Orleans–based *Southwestern Christian Advocate* provided some coverage of the black community, but it failed to become a paper for the entire black community, possibly because of its anti-Catholic and pro-Methodist stance. The *Louisiana Weekly* was secular and inclusive, however, and from the beginning espoused a clear mission. "We believe," the paper declared in its debut edition, "that in matters pertaining to race, a newspaper should not straddle. There is only one course for a newspaper to take in matters pertaining to Negro life and that is the right side." Acknowledging the historical community focus and collectivist ethos of African American newspapers, the debut editorial observed, "Negro newspapers are not the property of the individuals who have them in charge, but the property of the Negro public whose interests they should serve." As a member of the Associated Negro Press, the *Louisiana Weekly* had access to news concerning African Americans from across the nation, and being able to share that news strengthened the existing bonds of a shared racial identity.[32] The black writer and civil rights activist James Weldon Johnson stated it succinctly in an editorial: "They are race papers. They are organs of propaganda. Their chief business is to stimulate thought among Negroes about the things that vitally concern them."[33]

The *Louisiana Weekly* reflected Johnson's claim and remained steadfast and true to its stated aims, usually echoing the sentiments of the black community and helping to define vital issues. More than an organ of race chauvinism, it printed articles and editorials that challenged Jim Crow in its many manifestations. Not surprisingly, race relations articles and editorials were regular features. The weekly newspaper maintained continuous coverage and commentary on issues such as discriminatory voter registration practices, unresponsive white political leaders, the corrosive effects of incivility of white citizens, police misconduct, and racial segregation. The critique of prevailing race relations practices included what can be considered theoretical constitutional and legal issues as well. But enduring Jim Crow was a lived experience. The publisher, journalists, and editors of the *Louisiana Weekly* never forgot that fact and, by highlighting the realities of life under Jim Crow, built and maintained strong support throughout the entire community. One editorial, for example, criticized city officials and white community leaders for successfully blocking the opening of a theater for African Americans. According to the editor, the theater did not open "because of all the chicanery and political maneuvering of the white people [that] was brought to bear to keep a playhouse from opening for the colored brother so near the heart of the business section."[34]

Constant Dejoie and his staff did more than focus on the discriminatory practices of whites; they at times chided members of the black community for their failure to work aggressively for social change and for their misplaced priorities. "The Carnival season is here with all of its beautiful decorations and multitudes of visitors from every corner of the globe. This season means gaiety. The visitors are seeking pleasure. They will find it because New Orleans is noted for its hospitality and the many ways of entertaining," began an editorial that read like a typical celebratory piece extolling Mardi Gras. The editorial, however, was intended to politicize the African American community. "To the outsider within our gates everything appears to be as a smooth running piece of machinery," it continued, "but to us who toil here daily for our bread, can see deeper than the Carnival veneer of good times. Many members of the group will don gay costumes and add their voices and presence to the gaieties, while at the same moment something that is a vital necessity is being left undone."[35]

Such editorials suggest that the *Louisiana Weekly* was engaged in an ongoing conversation with African Americans in the city and hoped to cultivate progressive African American leadership from within and outside the professional class. "It may be, since law makers and educators neglect us," a frustrated editor stated, "lacking militant members in the higher professional groups to fight for us, we may look hereafter to the laboring men to protect our interests and make the way for us."[36] Good leaders, however, often needed better followers, and the *Louisiana Weekly* remained adamant about the need to cultivate greater activism within the black community. Consistent with the self-help tradition, the newspaper implored African Americans to do more to help themselves in throwing off the odious yoke of oppression and discrimination. In language that both Booker T. Washington and W.E.B. Du Bois might have used, one editorial maintained that "too long have we as a group sat supinely by and with weeping and wailing bemoaned our lot. And now must we remember that only when we act, act as men, act as thinking men, act, act, will we find ourselves the recipients of these things that are our just and legal right."[37] The decision to "act" helped African Americans in New Orleans gain important community development and individual goals. One such goal involved activities designed to improve health care opportunities for African Americans.

The architects and supporters of Jim Crow sought more than racial segregation; they wanted black economic subordination as well. As a result, most African Americans labored at the economic margins. This system affected the material wealth of individuals and families as well as institutions vital to the African American community. Low subsistence wages meant, among other disadvantages, inadequate health care. New Orleans, for all its citizens, was not a healthy city, and for those at or below the economic margins an illness could easily advance from serious to acute to fatal. Indeed, in the 1890s the death rate of African Americans actually increased from 36.61 to 42.4 per 1,000. Whites in the city, on the other hand, experienced a decline from 24.41 to 23.8 per 1,000. Health experts at the time understood that what today are considered lifestyle factors contributed to the differences. But differences in access to health care, especially hospitals, played a greater role. The Phillis Wheatley Club, an organization of black women, recognized the need for additional health care in the 1890s and sought ways to provide it. In 1896 the members organized the Phillis Wheatley Sanitarium and Training School for Nurses to meet some of the health care needs of New Orleans's black community. During its brief existence Wheatley leaders and supporters had to contend with two main problems: a shortage of medical personnel and inadequate finances. These problems were eventually too difficult to overcome, and the reasons why reveal some of the issues and challenges that African Americans in New Orleans encountered in their attempts to build race-specific institutions during a period of substantial economic, social, educational, and technological change.[38]

In 1901 New Orleans University assumed control of the hospital as part of its medical school, Flint Medical College. University trustees changed the name to Sarah Goodridge Hospital. In the ensuing decade, however, the inability of New Orleans University to maintain the level of medical education at Flint Medical College demanded by the American Medical Association—and to a degree an American public increasingly concerned with higher standards and professionalization—became apparent to school leaders and supporters. And any ambiguity regarding the ability to offer adequate medical education at New Orleans University was quelled with the release of a study conducted by Abraham Flexner for the Andrew Carnegie Foundation for the Advancement of Teaching. The report (*Flexner's Medical Education in the United States and Canada*), though highly critical of the state of medical education in the United States, became one of the foundational pieces of medical education reform and improvement in the country. Some of the problems noted in the study included inadequate or virtually nonexistent admission requirements, inadequate funding, and low academic and clinical standards. Two areas, however, were subjected to scathing criticism: commercial medical colleges and the sheer number of medical colleges. "It has, in fact," the study charged, "become virtually impossible for a medical school to comply even in a perfunctory manner with statutory, not to say scientific, requirements and show a profit." The result, the study's authors predicted, would be "but a short step from an annual deficit to the conclusion that the whole thing is wrong anyway." The anticipated demise of the commercial medical colleges, which the study called for, would of course reduce the total number of medical colleges. Further reductions would result when "universities realize that medical education is a serious and costly venture; and that they should reject or terminate all connection with a medical school unless prepared to foot its bills and to pitch its instruction on a university plane."[39]

In 1910, when the study appeared, some universities had already started that process, including Tulane, located in New Orleans. Although it was not acknowledged in the Flexner study, over the previous several years New Orleans University had also begun to upgrade its medical education at Flint Medical College. The improvements, however, were uneven, unsustainable, and short of the emerging minimum standards for medical schools. In January 1909 twenty-four students attended Flint Medical College, instructed by a teaching staff of fifteen. The study noted the college's "scant equipment in anatomy, chemistry, pathology, and bacteriology" for use in laboratory work. Clinical facilities consisted of the twenty beds at Sarah Goodridge Hospital. Funding from fees and a small appropriation from the Freedmen Aid Society of the Methodist Episcopal Church represented the school's only income. The study determined that Flint Medical College was "in no position to make any contribution of value" to medical education for African Americans. Flint and four other African American medical colleges were, according to the study, "wasting small sums annually and sending out undisciplined men, whose lack of real training is covered up by the imposing M.D. degree."[40] But there were exceptions to that dire assessment.

The report concluded that Howard University Medical College, in Washington, D.C., and Meharry Medical College, in Nashville, Tennessee (affiliated with Walden University), provided creditable medical education and should be supported and strengthened. The plan to close poor performing medical schools proceeded with support from private foundations and the Council of Medical Education of the American Medical Association. For Flint Medical College that process occurred almost immediately. In 1911 Methodist officials decided to end medical education at New Orleans University and closed Flint Medical College. They decided, too, to retain the nurse training program and health care at the renamed Flint-Goodridge Hospital. By the time it closed, the college had graduated 102 physicians. Many of the medical school graduates remained in New Orleans, and some of them provided support and leadership in the development of the city's African American community. Despite their presence, improved health care for black New Orleanians remained at times an elusive community goal, as it did for African Americans in other southern cities.[41]

African Americans in New Orleans were often caught on the proverbial horns of a dilemma. On the one hand, community development involving large financial outlays and the cooperation of public policy makers depended on the support of whites. On the other hand, the views and ideas of whites quite often failed to meet the goals of progress envisioned by the African American community. In addition, the continued insistence that with substantial white financial support, even from funding agencies located outside the South, came white administrative control produced challenges and problems. A case in point in New Orleans involved Flint-Goodridge Hospital. In the 1920s friction and tension developed between the white administrator of the hospital, Dr. T. Restin Heath, and African American students in the nurse training program. In 1925 the students decided to stage a strike to protest what they considered "unbearable conditions." The students gained little from the strike, but African American physicians received "a voice and recognition in handling the affairs at the institution." For some African American physicians and leaders in New Orleans, however, the limited "voice" was not sufficient.[42] They addressed the inadequacy by forming the New Orleans Colored Hospital Association, composed of physicians (including Rivers Frederick and R. J. Vinning) and community leaders (including Constant C. Dejoie, James E. Gayle, Joseph P. Geddes, and Arnold L. Moss). These individuals had been in the forefront of many community- and institution-building efforts in the city and believed they could raise sufficient money to start a hospital for African Americans. And indeed, they achieved some success, raising tens of thousands of dollars in donations and pledges. Plans progressed enough for them to acquire a building, before the effort stalled and became part of a larger campaign to improve African American access to hospital care. Just as African American physicians had grown dissatisfied with relations with the white leadership at Flint-Goodridge Hospital, nearly everyone affiliated with the hospital, including the patients it served, were dissatisfied with the outdated and inadequate facility.[43]

Methodist officials eventually decided to replace the old hospital with a new, modern one and to make it the centerpiece of a larger black community development project to close both New Orleans University and Straight University and to create Dillard University. This campaign, unlike the plans of the New Orleans Colored Hospital Association, garnered support from white leaders in the city. New Orleans had to raise $250,000 of the campaign goal of $2 million. To meet part of New Orleans's share and that of the African American community, in March 1930 the New Orleans Colored Hospital Association committed to transferring its assets (property, donations, and pledges) to the campaign for the new hospital. The proposed new hospital, the *Louisiana Weekly* confidently predicted, "will be a success and a benefit to the masses of Negroes who are unable to get the proper hospitalization because of the very limited facilities offered them."[44]

On 31 January 1932 the atmosphere was festive in the Uptown section of New Orleans. Band members and marchers milled about, awaiting their turn to assemble. The air was cool and the sky clear as spectators arrived and began lining the sidewalks. A visitor to the city might have assumed the activities indicated the start of one of New Orleans's many Mardi Gras parades, for it was indeed the Carnival season. But no floats, masqueraders, or intoxicated revelers lined the streets on this occasion. The participants and spectators for this event were witnesses for a different type of celebration, a significant event in community development in black New Orleans. The dedication ceremony for the opening of the new Flint-Goodridge Hospital attracted blacks and whites throughout the city. The presence of whites indicated the level of interracial cooperation that made the hospital a reality. Here again, however, white support from national and local leaders in the fifth decade of the Jim Crow era reflected for most of these leaders the belief that racial segregation and racial exclusion were permanent. In addition, many white leaders still acted on the correct observation that health conditions in the African American community directly affected the health of the entire city. Interracial cooperation meant different things to black and white leaders. Most African American leaders rejected the permanence of racial segregation even as they worked among themselves and with white leaders to develop and strengthen African American institutions. But they did share with white leaders the conviction that improved conditions within the African American community redounded positively to the larger community. Indeed, that thinking formed a core strategy of African American uplift ideology before and during the era of Jim Crow. African American leaders had to be flexible in their approach and vision, resulting in Washingtonian race-specific projects such as Flint-Goodridge Hospital and Du Boisian projects that challenged the Jim Crow order such as the NAACP.[45]

After the new hospital opened, Flint-Goodridge's administrators and medical staff began providing health care to the African American community. Albert W. Dent, a native of Atlanta, Georgia, and a graduate of Morehouse College, served as superintendent of the one hundred–bed hospital. Dent came to Flint-Goodridge with impressive credentials. Prior to accepting the job, he had headed a successful fund-raising effort at Morehouse College and before that had served as vice president and auditor for the Safety Construction Company in Houston, Texas.[46] Dent was considered a talented administrator and drew considerable praise from the local black newspaper at the time of his appointment. "The selection of Mr. Dent," a *Louisiana Weekly* editorial stated, "is an admirable one as this young man is regarded as one of the most capable business executives in the South."[47] Dent possessed good interpersonal skills and self-confidence, traits that served him well as head administrator of a unique organization. At the time of his appointment he also enjoyed the unwavering support of influential whites in New Orleans, especially Edgar B. Stern and his wife, Edith. Several years into his tenure as head of the hospital the Sterns' support had only deepened. The Sterns, he appreciatively noted in a letter to Edith Stern in 1938, had "been a source of much inspiration to me since I have been here, and I am grateful for the interest and support which you have always given."[48]

The board of trustees of Flint-Goodridge Hospital, in close cooperation with New Orleans's black physicians, selected an interracial medical staff to work with Dent. The decision, though hailed in contemporary accounts as evidence of better race relations, also reflected the limited access to effective medical education for African Americans in the era of Jim Crow. When Flint-Goodridge opened its doors in February 1932, few of the African American physicians in the city had served an internship. And of the thirty-three doctors on staff at Flint-Goodridge, only two possessed internship experience. Hospitals throughout the South usually denied black doctors access to training or practicing opportunities. In New Orleans the state-supported Charity Hospital, throughout the Jim Crow era, barred black physicians from practicing medicine at the hospital. Limited training opportunities for African American physicians extended, of course, beyond the South. Indeed, Dr. Daniel Hale Williams had led the successful effort to start Provident Hospital in Chicago so black physicians could have access to training.[49]

Faced with a trained but inexperienced group of African American physicians, leaders at Flint-Goodridge Hospital attempted a different approach. They persuaded doctors from Louisiana State University and Tulane University medical schools to serve as senior and junior consultants with the dual task of providing patient care and physician training. The trustees and leaders of the African American medical profession intended the arrangement to last only until African American physicians gained sufficient experience. They hoped that in time African Americans would head all of the departments. The selection of Dr. Rivers Frederick to head the surgery department when the hospital opened made African Americans leaders cautiously optimistic that the lack of leadership positions for African American doctors at the hospital would be temporary. Dent and Stern shared that view and worked to prepare for a transition to African American leadership in all the departments. Through focused training and advanced studies opportunities, the continued cooperation of white physicians and medical schools, and financial support from foundations, African American physicians eventually led all departments at the hospital.[50]

A native of Point Coupee Parish, Rivers Frederick came to New Orleans to attend Straight University and later Flint Medical College of New Orleans University. He decided to seek his last year of medical school training in the state of Illinois and received his degree in 1897. After stops in his home parish and several years residency in Central America, Frederick returned to New Orleans in 1908. He did so because of his "growing desire to return to the place of my birth in order to help train young Negroes for adequate service in the growing field of medical practice, badly needed among our people." Unfortunately, shortly after his arrival in the city, Flint Medical College closed its doors for the last time. Most African Americans who desired medical training had to travel to Nashville, Tennessee, to attend Meharry Medical College or to the nation's capital to attend Howard University. The opening of Flint-Goodridge Hospital, however, gave Frederick an expanded opportunity to train young African American doctors in his capacity as staff physician and chief of surgery. Frederick, and other physicians who labored under less than ideal conditions, provided African Americans with medical care not readily available anywhere else.[51]

THE SECULAR DIMENSIONS OF COMMUNITY DEVELOPMENT

Ambitious and motivated individuals such as Dent and Frederick helped to sustain and strengthen black institutions. Dent, for example, combined vision and administrative talent to produce innovative and efficient health care for black New Orleans. Dent realized that a one hundred–bed hospital could not meet the total needs of a growing African American community of over 100,000. He measured success, as did most African American leaders, not in terms of eliminating all problems but by how much they were reduced. Through his leadership at Flint-Goodridge Hospital he addressed specific health care issues such as high infant mortality, prenatal care, sexually transmitted diseases, and insufficient health awareness. In addition, Dent assisted in meeting the goals of the trustees and African American leaders that Flint-Goodridge would serve as a teaching and training hospital for African American doctors. This goal greatly assisted the advancement of health care because patients without access to Flint-Goodridge Hospital benefited from the improved training that African American physicians received.[52]

Before leaving Flint-Goodridge to become president of Dillard University, Dent amassed an impressive record. Through various community programs the demand for health services increased. The number of clinics grew from seven to thirty. In 1937, 20,000 patients received treatment at the various clinics. Consistent with the desire to make the facility a true community health center, one of the clinics, Medicine B Clinic, offered services at night twice a week. Other clinics included dentistry, gynecology, surgery, urology, and treatments for diphtheria, diabetes, and venereal disease as well as pediatric, well-baby, and ear, nose and throat services. To make the clinics as accessible as possible, Dent reduced the already low fee of twenty-five cents to ten cents in 1937. Dent retained the fee not so much to cover the cost of clinic visits "but rather to establish in the patient a sense of responsibility and self-reliance."[53] Even in something as vital as health care, African Americans leaders recognized the value of the self-help, uplift ideology because they believed that it was crucial for community development and personal advancement.

Often, however, business pragmatism influenced Dent's decisions at Flint-Goodridge as much as his continued belief in uplift ideology. Nonetheless, the decisions made for strictly business reasons frequently advanced and met the collective needs of segments of the black community. This was true of an innovative health plan Dent started in 1936. When Flint-Goodridge opened in 1932, hospital officials reserved twenty of the one hundred beds for indigent patients. Those beds were always filled, but the beds allocated for patients with the ability to pay sometimes operated at 50 percent capacity. Flint-Goodridge was a private hospital and depended on the collection of fees to meet a considerable portion of its operating costs. Dent first took steps to increase the number of private patients by convincing black public schoolteachers to join a hospital insurance program. For an annual premium of six dollars, members received health care when needed. Dent soon managed to enroll black postal workers as well, but the number of patients receiving free services remained at more than 50 percent. To address that problem, Dent instituted a program he called the "penny-a-day plan." "In order to reach the persons in the lower income levels," he later recalled, "a plan was devised during 1936 whereby complete hospital service could be secured by groups of employed individuals for $3.65 a year." The penny-a-day plan brought additional members into the insurance program. Community outreach programs and the offering of low-cost health insurance made Flint-Goodridge accessible to working-class blacks and prevented it from becoming a health care enclave only for the black middle class. African Americans throughout the city thought of Flint-Goodridge as "their" hospital and a vital component of black community development. Flint-Goodridge's large and modern facility on Louisiana Avenue stood as a visual reminder of black New Orleans's community-building efforts.[54]

By 1940 the development of institutions that in many ways made black New Orleans a community within a community did not produce a completely segregated society for African Americans. Throughout the Jim Crow period black and white leaders engaged in meaningful and constructive communication and cooperation, as the interracial work at Flint-Goodridge suggests. Usually the cooperative efforts involved government-sponsored programs and services such as schools, playgrounds, infrastructure improvements, and police protection. Another example of interracial cooperation was the establishment of the Urban League of Greater New Orleans in 1938. By 1930, historian Kevin K. Gaines has argued, some national African American leaders, including the intellectual and journalist Hubert H. Harrison and sociologist E. Franklin Frazier, had started to question the true benefits to black communities of groups such as the National Urban League. For leaders such as Harrison and Frazier, "racial uplift ideology and its assumptions could not keep pace with the whirlwind forces of change."[55] But most African American leaders in the

South, including those in New Orleans, did not see racial uplift ideology only as an idea imposed on them and as an accommodation to racial segregation and exclusion. For them it remained, as it had from the beginning, both a challenge and an accommodation to Jim Crow.

The opening of a branch of the National Urban League in New Orleans provided African Americans with another link to a national organization and a boost to their community-building efforts. Organized in 1911, the National Urban League established branches in cities to assist urban blacks, especially in the Northeast and Midwest. Urban League branches sought to improve employment opportunities and housing for African Americans. Although the Urban League avoided a direct challenge to white privilege and power, its pursuit of black economic advancement conflicted with policies designed to keep African Americans in their "place," especially in the South. The Urban League, to a greater degree than the NAACP, needed the support of white Americans, for whites controlled employment and most levers of the nation's local, regional, and national economy. In southern cities, where whites used economic measures to buttress white supremacy, Urban League members had to exercise caution, patience, and tact. And black leaders had to bide their time as they worked to improve race relations. By the late 1930s several black leaders thought the time had come to organize a branch of the National Urban League in the city.[56]

The impetus for the Urban League emanated from the existing institutional structure of black New Orleans. Albert W. Dent, superintendent of Flint-Goodridge Hospital, and Rev. Norman A. Holmes of Central Congregational Church provided early leadership. Both men believed African Americans needed a citywide organization that directly addressed economic and social issues. In transforming that sentiment into action, Dent and Holmes received cooperation from individuals and organizations within the community. The Council of Social Agencies, a white-run organization headed by Wilmer Shields, rendered valuable assistance throughout the organizing process. In addition, the National Urban League, through its southern field director, Jesse O. Thomas, supported the effort. The effort gained momentum when, on 6 March 1938, black and white leaders hosted an organizing meeting at St. Mark Fourth Baptist Church. Several speakers—Isaac Heller, a member of the Orleans Parish School Board; Archie E. Perkins, an educator; Bishop A. P. Shaw of the Methodist Church; Wilmer Shields; Jesse Thomas; and Bishop R. R. Wright of the African Methodist Episcopal Church—traced the history of the National Urban League, discussed some of the problems that needed attention in the black community, and requested support in starting a branch in New Orleans. The success of the movement, several leaders stressed at the meeting, depended on raising enough money to staff an office. In other words, blacks and whites had to demonstrate their commitment with money. Once again, black citizens displayed their support for community development and racial uplift. Before adjourning, the participants selected Rev. W. Talbot Handy to chair the campaign committee within the black community and Marshall Ballard Sr. to assume the same duties within the white community.[57]

Reverend Handy received and welcomed the assistance of black community activists, and he immediately started contacting individuals and organizations asking for their support. Black businesses, especially insurance companies, promised to assist in meeting the fifty-two hundred–dollar quota assigned to the black community. Labor groups such as the Railway Mail Clerks and the National Alliance of Postal Employees also made pledges. The Omega Psi Phi Fraternity was one of several fraternities and sororities that provided financial assistance. Reverend Handy also received help from black churches and religious leaders; several churches hosted neighborhood meetings designed to garner support for the Urban League. But the force that sustained Handy's effort and contributed to its eventual success was the persistent effort of dedicated activists, many of them black women. Mayme O. Brown, Lola Dixon, Wylene Saizon, Elouise Thornhill, and Mrs. L. L. Whitfield, for example, played prominent roles in the league's formation.[58]

Marshall Ballard achieved similar success within the white community but encountered different problems than those faced by Handy. Ballard operated within a community that not only recognized its own development needs but possessed the material resources necessary to address them. His task, then, entailed convincing white leaders that the program deserved their support and would benefit the city's whites as well as blacks. As a result, Ballard framed his appeal to emphasize the social welfare orientation of the league rather than its economic agenda, which stressed improved employment for blacks. He also directed his efforts at the city's small group of white moderates and liberals. In the late 1930s the terms *moderate* and *liberal* could be applied to white leaders and community activists in New Orleans who accepted the idea of varying degrees of black social, educational, and economic advancement, within the context of a segregated South. Some of them believed that white privilege and power could be maintained alongside black advancement, and some, no doubt, were willing to remove racial barriers entirely. If Ballard had compiled a list of white moderates and liberals in 1938, it would have been considerably longer than a similar list compiled in 1900. Ballard's organizing efforts brought him into personal contact with white leaders such as Rabbi Julian Feibelman, Isaac Heller, Rosa Freeman Keller, Archbishop Joseph F. Rummel, Edgar B. Stern, and John Minor Wisdom. These white leaders donated money and successfully derailed attempts to label the Urban League a communist organization, and several of them remained committed to achieving better race relations in New Orleans. Keller, for instance, contributed not only money but considerable time and social capital to the effort.[59] This group of influential whites put into practice in New Orleans what the white writer and truly racial liberal Lillian Smith thought was needed. "There is a grave need for the white man and the black man in the South to understand each other," she insisted. "It is a necessity today for the intelligent white to use all the imagination he can lay hold of in an attempt to put himself in the Negro's place and learn how it feels to be there."[60]

The work of Handy, Ballard, and hundreds of others culminated, in November 1938, in the opening of the Urban League of Greater New Orleans office at 1010 Dryades Street. Marshall Ballard served as the first chairman of the board of directors. Constant C. Dejoie was the highest-ranking African American on the board. He served along with three others as vice chairman. The other top four positions also reflected a commitment to interracial cooperation. Two African Americans served as secretary and assistant treasurer, Blanche Best and A. J. Sarre, respectively. The large board of directors included female and male leaders of both races. The board appointed Clarence A. Laws as industrial secretary. He directed the daily operations of the league with the assistance of an office secretary. Laws later became executive secretary, the league's top position in local branches, and helped to make the Urban League a valuable and complementary component of the development efforts of black New Orleans.[61]

When Booker T. Washington delivered his Atlanta speech in 1895, as contemporaries understood and scholars have demonstrated, he spoke to both black and white America. Washington knew, as did others, that the activities of African Americans did not occur in a vacuum and would invariably elicit a white response. New Orleans's black leaders during the first three decades of the twentieth century embraced parts of Washington's philosophy and several of his programmatic initiatives. Many, however, did so without accepting his philosophy of limitations, which assigned, at least for the foreseeable future, African Americans to the lower rungs of the nation's social, economic, and political ladder. Early-twentieth-century leaders such as Reverend Dunn, Bishop Jones, and Emile LaBranche shared Washington's appreciation of the interplay of black activities and white responses. They realized that efforts to gain full equality for African Americans entailed more than black community development and protest activities; such efforts also involved active participation in the affairs of the larger New Orleans community.[62]

Segregation and white hostility limited the opportunities for African Americans to engage in civic activities but did not eliminate them. African American citizens and their leaders attempted to take advantage of civic opportunities whenever possible and at the same time sought to expand their opportunities for broader engagement. Citywide charitable drives and poll tax campaigns were annual events that provided black citizens with opportunities for civic participation. Emergencies related to natural disasters (floods and hurricanes, for example) and the two world wars produced additional opportunities. African Americans, of course, were aware of the irony of participating in poll tax campaigns, given that the poll tax existed in part as a way to keep black citizens off the voting rolls. But revenues from the poll tax went toward education, and payment of the poll tax became a litmus test of civic responsibility. New Orleans's black teaching corps led the way in this effort by consistently reaching the goal of 100 percent participation. Normally one individual coordinated poll tax campaigns from each school. Black teachers, such as the sixty-four-member faculty at Thomy Lafon School in 1933, realized that paying their poll tax strengthened the claims of black parents and leaders for improvements in black education. Few of them understood this better than George Longe, who for many years served as chairman of the poll tax campaign for the black public schools.

Longe involved himself in a myriad of activities that reflected the collective aspirations and behavior of the larger African American community: individual initiative, community development, and black liberation. His behavior and career dramatically illustrated that African Americans during the Jim Crow era, while pursuing full citizenship and community goals, were equally committed to personal and professional advancement. To be sure, many of them accepted the view that the knowledge they gained, the income they earned, and the experience they received should in some way benefit their race. And in that sense they embraced the challenge implicit in the idea of a Talented Tenth. Nonetheless, Longe and others knew that their individual efforts would improve their standards of living, self-esteem, and community status. It was not necessary to forsake individual initiative to pursue liberation strategies. Indeed, the evidence strongly suggests that the collective striving of thousands of individuals for personal improvement made the black liberation struggle possible.

Participation in Community Chest drives produced results similar to those achieved in poll tax campaigns. African American leaders such as George Longe embraced opportunities to become involved with the Community Chest, for black New Orleanians derived benefits from their participation: the chest donated money to several black agencies, and being involved demonstrated civic spirit. Such participation reflected the deliberate and conscious nature of efforts by African Americans in New Orleans to strengthen their community. One piece of literature distributed in 1935, for example, contained a picture of an African American boy of about ten years of age carrying a much younger boy on his back. The caption at the bottom read, "He's Not Heavy—He's My Brother." And to the left of the photo and caption appeared the statement "Help the Chest, Help Our People."[63] That is not to suggest, however, that the majority of the city's African Americans gave to the chest expressly to demonstrate their civic spirit. A campaign chaired by Longe in 1935 was typical and stressed the level of financial support the chest provided to black agencies. But beyond financial support African Americans understood that helping their people also entailed the challenging and difficult task of improving elementary and secondary education.

5

Public Education

By 1900 the idea that African Americans needed at most only the equivalent of a primary and grammar school education and the right kind of manual and industrial training had become the dominant philosophy guiding black education throughout the South. Black education would not include training for careers or occupations that would enable African Americans to compete successfully with whites in the fast-changing industrial-technical economy of twentieth-century America. When white leaders and citizens thought of the ideal type of black education, they thought of Hampton Institute in Virginia and Tuskegee Institute in Alabama. School board members and political leaders in New Orleans wanted their city to join the rest of the South in providing African Americans with the "proper" kind of education. Education for black advancement throughout the South was replaced with attempts to make education a blunt instrument for enforcing white supremacy and black oppression. Through custom, law, and school board policy, whites in New Orleans attempted to establish what they considered African Americans' proper place in society. African Americans, however, rejected the policy of limited education and worked to expand educational opportunities. Less optimistic about achieving a nation or city of "one people" than they had been during the 1870s and 1880s but nonetheless determined to fashion an educational agenda to fit their needs, African Americans in New Orleans started the difficult work of gaining educational equity within the framework of "separate but equal."

Barred from politics through legal and extralegal means, segregated in or denied access to public accommodations, and employed in mostly menial jobs, many African Americans saw education as a way out of the quagmire. During the Jim Crow period the quest for improvements in education became the only sustained form of protest that the black community directed against the citadel of white political power and supremacy. Between 1900 and 1960 the tactics and strategies changed, but the goals and focus remained the same: improved schooling consistent with the principles of full citizenship and equality. Through the various organizations they formed to improve education for the black community, black leaders fought for specific objectives and refused to accept the mandate of white leaders to use education as a means of racial oppression. They had their own idea of their proper place in New Orleans society. Using protests, petitions, and constant pressure on school officials, African Americans won some victories. Their protest strategies centered on three areas. First, they sought to expand black educational opportunity by forcing school officials to provide black students with high schools as well as vocational and evening schools. Second, they fought for improved conditions within the schools — an upgraded curriculum, better facilities, and a smaller pupil-teacher ratio. Third, they attempted to obtain an all-black teaching corps. Although black leaders and parents achieved some of their education goals during the Jim Crow era, especially in the 1940s and 1950s, educational opportunities for African Americans remained unequal to those available to white students.

Racism and discrimination involved more than the emotional, ritualistic, and sadistic random killing of African Americans. Racial discrimination was organized, purposeful, and directed toward maintaining white domination. To that end school officials in New Orleans and throughout the South pursued policies of limited education for black southerners. By 1900 local school officials no longer expressed much concern regarding low black student enrollment or made references to maintaining equal school facilities for African Americans. The policy damaged black educational advancement in at least two ways. First, it occurred at a time when school officials had begun a significant expansion of educational opportunities for white students, which further widened the educational attainment gap between black and white children. In addition, the policy of limited education was not consistent with the desire of the black community to use improved education as an instrument to aid individual advancement and community development. The condition of black education reflected to a large degree the racial ideology of the dominant population.

White southerners had definite views concerning the kind of education African Americans should receive. Overcrowded schools, unsanitary buildings, rented annexes, and a general disregard for the educational needs of the black community stemmed from their desire to keep blacks in an inferior position in the social order.[1]

Moreover, as historian James D. Anderson has pointed out, other ideological currents influenced black education. Anderson maintains that the debate "was not in any significant sense a conflict between extreme racists and moderate racists. There were racists, extreme and moderate, who both supported and opposed the idea of universal public schooling for blacks and whites. There were also extreme and moderate white supremacists who favored a racially restrictive form of universal education." What, if not race, determined black educational policy in the South? According to Anderson, "conflicting conceptions of the relationship between political economy and universal education" were key. Southern reformers and their northern allies placed their faith in the conforming powers of education. By contrast, the agriculturalists had no reason to abandon their traditional and effective methods of coercion and force. New Orleans's urban environment, however, did not possess an agriculturalist-reformist dichotomy. The debate in New Orleans centered on whether black education would serve as a means to improve the socioeconomic position of blacks or as a brief way station to inculcate social deference and rudimentary skills in reading, writing, and arithmetic for a lifetime of manual or menial labor. Racism was the key variable that united most whites in New Orleans in supporting limited education for blacks.[2] But despite the persistence of racist ideology, alternate views on black education existed. Three main views regarding black education usually framed the debate in New Orleans during the Jim Crow era. Most African Americans, of course, thought black students should receive an education comparable to that of whites. They articulated their opposition to limited black education clearly and often. Some school officials and city leaders advocated and supported improved black education, although their support stopped short of a belief in providing equal facilities and the same curriculum for blacks and whites. Another group, as personified by white civic leader and school board member James Fortier and accepted by large segments of the white community, wanted a continuation of the policy of limited education for blacks — education at the elementary level with some manual training. Nonetheless, despite white opposition, black education progressed throughout the period, yet it always trailed the gains made by whites.

Such progress was at times painfully slow and was made more difficult because of a decision by the school board in 1900. That year the New Orleans public school system reached an educational nadir for African Americans. In response to a request by black parents and leaders to extend kindergarten classes to several black schools, several school board members believed such a discussion provided a "favorable moment at which to call attention of the board to the work of our colored schools and suggest a change in the curriculum and character of work to be done in these schools." The task of making the most of the "favorable moment" fell to the board's elementary school committee, which recommended the discontinuation of grades 6, 7, and 8 in the black schools. And in grades 1 through 5 the committee wanted "to make that education useful, thorough and practical as far as it goes, and to fit him or her for that sphere of labor and social position and occupation which they are best suited and seemed ordained by the proper fitness of things." The school board adopted the recommendations and instructed the superintendent to put the new policy into effect for the 1900–1901 school year. Four years after the separate-but-equal decision in the *Plessy v. Ferguson* case, two years after the state's constitutional convention substantially accelerated black disfranchisement, and one year after the Supreme Court's decision in *Cumming v. Richmond County Board of Education,* it was not difficult for the black community to connect all the political dots. "Disfranchisement is evidently the gateway to complete subjugation" of African Americans, the *Southwestern Christian Advocate* had asserted, but "it is left to the City School Board to take the latest and most decided step towards the Negro's consignment." Few blacks or whites, but with different interpretations, would have disagreed with the *Advocate*'s position.[3] At the same time, however, African American parents and the black community had to guard against educational apathy and not allow white leaders to dampen their resolve for expanded educational opportunities. Members of the Phillis Wheatley Club, for example, many of them educators such as Sylvania F. Williams, accepted that challenge and regularly urged black parents to register and send their children to school. They knew that increased black school enrollment would strengthen their demands and hopefully place some pressure on school officials to improve black schools.[4]

The refusal of the school board to allocate sufficient revenues to black schools serving the five permitted grades accounted for their poor condition, but it raises several important questions. What philosophy or policy guided school board members in their budgetary decisions? How many members had clearly defined ideas on the desired purpose and scope of black education? To what degree did the articulated educational aspirations of African Americans influence school board policy? Several members and school officials used the school board meetings as a forum to voice their views on black education and race relations. At the beginning of this period several board members maintained that New Orleans should duplicate the policy of other southern cities and limit black education to the primary grades, emphasizing manual and domestic training. Advocates of the primary-manual training school philosophy attempted to fashion a program for the present as well as the future. When Sol Wexler, who was emblematic of this type of thinking, resigned his position as president of the school board in 1916, the belief that the educational needs of black students differed from those of white students still prevailed. Wexler admonished his soon-to-be former colleagues to "not neglect the negro in providing educational facilities. The welfare of the South can be greatly increased by better educational and uplift work among our negro population. Give them the rudiments of a good education up to the eighth grade, with specially selected subjects, and particularly teach them the domestic sciences, manual training and the vocations which will enable them to become more useful citizens and taxpayers." Several years later another school board member, James Fortier, echoed Wexler's sentiments. Fortier, a white supremacist, thought "it absurd to follow any plan for the education of the negro which involved anything beyond reading and writing and the teaching of the trade; that the negro's place in life was to do the heavier manual work; that it was absurd to attempt to teach negroes the beauties of Roman and Greek history." Fortier wanted school officials to build schools that featured only manual training. Years after the death of Booker T. Washington, his legacy of promoting industrial education for African Americans continued to influence the educational policy of most whites.[5]

Of the men who served as superintendent during this period, the one who said the least about black education probably revealed the most. Warren Easton, who had the longest tenure of the superintendents, failed to mention the needs of black students in his annual reports from 1900 to

1910. His omission indicated the low or nonexistent priority given to African American education. During Easton's years in office African American education reached its lowest point. His actions alone did not contribute to that condition, but his policy of active neglect did little to arrest the trend. After the death of Easton in October 1910, Joseph Gwinn became superintendent. Almost immediately he found himself involved in a tempest regarding the South's racial norms. After assuming office, Gwinn called a meeting of all the teachers, both black and white. Unlike previous meetings, some blacks and whites sat in the same section, which drew condemnation from the school board. Effectively chastened, Gwinn assured his superiors that "all meetings of teachers called by the Superintendent shall be for white teachers alone or for colored teachers alone" and promised to "also discontinue the practice of holding joint meetings of white and colored principals." He wanted his position on race relations clearly understood. "In this connection," he stressed, "I wish to state I am now and have always been opposed to any action which tends toward or seems to tend toward the breaking down of the color line as it has been established and maintained in our community."[6]

Despite Gwinn's declaratory allegiance to segregation, during the years that he led the school system he demonstrated some awareness of the need to improve black education. His opinion on, and support for, black education did not mirror that of the black community, but it marked a new departure from the twenty-two years of active neglect the black community had experienced under Easton. Gwinn maintained that manual and industrial training represented the ideal type of education for the minority population. Nonetheless, he conceded that "provisions should be made for the smaller class who are going to enter the teaching or other professions." Black education not only suffered because of the narrow instructional limits whites attempted to impose; whites also refused to adequately fund the programs they had outlined. Gwinn at least sought more funding and included black schools in his annual reports. Although such statements as "There is pressing demand for an evening school for colored youth" merely reiterated the many petitions and statements of the black community, African Americans benefited from having someone in office not totally hostile to their educational interests.[7] Nicholas Bauer became superintendent in 1923, succeeding Gwinn. Bauer, a native and lifetime resident of New Orleans, continued the course charted by Gwinn. He occasionally met with African American parents and leaders and once vowed "that he would never be satisfied until every child in New Orleans, both white and colored . . . [received] full and adequate educational facilities."[8]

The policy of educational neglect and limitations pursued by Fortier and other board members affected the quality and quantity of school facilities, and white protesters frustrated many attempts by school officials to provide African Americans with additional facilities. White protest usually centered on plans to convert existing white schools to black use. The historical residential patterns in New Orleans caused a dilemma for segregationists and school officials. In-migration and intracity relocation kept the racial composition in some neighborhoods in a state of constant flux. The sword cut both ways: whites moved into black areas, and African Americans moved into white areas. Several incidents illustrate this point. Using money from the John McDonogh Fund, city officials had built a school for African Americans living in the community of Algiers. In 1904, responding to an "increasing number of white children in the vicinity of McDonogh No. 5," school officials proposed building another school and transferring the black students. On 14 April 1905 the board adopted a resolution to convert the school and build one for African Americans in another section of the city. This decision represented a form of indirect urban planning along racial lines because adequate school facilities attracted additional residents. African Americans protested the change because school officials planned to build a school of lesser quality and wanted to transfer the black students to a rented church until the completion of the new school. Board members heard their protest but decided to follow the original plan. School officials had the sometimes difficult task of operating a dual education system with limited resources amid black demands and white protests.[9]

African Americans usually found themselves on the other side of the argument, favoring school conversion. Between 1900 and 1945 African Americans attended several schools that formerly housed white students. The board, for example, converted Zacharie, McDonogh Nos. 13, 17, and 20, and Benjamin Schools for use by African Americans. To prevent the conversions, whites used several arguments in addition to the appeal to white supremacy. Julia Volz, chairwoman of the Fourth Ward Civic League, spoke out against the conversion of McDonogh No. 17 because she believed that "when Bienville founded the city of New Orleans he certainly did not found it for the colored people." Few opponents of conversion used this kind of flawed historical approach. Typical statements argued that property values would decline or that area businesses would suffer.[10] And because black education and school conversion plans existed within the larger framework of race relations in the city, gaining additional school facilities for black students sometimes involved more than sufficient school board revenues. Early in the twentieth century whites in New Orleans attempted to expand the spatial separation of the races; as a result, they developed a heightened sensitivity to black schools in areas with a significant white population. Residential patterns that had developed over centuries came under scrutiny. Not only did whites seek to prevent black encroachment; in some cases they attempted to remove African Americans from schools and institutions they had occupied for several decades. One of the more contentious examples involved attempts by school officials to build a replacement for the Bayou Road School.

The Bayou Road School incident provides a typical example of the difficulties African Americans encountered in their fight for improved schools, but it also reveals the black community's determination to oppose the limitations of Jim Crow. African Americans living in the Sixth Ward, a working-class neighborhood below Canal Street, had attended the Bayou Road School since the 1880s. By 1910 the school, located at the intersection of Bayou Road and Derbigny Streets, was one of a few still operating in a rented building. It was also overcrowded and in a state of physical deterioration. The Bayou Road Parents' Club informed the board of the problems and requested immediate improvements and additions to accommodate the pupils. The board refused to commit itself to constructing a new building but promised to rent another building for use as an annex and to make some repairs to the present structure. When white residents in the neighborhood learned of the proposed annex, they protested. After referring the protest to the Committee on Teachers and Instructions, the board decided not to alter its plans. The board members refused the request because, they claimed, the lease for the building had already been signed and because "Bayou Road Colored School has been established there for a number of years."[11]

The addition of the annex alleviated the problem of overcrowding but left the board with another rented building in need of substantial repairs. Conditions at the school worsened and evoked a strong letter of condemnation from the city's board of health. In response, John Wegmann, the chairman of the Committee of Buildings and Grounds, inspected the facility. Wegmann acknowledged the bad conditions but thought the health board official had exaggerated and possibly overdramatized the conditions. Nonetheless, Wegmann considered the buildings unsuitable for school purposes. "It is the best we have . . . and I can conceive of nothing that can remedy the situation, unless it be the building of a new school somewhere in the neighborhood," he explained. Wegmann examined and quickly dismissed the possibility of using McDonogh No. 18 School, an abandoned white school located about a mile and a half from Bayou Road, as a replacement. He considered it to be in worse condition than Bayou Road. In February 1914 the board finally initiated plans to build a new school to replace the two rented buildings. School officials examined seventeen possible sites before deciding to purchase a large tract of land that encompassed the old school. Several factors influenced the board's decision, but an important consideration was its belief that using part of the old site would prevent "a protest from neighboring property owners." That thought proved more hopeful than prophetic; a sustained and angry protest by white residents in the area eventually developed.[12]

Almost a decade passed before school officials actually built the new school. Several factors contributed to the delay. When school officials first made the decision to replace Bayou Road, the city had responsibility for building schools and acquiring sites. But in 1914, despite a "strong plea" from the board because of conditions at Bayou Road, members of the New Orleans Commission Council stated that the city could not afford to purchase the site for the new school. Consequently, board members voted to lend the city enough money to make the purchase as well as to build another black school. Using funds from the board, the city purchased both tracts in the summer of 1914. After acquiring the land, however, the city still did not build the school because of a lack of funds. Meanwhile, the situation at the Bayou Road School grew progressively worse. Officials from the board of health closed the school in September 1914 and refused to reopen it until the board made needed repairs. A year later, on 29 September, a storm tore into the city and damaged most of the schools, including the annex to Bayou Road. Work crews under the supervision of board and city officials eventually managed to repair most of the damaged schools, but several, including the Bayou Road Annex, had to be demolished.[13]

The effects of World War I came to the city, then receded, and the Bayou Road School remained as overcrowded and dilapidated as ever. Finally, in 1922, construction started on the long overdue replacement for Bayou Road. Almost immediately, intense opposition developed and exposed the state of race relations in New Orleans. Numerous whites appeared before the school board and left little doubt that they expected and demanded the bulk of the community's resources. Any concessions made to African Americans had to occur after city leaders satisfied the needs of the majority population. White opposition to the building of Bayou Road centered not only on its location but also on the scale of the project. School officials planned to build a school comparable in quality to schools built for white students. The first protest came in July 1922, when a group of whites from the neighborhood around Bayou Road attended a meeting of the school board. One protester complained that the location was not in a black area, another that property values would decline, and another suggested that the board either build another school in a neighborhood with a large black population or convert an older white school into a school for blacks and give the new school to whites. School board president Daniel Murphy stated "that no matter where the board decided to locate a colored school protest would arise." The meeting ended without a final decision by the board.[14]

At a January 1923 board meeting white citizens again voiced their opposition to the school. "To put from eight hundred to a thousand negroes in that section almost entirely inhabited by white people," according to one spokesman, "would be a very serious disadvantage to both races." Another white speaker thought it absurd for white students to attend McDonogh No. 9 "while the negroes would be given a school that was really a monument."[15] None of the speakers convinced a majority of the board to deny African Americans use of the new school. School board president James Fortier, who had not entered into the discussion, relinquished the chair so that he could speak and used his opening remarks to emphasize his deep conviction on the subject. He lived, he began, in the Sixth Ward, only "about twenty-four squares from the proposed school, but if he lived seventy-five squares he would be vitally interested as though he were a resident directly across the street." According to Fortier, the issue "concerned the development and the growth of the entire city." Fortier did not want to see black homes or schools in predominantly white areas and lamented the Supreme Court decision in *Buchanan v. Warley,* which had declared residential segregation laws unconstitutional. In the absence of legal authority, Fortier contended, it became important for agencies such as the school board to prevent blacks from living in white areas.[16]

Fortier recommended three possible uses for the school, and none of his suggestions included use of the school by African Americans. He wanted it used as a junior high school, an annex to Esplanade High School, or an industrial training school. Percy Moise asked Fortier what he planned to do about the eight hundred black students scheduled to attend the school. Fortier thought school administrators could devise a plan to house the black students in other locations. Moise again voiced his support for the protesters but wanted a concrete plan to provide for the students. He reminded the protesters that the board had adhered to the established practice of building replacements for black schools on or near the original site and that many of them had purchased their homes "with the knowledge that the negro school existed in their midst." Moise was willing to concede to white sensibilities by borrowing money to build another school for African Americans in a different area. In the interim, however, he wanted to proceed with the scheduled opening of the school as a school for African Americans. Fortier disagreed with Moise's position and wanted an unequivocal declaration from the board that African Americans would not enter the school. Fortier viewed potential black enrollment as a threat to segregation and white supremacy. But this time the familiar embrace of white solidarity that usually accompanied the phrase *threat to white supremacy* failed to elicit the usual response. Moise made a motion that passed four to one to continue the plan for opening the school for African Americans with the understanding that if the board received a workable plan to house the students, school officials would transfer the students immediately. Only Fortier voted against the motion and remained determined to keep African Americans out of the school.[17]

Fortier, expecting persistence more than justice and fairness to triumph, called a special meeting less than a week after the board had voted against his plan. There he unveiled the idea of "placing these pupils on part-time for the next five months, while a comprehensive policy was being devised to cover the entire field of negro education." Moise stated his objections in strong terms, and the meeting ended without a vote. Undeterred and correctly sensing that a viable plan would break the opposition, Fortier came to the next meeting better prepared. He recommended placing the students in several schools in the area. Fellow member Daniel Murphy declared his faith in Fortier's sincerity but nevertheless supported allowing African Americans to use the new school because it "was the first move on the part of the board to give the negroes a real substantial building." When Superintendent Gwinn stated that the area schools could accommodate the students by placing them on part-time status, board members Mrs. Arthur Baumgartner and Fred Zengel reversed themselves and supported Fortier. Baumgartner made a motion to defer the opening of the new school until Fortier had an opportunity to present his plan. The motion passed by a three-to-two vote. Moise and Murphy cast the dissenting votes.[18]

Leaders in both the black and white communities were busy before the next meeting of the board. Walter L. Cohen, Emile LaBranche, and other black leaders called a mass meeting to protest the board's decision and to formulate a response. Members from the Colored Educational Alliance, New Orleans Branch NAACP, the National Progressive Association for Negroes, and many interested black citizens attended the meeting. Their lack of suffrage left them and the black community with few options. They could not threaten school board members with political reprisals but did denounce the board's position and drew up a petition of protest. They chose LaBranche to serve as their chairman and spokesman and decided to present their petition at the next board meeting. Some of the board members were also busy several days before the next meeting. Baumgartner and Zengel decided to personally inspect conditions at three of the schools scheduled to receive the influx of new students from Bayou Road. Both of them emerged from the inspection obviously concerned by what they had observed and would later share their findings with the other members. The black community also received unexpected support from the *New Orleans Times-Picayune:* "Time and reflection have only served to confirm this newspaper's belief that the closure of the school and consequent denial for an indefinite period of elementary education to Negro children whose fathers and grandfathers learned their letters in the place now closed to them amounts to a grave injustice. Let us close the incident in the right and wise way by adopting the course counselled by every consideration of justice and equity."[19]

On 9 February 1923 a large crowd of blacks and whites assembled for the regular scheduled meeting at the school board office. LaBranche presented the petition from the black community. He maintained that African Americans in the area had needed a new school for decades and confined his arguments to the educational needs of black students. Two white speakers believed that the use of the new school by African Americans threatened the system of segregation and white supremacy. Other white speakers expressed similar opinions before Fortier gave his views.

He criticized the newspaper articles supporting the board's original plan and declared that the time had come to reassess black education. Fortier wanted the board to develop a comprehensive plan to provide African Americans with vocational and manual training. Fortier also angrily criticized African Americans in attendance who, he thought, had the audacity to appear before the board and question its decisions. And he admonished his fellow members for establishing a dangerous precedent by reacting to the protests of African Americans. Fortier's position was clear; he wanted the school used for whites. Fortier could not comprehend the board's attempt to provide a modern school for blacks, when, for example, "our white boys of the Warren Easton High School are crowded and put into the basements." Despite his advocacy of a policy that ran contrary to the educational needs of the black community, Fortier suggested that his proposal would foster friendlier relations between blacks and whites. In his view the needs and aspirations of the black community did not enter into the prescription for improved race relations.[20]

Apparently, neither Fortier nor the various groups realized that Baumgartner and Zengel had changed their position. Baumgartner asked Fortier if he had visited any of the schools. He replied that he had not. Baumgartner then stated that she and Fred Zengel had visited the schools within the last week. She considered the conditions at the schools deplorable. "We found the Valena C. Jones crowded to a great extent. We found them in dark rooms in cottages rented by the board some time ago. We found the children three and four in one desk. I saw a condition in the Valena C. Jones [School] that I never knew existed in a school room before." Despite the horrible conditions at Jones, Baumgartner reported they were better than what she had seen at Bienville. Zengel supported Baumgartner's bleak assessment and thought Fortier's plan to add more students to those schools was impractical. After subsequent discussion failed to produce any new points, the board adopted a motion by Zengel to open the school for black students within a week. Only Fortier voted against the proposal. What seemed a favorable vote for the black community was actually only a compromise. School board members also declared their intent to build a replacement for the school and locate it in a predominantly black neighborhood. In an irony probably lost on most contemporaries, the school board named the new Bayou Road School after Joseph A. Craig, the black Reconstruction school board member who in 1877 had voted with the white majority to resegregate the public schools. In 1927 school officials finally transferred the black students to a new facility and transferred the name of the school with them.[21]

Another indication of the inequities of school board policy can be understood by examining the number, condition, and value of various schools. In the 1901–2 school session blacks had twelve schools and whites sixty. In 1910 New Orleans had sixteen black schools and sixty-eight for whites. Moreover, school officials generally spent more to maintain white schools than to maintain black ones. Whites also benefited disproportionately from new construction. Between 1900 and 1910, for instance, school officials erected twenty-one schools. More white schools already existed than those for African Americans, yet only three of the new schools served the black population. The estimated site and building value of the new black schools averaged $25,000. By contrast, the value of the new white schools averaged $42,500. The three black schools were frame structures, but twelve of the eighteen white schools were brick. Whites not only were allotted more schools; they also had substantially better schools.[22] Ten years later the superintendent's report for the 1920–21 school year revealed similar statistics. Out of the eight-six public schools in the city, fewer than twenty served the needs of black students. Again, city leaders had erected new schools; fourteen new schools opened between 1910 and 1920. Only one, however, served black students. Black and white leaders knew that the number of available schools often affected how many black students enrolled and that limited facilities contributed to lower enrollment. After 1920 black school enrollment consistently exceeded available facilities, which placed additional pressure on school officials and provided them with tangible evidence of black educational interest. Greater enrollment and interest also placed pressure on black leaders to fight for better schools. To meet the educational needs of the black community, black leaders had to become more aggressive in their attack on the status quo.[23]

The need for additional black schools persisted throughout the period. The Colored Educational Alliance, the NAACP, and the city's various black civic organizations kept the need for more and improved black schools before school officials. In the main the school board was a reactive body, seldom making decisions until some type of community interest or pressure developed. In matters related to black education, this tendency was even more evident. Black activism, therefore, became a crucial element in the campaign for improved schools. African Americans residing in the less-developed sections of the city fared worse in the quest for schools. Residents in the Milneburg area, an outlying district near Lake Pontchartrain, on several occasions petitioned school officials, without success, for a school. Others living in the more populous areas also kept their needs before the board.[24]

African American leaders often couched their appeals for educational improvements within the context of civic improvement. A 1913 petition from the Colored Educational Alliance requested that several annexes and new schools be erected. The petitioners pointed out that money spent on black education would benefit the entire community. In a city that often displayed hostility to any form of black education beyond the primary level, it made sense to link the educational aspirations of African Americans to the development of the larger community. African Americans emphasized that they wanted a fair share of the community's educational revenues. "Fair and equitable" meant the resources spent on black education should approximate the percentage of the population that was black.[25] Adherence to the second part of the separate-but-equal doctrine had long ago succumbed to racism and budgetary constraints. Leaders such as Rev. Henderson Dunn and Dr. Joseph Hardin hoped that investigating and exposing the conditions in the schools would lead to improvements. They also used the many investigations as a means to keep the black community involved in educational issues. African Americans gained many educational victories, and parental and community interest increased because of the emphasis placed on education by African Americans leaders. When African Americans petitioned for better school buildings, they often sought not an upgrade from adequate to good or good to better; rather, they had to fight to make deplorable schools simply adequate.[26]

Renting buildings served only as a temporary measure; modern brick structures represented the real answer to the problem. School officials rarely allocated enough money for such permanent solutions. When officials finally transferred students from "the broken down church building which formerly housed Fisk Branch School," conditions improved marginally. A school hygienist still considered the building unfit for a school. One report concluded that "all of the rooms are filled with desks. The windows have not been changed, but are the same windows usually found in residences. No desk space for the teacher is possible." As late as 1927, African Americans had only one modern school building, Joseph Craig, located in Faubourg Treme, the city's oldest black residential area. Most of the other schools were wooden structures in poor condition. A large delegation of African Americans, including Hardin and members of the Seventh Ward Civic League, appeared before school officials in 1928 to discuss conditions at one such school, Valena C. Jones. Hardin presented pictures of the school that supported his statements, and Superintendent Nicholas Bauer informed the board that conditions were as bad as Hardin indicated. Bauer recommended immediate relief and suggested the construction of a modern school for that section of the city. The board members assured the group that relief would follow, and this time they kept their promise.[27]

Several months later school officials accepted bids for the construction of the new school at Annette and Miro Streets. In October 1929 over two thousand individuals attended dedication ceremonies for the new Valena C. Jones, "considered one of the best equipped school buildings in this section of the country." The lengthy program included speeches by Superintendent Bauer, board member Isaac Heller, community leader Hardin, and Jones's principal, Fannie C. Williams. Heller gave the keynote address and used the theme "The New Negro" as his topic. Williams encouraged the crowd to tour the school and "note the modern equipment, which includes a radio in the school auditorium, an electric refrigerator and gas stoves and ovens in the domestic science room, a fire-chute, and a well-equipped infirmary." Doubtless, many parents in attendance shared Williams's joy, heightened by the realization that the school had begun in the early twentieth century in a "lowly tenement house."[28] The new Valena C. Jones School was a response to greater enrollment but also would contribute to additional enrollment increases (table 5.1).

Schools recently built often became overcrowded. The new Thomy Lafon School, erected in 1906, was overcrowded a year later, which necessitated an annex. McDonogh No. 32, built in 1907, had to conduct some of its classes in a rented church building that constantly needed repairs. Renting church buildings, though popular with school officials, worked a hardship on teachers and students. Unlike residences, school officials could not build partitions or even place desks in the rented churches. Although vacant during the week, the buildings had to be in condition for use by their congregations on Sundays. When the board could not find suitable buildings to rent or did not have the funds to construct annexes, officials forced black students to attend school only part of the day. The idea of part-time classes developed slowly but became widespread in the

Table 5.1. New Orleans Public School Enrollment, 1900–1940

YEAR ENDING	BLACK	WHITE	TOTAL
1901	5,509	26,038	31,547
1902	5,072	26,133	31,205
1903	4,856	26,228	31,144
1904	4,949	26,751	31,700
1905	4,558	27,331	31,889
1906	4,847	27,125	31,972
1907	5,659	28,605	34,625
1908	6,295	31,710	38,005
1909	6,717	33,687	40,404
1910	6,616	36,117	42,733
1911	7,674	38,151	45,825
1912	8,105	38,499	46,604
1913	8,367	40,080	48,447
1914	8,706	39,161	47,867
1915	8,736	40,244	48,980
1916	9,656	41,835	51,491
1917	9,401	41,647	51,048
1918	9,685	41,836	51,521
1919	9,362	40,182	49,544
1920	10,984	40,611	51,595
1921	12,997	40,923	53,920
1922	15,256	44,662	59,918
1923	16,103	47,325	63,428
1924	16,128	47,087	63,215
1925	17,052	47,401	64,453
1926	16,500	47,952	64,452
1927	19,625	48,731	68,356
1928	21,025	50,164	71,189
1929	21,912	52,927	74,839
1930	23,018	52,891	75,909
1931	22,572	56,834	79,406
1932	24,987	55,948	80,935
1933	25,130	57,364	82,494
1935	26,640	58,968	85,608
1936	29,256	59,587	88,843

Table 5.1. New Orleans Public School Enrollment, 1900–1940 (continued)

YEAR ENDING	BLACK	WHITE	TOTAL
1937	29,062	57,496	88,558
1938	27,537	54,797	82,334
1939	28,322	54,140	82,402
1940	27,787	53,657	81,444

Source: New Orleans Annual Report(s), 1900–1920; New Orleans Statistical Report(s), 1921–40, OPSB Collection.

1920s. Students at McDonogh No. 6, however, had their school day shortened as early as 1915. In the beginning of the 1922–23 school year 5,396 black students attended school part-time. By contrast, only 192 white students had less than a full day of school. School officials attempted to limit part-time classes to the primary grades, but that often proved impossible as the number of African Americans in grammar and secondary schools increased. Students forced to attend part-time averaged two and a half to four hours of school per day. No official policy or regulation existed regarding the length of the school day for students attending classes part-time. School officials reacted to conditions as they arose.[29]

One of the more glaring examples of the school board's policy of limited educational opportunities was the lack of high school facilities for African Americans. School officials at least acknowledged a need for vocational training and agreed that the public school system should provide it. Of course, they did very little to make such training a reality. But for decades school officials did not even admit there was a need for a black high school, and black leaders usually had more success achieving educational improvements that met the school board's view of the proper education for African Americans. The board's decision in 1900 to reduce black education to the fifth grade temporarily forced African Americans to abandon their efforts to secure secondary schools. It made little sense to launch an aggressive push for a high school when public education ceased after the fifth grade. Then, too, Southern University located in New Orleans still offered high school courses. Between 1900 and 1910 African American parents and leaders worked to regain grades 6 through 8.

The closing of Southern University in 1913 and its removal to Baton Rouge in 1914 led to a change of strategy. Many whites and blacks thought Southern University's location in an urban area prevented it from becoming an agricultural training school for African Americans from throughout the state. Black leaders in the rest of the state argued that New Orleans had three other black universities and that this fact alone justified the removal of Southern. State officials, including Governor Luther E. Hall, his predecessor Jared Sanders, and state superintendent Thomas H. Harris, eventually supported the move from New Orleans. Joseph S. Clark, a black educator who would later become president of Southern University, also actively worked for its relocation. Most African Americans in the city opposed the move, but support for the change did emerge from individuals affiliated with Straight University. According to one account, Straight University officials acted because of self-interest — the elimination of a rival free university.[30] In July 1913, as soon as it appeared doubtful that Southern University would remain in New Orleans, African American leaders asked school officials to "make arrangements for a colored high school, as the pupils formerly attending Southern University are now deprived of the State High School." The board agreed to add the seventh grade in 1913 and the eighth the following year but still refused to open a high school.[31] Between 1914 and 1917 various groups of African Americans repeatedly petitioned the school board for a high school. Each time board members denied the request, but African Americans persisted in their attempts to sway the board. Education could not aid individual advancement and black community development without public secondary schools. The idea of social mobility for blacks contradicted whites' belief in the inherent inferiority of blacks. Segregation forced New Orleans's white leaders to concede the need for a small number of blacks to receive academic high school training. They recognized that a separate black community needed physicians, teachers, lawyers, and clergy, but they nevertheless refused to allocate public funds to provide the educational foundations for an emergent professional class.[32]

In January 1917, 823 New Orleans children completed the eight-year elementary school course of study in the public schools. Many of them looked forward to attending one of the four public high schools — Esplanade, Francis Nicholls, Sophie Wright, or Warren Easton — all recently built and reflecting Progressive era attitudes on the importance of secondary education. The four schools represented a capital outlay of nearly two million dollars. The city's architect, E. A. Christy, and Superintendent Gwinn had visited several cities to learn of the latest in school design and equipment. They wanted to ensure that New Orleans would have high school facilities unsurpassed in the South. Care also went into formulating curricula for the schools. Warren Easton High School offered college preparatory courses as well as commercial classes in bookkeeping, banking, and typing. Sophie Wright High School and Esplanade High School were college preparatory schools for girls. Francis Nicholls High School offered vocational training for females. Seventy-one of the 823 students who completed the eighth grade, however, could not attend any of the four public high schools because they were African Americans.[33]

But in September 1917 the situation changed. Years of persistence and agitation by African American parents and education leaders and an increasing number of black grammar school graduates finally convinced the school board to open a high school for African Americans that fall. For this venture school officials did not plan any fact-gathering trips or appropriate a large capital outlay. They simply converted the white McDonogh No. 13 Elementary School to black use. African American parents and students would have preferred a modern high school in a less commercial part of the city. They accepted the building because they were realists and viewed the gain as a small victory in a continuous struggle for improved educational opportunities. The school opened in 1917 as McDonogh No. 35 and would eventually win acclaim for academic excellence. John Hoffman, a native of Tougaloo, Mississippi, and a graduate of Wilberforce University and Michigan Agricultural College, served as its first principal. The curriculum at McDonogh No. 35 featured the traditional college preparatory courses. To graduate, students had to complete a combination of required and elected subjects in English, Latin, history, science, music, mathematics, and physical education. "Credit for these subjects," according to a resolution adopted by the board in September 1917, was "to be given on same basis as in the white high schools." Except for the general science textbook, black students used the same books as white students. Eighty-two students enrolled for the fall semester, and an additional sixty-one began in the spring. Only one spring graduate from the elementary school failed to enroll at McDonogh No. 35 in the first year. A need had existed for a black high school, and African Americans availed themselves of the new opportunity.[34]

Like the leader of any pioneering effort, McDonogh No. 35's principal wanted the school to show immediate signs of success. Assessing the first year of operation, Hoffman noted that "from the beginning, both pupils and teachers have joined in their efforts to set a high standard of efficiency and promote a spirit of good will in the school." From the start, however, the school faced a dilemma — or, rather, a crisis of identity. Although McDonogh No. 35 was established as a college preparatory school, Hoffman wanted it to "meet the larger needs of the community." As the only black public high school in the city, Hoffman believed it should offer a diverse curriculum. He sought to expand the offerings to include vocational education and thought "that courses in Wood Working and Domestic Science will be extremely desirable for our pupils." In later years he advocated introducing courses in plumbing, printing, and automobile mechanics. Citing the opportunities available for employment in those fields, he believed "that the majority of the boys will greatly benefit by such a chance to fit themselves for practical service." By 1927 vocational classes had become part of the curriculum, and a contemporary observed that "the manual training department of the Negro high school made all the work desks for the whole system, [and] the cooking department takes care of the daily lunches."[35]

Emphasis on vocational training did not hinder the school's academic development. Like much of black community development during the period when Booker T. Washington's views regarding industrial education were seemingly triumphant, African Americans leaders such as John Hoffman, without irony or inner conflict, stressed academic attainment with the same zeal that they advocated vocational expansion. They borrowed freely and often from both the expansive view of black education advocated by W.E.B. Du Bois and the more utilitarian idea of black education championed by Washington. So, at the conclusion of the first year Hoffman could boast of the "excellent showing made in the Department of Science." He credited its success to the teachers and students who "worked enthusiastically during the entire year to build up a first-class department." The mathematics department drew praise for helping students develop "clear and concise reasoning" skills. The history classes "awaken in the pupils a higher sense of duty and patriotism through a knowledge of the development of civilization and nations." Hoffman expressed less satisfaction with the English instructor and wanted "a teacher of marked ability and special training in English." To enhance the academic environment, the students formed a debating society and attended lectures presented by guest speakers. As the school grew, the board hired additional teachers. The popularity and success of the high school soon produced overcrowding and a renewed commitment by African Americans to secure additional high school facilities (table 5.2).[36]

In addition to the desire for additional secondary schools, African Americans also wanted educational facilities for students unable to attend school during traditional school hours. Many black children failed to attend school for the same reason as many whites: they simply lacked interest. On the other hand, large numbers of New Orleans's black and white youths worked and could not attend regular day school. In 1910,

Table 5.2. Trends in Black High School Enrollment, 1918–1940

YEAR ENDING	TOTAL
1918	143
1919	255
1920	372
1921	565
1922	613
1923	766
1924	509
1925	454
1926	694
1927	869
1928	902
1929	1,226
1930	1,372
1931	2,182
1932	2,425
1933	2,578
1934	2,811
1935	3,286
1936	3,682
1937	4,006
1938	4,111
1939	4,274
1940	4,568

Source: New Orleans Annual Report(s), 1920–21; New Orleans Statistical Report(s), 1924–40.

45.7 percent of blacks age seven to twenty attended school, compared to 54.2 percent for the entire city. In 1920 approximately 58 percent of African Americans in that age group attended school. Figures for the entire city were slightly better, at nearly 60 percent. Several educational trends at the beginning of the century involved attempts to boost school attendance through expanded educational access. The start of evening schools significantly extended educational opportunities for white youths in the city. School board members voted to start an evening school at McDonogh High School No. 1 for the 1903–4 school year. The school opened on 2 November with 142 students. Enrollment reached 180 before the end of the session five months later. In addition to classes in English, reading, math, geography, and history, students received instruction in typing, bookkeeping, and stenography. Increased enrollment led Superintendent Warren Easton to request additional evening schools. When the 1911–12 school year started, nine evening schools operated throughout the city, although none of them admitted African American students.[37]

The evening school curriculum for white students offers a vivid look at the relationship between educational access and enhanced employment opportunities. The curriculum expanded from the initial three commercial courses to include classes in manual and industrial training, domestic science, and additional commercial classes. When necessary, school officials fashioned a curriculum to meet a specific need or objective. During the winter of 1907–8, for example, whites in New Orleans became upset by what many regarded as an inordinate number of African Americans in the federal civil service. Some white citizens charged that the area black colleges provided their students with special instruction to prepare them for the federal exam. Superintendent Easton immediately organized a class at one of the evening schools to prepare white students for the test. He soon reported "excellent results by pupils of the Civil Service Class of Evening School No. 1." Seven of the eight evening school students who took the test passed; one of them earned the highest grade on the letter carrier exam.[38] Easton's quick response to the vocational needs of the white community was not extended to the needs of the black community. Expressing the frustration many African Americans experienced because of the board's refusal to provide evening schools, an editorial in a religious newspaper "question[ed] the right of a people to rule who are so nearsighted and thoroughly selfish as to refuse the petition of an element of the citizenship that is loyal, though poor and helpless."[39]

African Americans did not benefit initially from the expanded educational opportunities associated with evening schools but welcomed the new program. They knew, as one scholar has observed, that "the southern educational revival widened the gap between the schooling of whites and blacks at the same time that it extended opportunity for both groups." Once a new program for whites became operational, black leaders and parents demanded that African American students have access to the same program. Constant denials by the board failed to lessen their resolve, and persistence often produced favorable results. In November 1918, after countless appeals and petitions, the school board established an evening school for African Americans. Despite its restrictive admission requirements — males had to be employed six hours a day, and instruction could not extend beyond the fourth grade level — the evening school experienced immediate success. Enrollment reached 398 during the first year of operation (table 5.3).[40]

The early-twentieth-century debate led by Washington and Du Bois regarding industrial or academic education for African Americans had little relevance to black education policy in New Orleans because school officials refused to adequately fund vocational training for black students. Despite the opening of McDonogh No. 35 and the start of evening schools, exclusion or limited educational opportunities served as the operational philosophy of school officials. James Fortier and other school board members consistently expressed the belief that African Americans should receive, almost exclusively, manual, industrial, or domestic training, but budgetary problems prevented them from putting the idea into practice. Indeed, even in white schools, vocational training developed slowly because of a chronic shortage of revenues.[41] But white leaders wanted industrial training for white students and frequently pressured school officials to furnish it. Joseph Kohn, a businessman and president of the chamber of commerce, offered to donate one thousand dollars toward the purchase of industrial training equipment. Kohn later extended the same offer for equipment for a black school. The board accepted both offers. And efforts to secure industrial education received the enthusiastic support of the various superintendents. Warren Easton, for example, actively sought to start an industrial program as early as 1901. With plans still dormant several years later, Easton informed school board members that industrial education was not a "fad" and suggested they establish a program in the high schools

Table 5.3. Trends in Black Evening School Enrollment, 1919–1940

YEAR ENDING	TOTAL
1919	398
1920	922
1921	2,321
1922	2,824
1923	2,277
1924	2,021
1925	2,527
1926	2,023
1927	3,890
1928	4,203
1929	4,402
1930	4,754
1931	4,710
1932	4,702
1933	4,754
1934	3,581
1935	4,780
1936	4,808
1937	3,282
1938	2,413
1939	2,764
1940	2,166

Source: New Orleans Annual Report(s), 1918–21; New Orleans Statistical Report(s), 1924–40.

or in a separate vocational training school. In 1910 school officials finally decided to offer industrial training in several white elementary schools.[42]

Most white citizens and leaders agreed that African Americans needed industrial or vocational education; indeed, many white leaders insisted that was all the schooling they needed. African American leaders and parents also embraced vocational education but wanted a full range of educational options. They knew that even in a race-neutral society varied intellectual abilities and vocational interests necessitated a diverse school curriculum. The idea that schools should prepare students for work was a cardinal principle that everyone accepted. So the struggle for industrial and vocational education remained an integral part of the overall strategy to improve the lives of individuals and develop the black community. The occupational status of African Americans in New Orleans necessitated such an approach, and it could be justified because the majority of African American males employed in the city worked as unskilled laborers. In 1920, for example, African Americans constituted 27 percent of the population but nearly 45 percent of those engaged in domestic and personal service. Looked at another way, more foreign-born white males had professional jobs than African American males (619 to 462). Yet African Americans outnumbered foreign-born whites nearly four to one (100,910 to 25,992). In 1950 the city's black laborers outnumbered white laborers almost two to one. Earning capacity, of course, depended on occupational status. As a consequence, in 1944 black median income was 50 percent less than that of whites. African American leaders and parents attempted to enhance and expand the occupational options of youths through vocational training.[43]

Eventually, Joseph Kohn raised his initial offer from one thousand dollars to twelve hundred dollars for industrial equipment in a black school. Citing a lack of funds, school officials nevertheless failed to take advantage of the offer, notwithstanding the requests from African Americans and the recommendations of the superintendent. "Facilities for trade and industrial education are needed for the colored youth in the upper grammar grades," Superintendent Gwinn stressed in 1912. On another occasion he admitted that "nothing has been done to supply facilities for industrial education for the negroes. All recognize the great need for this training for the youth of that race."[44] At one point the board considered building an extension to the Thomy Lafon School to house several industrial classes. Board members abandoned that plan, citing the expense of what was actually a relatively modest construction cost of $2,250. At the same time they had appropriated $100,000 for the vocational training of six thousand white students. Finally, in 1918, school officials authorized the construction of a three-room annex for manual training at Lafon. Several years after making his pledge, Kohn sent the board a $1,200 check. Eighteen years into the twentieth century, black school-age children in New Orleans finally started receiving their supposedly "proper" education. By 1927 additional black schools, including McDonogh No. 35, offered manual or domestic training. Female students received instruction in areas such as sewing and cooking, and males learned printing, carpentry, and bricklaying.[45]

Vocational instruction in various elementary schools and at McDonogh No. 35 High School only provided a partial solution to the problem of inadequate vocational training for African Americans. School officials consistently acknowledged the need for a trade school for elementary school graduates. Whenever the subject came before the board, however, the board refused to act, citing insufficient funds. And board members used the knowledge that some members of the black community opposed building a trade school to justify their delay. John Guillaume, president of a proprietary business college, argued that African Americans needed academic high schools more than a trade school. "A trade school building is not our greatest need in the line of school facilities," Guillaume stated in a letter to Superintendent Bauer. In an editorial titled "We Need It," the *Louisiana Weekly* disagreed with Guillaume: "The trade school idea is a good one; if not, the white children would not have two in our city while we are getting one. If the idea is good for the opposite group, where they have one hundred chances to our children's one for positions by which they are to earn their daily bread, then why condemn something that will have a tendency to put our children on an equality with those of the other groups." The majority of the black community shared that view.[46]

Into the financial void, and to the relief of the black community, stepped representatives of the Julius Rosenwald Fund. School officials had attempted to get money from the Rosenwald Fund as early as 1923. Interest by the fund coincided with the school board's issuance of $3 million in bonds for school construction. The board voted in February 1930 to use $275,000 from the bond money to construct a black trade school. At the time the figure represented the largest amount of money ever allocated by the board for a black school.[47] Rosenwald Fund officials then pledged $125,000 to the proposed $400,000 project. Blacks welcomed the financial support and noted with some satisfaction statements made by Dr. Franklin Keller, an executive of the fund. In February 1931 Keller met with leaders of the black community to discuss the trade school project. He assured the delegation that "in New Orleans there will be as fine a trade school for Negro children as there is now for either whites or negroes anywhere in the United States." Keller attempted to allay the concerns of African Americans regarding the type of courses to be offered. He maintained the trade "school will continue to introduce new courses of study along with the development of new trades during the constant revolution of industry." He cited the city's need for bricklayers and automobile mechanics and argued that the trade school should train blacks to meet those and other labor needs of the community.⁴⁸

Viewing vocational education in a broader context, African Americans wanted vocational courses to go beyond the narrow dictates of the New Orleans labor market. World War I and the northern migration of African Americans convinced many black leaders of the need for training local African Americans for a national labor market. The South's hold on the black population was not as firm in the 1930s as it had been prior to World War I. "If the school disregards equipping the Negro for the needs of the forty-eight states," charged the *Louisiana Weekly*, "and holds to the theory that brick-laying and plastering is sufficient thereof, we are compelled to ask 'to what aught is this waste?'"⁴⁹ The black community did not feel constrained by the policies or actions of the majority population. They knew the proper education of black children involved a struggle of seemingly endless duration. Many whites, on the other hand, wanted a very limited vocational curriculum for African Americans. Because race antipathy prevented the inclusion of African Americans in most local skilled unions, white workers had a vested interest in suppressing the development of black skilled workers. Attempts at black-white worker solidarity had already succumbed to the "color line." Board members such as Isaac Heller, who displayed some sympathy for black education and led the campaign within the school board for a black trade school, had to contend with the thinking of the white community. A month after school officials announced their intention to build a trade school, Heller tried to mollify white fears with the assurance that the school would not increase occupational competition between blacks and whites. He maintained that the trade school curriculum would reflect traditional black employment patterns. Although he spoke in general terms, his statements probably prevented the formation of organized and sustained white opposition.⁵⁰

Conflict and concern over the proposed curriculum became moot when school officials allowed the project to die a slow death. With the assistance of the Rosenwald Fund and the money from the bond issue, school officials had sufficient revenues to erect the trade school. To the chagrin of the black community, the school board purchased a former hospital building on Carondelet Street to serve as its central office. Part of the money for the acquisition came from the funds set aside for the trade school. Why did the board suddenly change policy? Support for the project among board members was tepid at best and rested to a considerable degree on the efforts of Heller and Superintendent Bauer. A $400,000 school for blacks, even if it promised to train them for the "right" jobs, was too large an expenditure for black education. Additionally, the lingering fear of potential job competition between the races convinced the school board to abandon the project, and the effects of the Great Depression all but eliminated reconsideration of the project for several years.[51]

In the meantime the board, with bitter irony, or disdain, decided to build an inexpensive elementary school on the site previously purchased for the trade school. The new school, constructed in less than two months, alleviated overcrowding at three schools in the area. Ordinarily, black leaders and parents expressed joy at the addition of new schools. This time they knew that they had lost more than they had gained. With justifiable indignation many African Americans shared the opinion expressed in a *Louisiana Weekly* editorial: "Did they decide to give a 25,000 dollar temporary building on a site selected for a trade school in order to avoid erecting the needed trade school?" African American leaders nevertheless continued the effort to secure a trade school. Throughout the 1930s the Colored Educational Alliance, the New Orleans Branch NAACP, and the Federation of Civic Leagues kept the issue before the school board. Funding through the federal Works Progress Administration eventually made the trade school a reality. In 1940 construction started near the previous site, which had been purchased amid much fanfare and hope. In honor of the man who a half-century earlier had placed his life's energies into the promotion of industrial education, the board named the school Booker T. Washington.[52]

6

Business and Labor

The start of rigid racial segregation in the South occurred at a time in the nation's development when businesses and businessmen enjoyed the esteem and adulation of most Americans. Despite social, political, and economic discrimination, African Americans also embraced the pro-business ideology and championed an entrepreneurial spirit. Operating businesses from insurance companies and funeral homes to small retail stores and service businesses, black New Orleanians entered the business world. They were aware, however, that the same system of racial segregation that provided business opportunities also made business success that much more difficult. Acquiring sufficient capital and credit to start, sustain, and expand businesses was often the most difficult challenge. So, too, was the problem of limited training and experience in business organization and management. A study published in 1932 maintained that "the prospective white business man can usually find an opportunity to become thoroughly acquainted with the business he expects to enter." On the other hand, the study concluded that "the limited number of really successful Negro units in all fields of business endeavor makes it impossible in most cases for the prospective Negro merchant to learn adequately the game in enterprises operated by members of the Negro race."[1] That assessment was accurate for New Orleans not only in the 1930s but throughout the entire era of segregation. Despite the obstacles, many hopeful African American businessmen were optimistic and shared the view of national leaders that the segregated black community provided a near-monopoly for industrious black capitalists.

The urbanization of the United States, which quickened considerably between the two world wars, affected the lives of many Americans, including African Americans. Their migration patterns brought them to northern as well as southern cities such as New Orleans. By 1930, for instance, in thirteen southern cities the African American population exceeded 25,000, and four cities had at least 90,000 African American residents. Population figures for New Orleans during the period reflected the overall urbanization patterns. In 1900 African Americans constituted 27.1 percent of the city's population, or 77,714 of the 208,946 total. In 1930 New Orleans led all Lower South cities with an African American population of 129,632. By 1950, 181,120 African Americans resided in the city (table 6.1). Proponents of a black subeconomy focused on aggregate increases, for numbers translated into potential customers and clients for businessmen and professionals.[2] And if Booker T. Washington and W.E.B. Du Bois had different ideas regarding the political response of African Americans to racial segregation, disfranchisement, and second-class citizenship, they both championed the idea of black economic development. For Washington his founding and support of the National Negro Business League was but one manifestation of his belief in black economic development as a key to both individual and group advancement.[3]

African American business success depended in part on the economic status of African Americans. And many white-owned businesses ignored African American consumers because of their low earnings and purchas-

Table 6.1. New Orleans Population

YEAR	TOTAL	BLACK	WHITE	ALL OTHERS
1890	242,039	64,491	177,376	172
1900	287,104	77,714	208,946	444
1910	339,075	89,262	249,403	410
1920	387,219	100,930	285,916	373
1930	458,762	129,632	327,729	1,401
1940	494,537	149,034	344,775	728
1950	568,680	181,120	386,760	800

Source: U.S. Department of Commerce and Labor, *Thirteenth Census of the United States, Abstract with Supplement for Louisiana; Fourteenth Census of the United States, 1920, vol. 4: Population; Fifteenth Census of the United States: 1930, vol. 3, pt. 1: Population; Sixteenth Census of the United States, 1940, vol. 2, pt. 3: Population; United States Census of Population: 1950, Detailed Characteristics, Louisiana.*

ing power. They also made little effort to understand the African American market or misunderstood it because of notions of racial differences. The insurance business emerged as one of the more successful African American businesses in New Orleans during the Jim Crow era because white firms for a time virtually ignored that market. In addition, racial and residential segregation fostered the development of a viable black insurance industry in southern and northern cities.[4] The black insurance industry grew in New Orleans, black civic and economic boosters proclaimed, because "the advantages of insurance were so evident that experienced salesmanship was not an actual necessity, and growing racial solidarity made the advent of Negro companies welcome." Racial solidarity may have created the market, but it took capital, business acumen, and a certain degree of luck to start and maintain a profitable insurance company.[5]

In 1907 Unity Industrial Life became the first black insurance company chartered in the city. Organized by Dr. Prudhomme Dejoie, George Geddes, and William Robinson, Unity experienced some of the difficulties that plagued many black businesses throughout the South and in northern cities as well. In the spirit of the Progressive era the Louisiana legislature passed a law to regulate industrial life insurance companies and required companies to post a five thousand–dollar bond to operate in the state. Many of the city's black mutual benefit associations that provided small death benefits to the families of members in good standing did not have adequate capital to pay the bond. Dejoie and other community leaders also realized that the small, personal mutual aid societies were becoming obsolete, and the 1906 law provided a needed spur to the development of new types of business organization in the black community. As a result, three small mutual aid societies combined their resources to form Unity. The Dejoie family emerged as one of the driving forces in its development. For several years the firm concentrated on the New Orleans market but eventually expanded into surrounding parishes, and by 1933 Unity Industrial Life had fifty-four thousand policies throughout the state.[6]

In 1910 the relative success of Unity provided the incentive for the formation of the second black-owned insurance company, Peoples Benevolent Industrial Life. Several of the organizers included the city's most prominent Republican politicians, Walter Cohen, Samuel Green, and James Lewis. Religious leader Alfred Lawless and educators Albert Wicker and Arthur Williams were members of the advisory board. Peoples owners appealed to race pride in their attempts to gain business. "We believe the time has come when the colored people should contribute their support to a concern of their own, whose benefits are shared among them," the company claimed in one advertisement. But Cohen and his staff understood that appeals to race pride had limits and asked African Americans to support the company because Peoples would "give . . . as much, if not more, than any other institution of like character."[7] The decision to include *benevolent* in the company's name reflected another conscious marketing strategy. The name evoked the personalized and meaningful relations that African Americans enjoyed as members of numerous benevolent and mutual aid societies.[8] And during the early years of its operation, Peoples faced more competition from the continued popularity of those societies than from other companies in the emerging black insurance industry. Competition within and outside the new industry did not deter others from entering the market. Within the next decade Liberty Industrial Life and Louisiana Industrial Life opened.

The establishment of these insurance companies benefited the black community in several ways. First, they represented a main source of capital formation in the black subeconomy. Second, they provided some African Americans with managerial experience. Third, they aided the development of other black businesses by using black suppliers. Fourth, the insurance companies gave financial protection to a group generally ignored by white insurance firms. Fifth, they demonstrated to the community that African Americans could operate successful businesses. Finally, they provided clerical and sales employment opportunities for African American males and females. Enterprising African Americans in urban areas throughout the South also viewed black business development as crucial to countering the negative opinions that most white southerners had of their race. Under the leadership of Charles Spaulding, for instance, the Durham-based North Carolina Mutual Life Insurance Company became one of the most successful black-owned businesses in the South. Spaulding possessed not only intelligence but also the necessary drive and energy needed to succeed in the insurance business. Eventually, North Carolina Mutual expanded into other businesses such as real estate and banking. None of the New Orleans insurance companies approached the scale of such black-owned firms as North Carolina Mutual or Atlanta Mutual. What was important, however, was the effect the black companies had on community and economic development. Uplifting the race and promoting racial solidarity were two reasons African American entered business, but it is also important to stress the economic aspect of their efforts.⁹

An examination of one company that started in the 1930s, despite the continuing Great Depression, is instructive. Dr. Jesse O. Sheffield was a pivotal figure in the origins and growth of St. John Berchman's Industrial Life Insurance Company. Sheffield, a native of Texas, graduated from Bishop College in 1920, completing a course of study that prepared him to teach industrial arts or vocational training. His diploma indicated a proficiency in mechanical drawing, cabinetmaking, carpentry, painting, varnishing, and glazing. At Bishop College, Sheffield also completed a "scientific" course of study and earned a bachelor's degree one day after receiving his degree in teacher training. Over the next four years he attended Meharry Medical College, graduating in 1924. By the end of that year he had moved to New Orleans and had passed the Louisiana medical exam. And like most physicians, both black and white, Sheffield considered a city practice more rewarding and remunerative than one in a rural area. He had earned his medical degree at considerable sacrifice; to pay his way through medical school, he had worked on trains and tour boats. From 1924 until his death in 1953 Sheffield lived the life of a physician-entrepreneur. In addition to establishing his medical practice, he opened Sheffield's Cut Rate Cash Grocery Store. Sheffield's most ambitious business venture, however, involved the establishment of St. John Berchman's. An initial attempt to open an industrial life insurance company in 1935 failed because Sheffield and his group could not raise the ten thousand dollars in capital required by state law. Locating investors proved difficult during the best of times, and attempting to start a business during the Great Depression made the task even harder. Rather than abandon the effort, the investors decided to amend their charter to meet the smaller financial requirements of a mutual company and opened in 1936.¹⁰

Sheffield entered the insurance business because in addition to providing death benefits, Berchman's also offered a health insurance program. In fact, the majority of the policies covered physician and drug costs. For a monthly premium policyholders received free care by a physician as well as medicine. Patients had to use doctors affiliated with Berchman's, and the policies did not cover all medical tests and hospitalization. Despite its limitations, that type of coverage gave many black New Orleanians access to medical care that otherwise would not have been available. Of course, it also assured Sheffield and other black doctors a steady stream of patients. Apparently, both groups benefited. Berchman's, according to an inspector's report, treated its policyholders with fairness and settled claims promptly. Berchman's investors remained committed to the original idea of a stock company and succeeded, in 1940, in gaining enough capital to reorganize as an industrial life insurance company. That July he got married, and his wife, Gertrude, later became an investor and member of the board of directors. By that year, too, several members of Sheffield's family had invested in the company. Other important investors and officers of Berchman's during the 1940s included Joseph Arceneaux Jr. and Sr., Julia Buckhalter, Dr. J. J. Donasier, Bonita Flenoy, Emile Labat Sr., and Bonita Nelson,. Sheffield served as president of Berchman's and was the person most responsible for the company's success. By 1950 Sheffield and his family owned nearly 40 percent of the company's stock. He knew that the company's success or failure would affect not just the black community but trusting and supportive family members as well.[11]

After the reorganization in 1940, Berchman's enjoyed several years of growth. Premium income, for example, increased from $49,933 in 1941 to $70,033 in 1944. In the mid-1940s premium income declined but had stabilized at about $59,000 by the end of the decade. It is possible that the decline in premium income reflected a business decision by management and not a decline in the company's fortunes. Premium income revealed the number of policyholders and the amount of coverage in force. A crucial test of an insurance company's profitability was its benefits paid–to–premium income ratio. In 1944, when Berchman's reached its peak premium income, it also experienced its largest payout to policyholders, $24,203. In 1950, by contrast, the company collected $58,588 in premiums but only paid $9,160 to policyholders. Sheffield, on the other hand, may have gauged success according to the number of policyholders and the amount of premiums collected. After two straight years of decline, Sheffield searched for answers. He thought he had found them in the conduct of several physicians affiliated with the company. "There is a general feeling going around that there is no need for one to carry a Doctor and Medicine policy with St. John Berchman's Industrial Life Insurance Company," he informed his medical care suppliers, "because you have to pay the doctor anyway." As a result, he contended, the company was losing policyholders. The remedy was clear: "discontinue charging for [most] examination[s]."[12]

Owner-managers of small businesses required steady involvement, analytical skills, and leadership abilities. Sheffield possessed these traits and needed to demonstrate them regularly as he attempted to keep his business solvent. At times Sheffield provided encouragement to his employees, imploring them, for example, to "pull together and cooperate for the success of the company." At other times he did not hesitate to fire employees who he believed "did not have the interest of St. John Berchman at heart." Consistent with the belief in the value of the "company man," which had become the desired management type by 1950, Sheffield wanted loyal and experienced employees who worked tirelessly for the benefit of his company. When he found them, and when opportunities became available, he promoted them to better positions. In this way Sheffield pursued his own individual advancement yet promoted community development by assisting others in achieving their goals. The survival of small companies such as Berchman's remained important to black community development, for their success would determine the viability of the whole idea of a black subeconomy. By 1950 astute African American business owners knew that appeals to race pride and solidarity, which business leaders such as Walter Cohen and Prudhomme Dejoie had used at the start of the century to gain support for black insurance companies, were no longer adequate and had to be supported with performance, value, and service. Nonetheless, persistent patterns of discrimination made black New Orleanians totally dependent on black businesses for employment in sales, management, and clerical positions. In 1947 Berchman's had ten office workers, including an office manager, and employed agents throughout New Orleans. The company paid, in salaries, bonuses, and commissions, $38,992 to its employees and officers that year. Community leaders knew that in the absence of several large black-owned companies in the city, the development and support of the thousands of small companies was that much more important.[13]

Another feature of Jim Crow was the refusal of whites to enter certain kinds of service businesses in the black community. Black-owned funeral homes operated totally free from white competition. Funeral homes had to deliver a level of personal and sensitive service while demonstrating a degree of caring that white owners of funeral homes would not provide. Several firms outpaced their competitors and became the leading black funeral home businesses in the city. And most of the top firms started early in the Jim Crow period. Blandin, George Geddes, Geddes and Moss, Henderson, Labat, and Rhodes funeral homes were all operating by 1910.

Funeral homes were usually family owned and operated and offered only limited employment opportunities to the larger black community. But the families involved in that type of business experienced economic success that placed them in the vanguard of the black middle class.

Advertising, personal contacts, and quality service sustained the growth of the black funeral homes. Owners also depended on several cooperative business initiatives for their continued success. Like the horizontal forms of business organization that helped transform the nation's economy around the turn of the twentieth century, several funeral home owners were involved in other small businesses and associations that funneled customers to them. Duplain Rhodes, owner of Rhodes Funeral Home, served as president of St. Mary's Benevolent Association for several years. This benevolent and mutual aid association paid Rhodes's company a flat fee for members' burial expenses. George Geddes, one of the most prosperous funeral home owners, was one of the original organizers of Unity Industrial Life Insurance Company. Funeral home owners also faced competition from companies seeking a greater share of their business. Sheffield, for example, eventually led St. John Berchman's into the funeral home business.[14]

By the 1950s, the last of the Jim Crow decades, the insurance companies and funeral homes remained the most successful black-owned businesses. Less prosperous but more numerous were the retail stores and service-related enterprises. The retail businesses included restaurants, grocery stores, produce markets, meat markets, furniture stores, and clothing stores. Dryades Street and North Claiborne Avenue served as commercial hubs for the African American community. Nevertheless, and consistent with the diverse housing patterns of the city, blacks owned and operated businesses throughout most areas of the city. The retail businesses, like the insurance companies and funeral homes, depended on the black community for customers. Yet to a much greater degree than black insurance companies and funeral homes, they had to contend with competition from white-owned businesses. Securing and maintaining the loyalty and business of African American consumers were challenging for varied and complicated reasons having to do with economics and psychology. African American consumers often made decisions on what businesses to support based on rational economic choices related to price, quality, selection, and convenience. Many white businessmen possessed more capital and experience than their black counterparts and often provided better goods at a cheaper price. The choice for many African Americans in the city may have been regrettable but was simple enough to understand; operating at the economic margin and needing the best bargain possible, black consumers often shopped at white-owned stores.[15]

Most African American retail businesses could not adequately compete with businesses owned by whites. With better capital, more experienced management, superior relationships with wholesalers and distributors, and a developed business culture, white-owned businesses enjoyed clear advantages. The results were apparent and predictable: "Very often the Negro small businessman is little more than a laborer in his own place. Though many have risen above this category, the majority of them are still struggling along on a narrow margin of success."[16] This slim margin failed to dampen the spirits of many aspiring business owners, and throughout the period African Americans continued to enter the retail business. In 1929, for example, African Americans in New Orleans owned a total of 771 retail stores, and only Chicago, with 815, and Philadelphia, with 787, had more. No other city had more than 400 black-owned stores. Together, the stores generated $2.3 million in sales, and their combined end-of-the-year inventory totaled $130,140. Of the 771 retail stores 479 were restaurants and produce stores and accounted for $1.16 million of the net sales for that year.[17] And in the 1930s the black-owned retail stores faced not only white competition but the overall effects of the Great Depression. In a six-year period, 1929–35, 482 retail businesses failed, and the remaining ones had combined net sales of $574,000. Some store owners, after losing their businesses, never again entered the entrepreneurial class. But many others persevered with dogged determination and resourcefulness and managed to keep, though at times precariously, a hand on the business ladder. Joseph James was one such individual, whose career provides insight into the vagaries of business formation for black New Orleanians.

James's emphasis on economic prosperity as part of black community development gathered momentum in the 1920s and reflected the growing conviction among African Americans that they could succeed in all facets of American life. Black New Orleanians, led by a vocal black leadership class, viewed the period, like many blacks and whites across the country, as "glorious and rosy years." They had, of course, some reasons for their optimism. The nation's economy appeared strong in the mid-1920s, African Americans registered an increase in business ownership, and the number of African Americans employed showed gains. And if black New

Orleanians failed to see the Great Depression over the horizon and the fragility of a separate black economy, they were not alone.[18] James and his family moved to New Orleans in 1919 from St. James Parish. He entered the city at a time when black leaders believed "the New Orleans Colored business man is making rapid strides forward and that he has an eye for the opportunity latent in the tremendous economic strength which numbers and wealth of the New Orleans Negroes give to him."[19] Between 1900 and the onset of the Great Depression the number of black-owned businesses climbed nearly 300 percent, and despite the movement of African Americans from the South, the majority of the businesses were located in the South. James remained in New Orleans and demonstrated through his actions his determination to enter the business class. So, with enthusiastic faith in his abilities, the potential of the black community to support businesses like his, and the vigor of America's economy, James entered the business world.

In 1925 James owned a grocery store in the Uptown section of the city with two of his brothers, Morris and Eddie. The establishment was small, with inventory, furniture, and equipment assessed at approximately fifteen hundred dollars. The brothers served as managers-workers, with assistance from other family members. They soon abandoned their first location and opened the next store at one side of a double house rented by Joseph. The relocation had no appreciable effect on the amount of business sales or the type of inventory carried. Their customers were individuals with modest incomes who often had to purchase items on credit. Like many small store owners, the James brothers had to provide credit or lose customers. While necessary and helpful in fostering a sense of community, this practice created problems. The store had the usual recurring expenses of rent, utilities, payments to wholesalers, and taxes. Often faced with a shortage of operating capital and with few capital sources available to him, James sometimes borrowed small sums of money at exorbitant rates of interest. One source "engaged in the business of making small loans," for instance, loaned the money to James at 3.5 percent interest a month, a lucrative business indeed.[20]

Joseph James and his brothers realized that their retail business would not provide them with adequate income, so they usually worked other jobs to supplement their small profits from the store. Eventually, Joseph secured employment as an insurance agent with Unity Life Insurance but remained committed to owning some type of business. His business ventures remained marginal at best, so it seems likely that something other than the prospect of wealth motivated him. James had two children. Sending them to private schools, which he did, was not sufficient to provide the life he wanted for them. He attempted to imbue in his children the value of education and business ownership. To a degree he succeeded, for both of the James children later owned small businesses. They both had benefited from observing their father's business activities, just as he and his brothers had learned the value of property ownership from their parents. The community development efforts of black New Orleanians involved preparing future generations for the task as well.[21]

The success of retail businesses such as Joseph James's depended on many factors: local permits, sufficient capital, managerial expertise, and adequate supplies. Many African Americans avoided some of these potential obstacles by owning service businesses. In addition, ownership of such businesses often fulfilled the vocational and professional interest of the individual. Throughout the Jim Crow period barbershops, beauty parlors, and dry cleaners constituted the majority of the service businesses owned and operated by African Americans. Most operated free from white competition, but dry cleaning and laundry businesses proved a notable exception. A few dry cleaners nevertheless successfully competed against white-owned dry cleaners and gained white and black customers. Butler Cleaners and Dorsey's Valetria were two such businesses.[22]

One service business, however, enjoyed a near total monopoly on black customers—beauty salons. Early in the twentieth century black female hair care developed into a lucrative business, not just for Madame C. J. Walker, one of the pioneers in black female hair care and skin preparation, but for tens of thousands of black beauticians. Born Sarah Breedlove in Louisiana in 1867, Madame Walker eventually headed a prosperous company and had a net worth of more than a million dollars but experienced a challenging and difficult early life that in many ways mirrored the lives of countless African American women. A widow with a child to support by the age of twenty-two, she worked as a washerwoman in her native state and in Mississippi. In the difficult post-Reconstruction period many African American women favored that occupation because it allowed a measure of autonomy and allowed them to work from home, enabling them to care for their children and home. This is not to suggest that the work was easy, and indeed, such an arrangement usually increased their overall work obligations. It was likely the cause of some of the stress and worry that the future Madame Walker experienced, causing her scalp problems and hair loss at a young age. She sought relief and experimented with different ingredients before finding a combination that healed her scalp and restored hair growth. She shared the mixture with friends and saw similar results. She started selling the product door-to-door and eventually opened several beauty salons, which developed into a chain in the United States and the Caribbean.[23]

In New Orleans the developing hair care and skin business was under the control of African American women. The "beauty culture industry," as one scholar observed, "was widely recognized as providing economic opportunities for black women who wished to escape domestic labor."[24] In New Orleans their methods of operation varied. The majority worked from their homes, often scheduling customers around their responsibilities as wives and mothers, resembling in some ways the work arrangement of washerwomen. Some operated their businesses away from home, indicating a degree of independence and a commitment to a profession. Only a small number managed to move beyond being owner-operators and expanded their shops enough to hire one or more workers on a regular basis. A very few employed workers and started beautician schools. Mrs. M. J. Spotts owned Crescent Hairdressing College and advertised it as the "largest and most thoroughly equipped hairdressing college in the country, owned and managed by colored people." In 1912 she operated her main school on Dryades Street and a branch on Tulane Avenue. The demand for hair care training remained strong, and in the middle of the period, 1930, the city had 261 black beauticians. Later Necola Beauty School and Katie Beauty School trained many of the city's black beauticians.[25]

Katie Wickham, the owner of Katie Beauty School, was both a business owner and community leader. For several years Wickham served as the vice president of the local NAACP branch and participated in many voter education drives. The idea that "the lessons and tactics black beauticians learned through their engagement with state-run beauty boards allowed them to develop boldness when engaging with the state" is consistent with the community leadership exhibited by Wickham.[26] In addition, her school and beauty shop often served as a center to disseminate protest information. Indeed, in her beauty shop Wickham fostered the type of female bonding that scholars have identified as a crucial component of black women's efforts to oppose victimization and oppression related to race and gender. Wickham's students and customers belonged to diverse

BUSINESS AND LABOR

class and religious groups, and the bonding that occurred within the context of black hair care helped to blur and transcend differences that could undermine community unity. Wickham's influence extended beyond New Orleans; she served as president of the National Beauty Culture League, an organization started by Madame C. J. Walker.[27]

Another service business with considerable female participation was dressmaking. Some females considered themselves "fashionable dressmakers," and others, out of modesty or honesty, advertised themselves merely as "dressmakers." Patterns of operations similar to those prevailing among beauticians existed in the dressmaking business. The majority of the dressmakers worked from their homes and relied on a small customer base. Even more than beauticians, dressmakers could structure their work around other responsibilities and interests. They also had more opportunities for creative expression, transforming ordinary dress patterns into fancy and "fashionable" ones. The creative aspect of the job was no small consideration for some of the women who worked as dressmakers. Through their daily work they gave an affirmative answer to a rhetorical and important question raised by the African American writer Alice Walker: "How was the creativity of the black woman kept alive?" It was kept alive in part through fashionable dresses and other acts of creativity that African American women managed to incorporate into their everyday duties and responsibilities.[28] Dressmaking and hair care were not the only fields dominated by African American women. They also maintained a presence in certain other professions.

Black females and males achieved some gains in several of the professional categories and registered growth in most others during the Jim Crow period (table 6.2). Those professions that serviced a largely black clientele—teachers, nurses, physicians, and dentists—experienced the highest growth. The number of black physicians increased between 1900 and 1950, despite the closing of Flint Medical College of New Orleans University in 1911. After Flint closed, Meharry Medical School in Nashville, Tennessee, trained most of the new physicians and dentists who established practices in the city. Several factors accounted for the black community's ability to lure physicians and dentists to New Orleans. The urban setting, the size of the black population, and the presence of a black hospital made the city an attractive place to start a career. Black physicians and dentists, sometimes laboring under adverse conditions, rendered a needed medical service to African Americans in New Orleans.[29] As the number of black physicians increased, so did the number of black nurses, although the level of training received by nurses was uneven during the first three decades of the century. The 1920 census, for example, reported 439 untrained nurses and only 60 trained ones. Many of the individuals who considered themselves nurses mainly performed midwifery functions. The demand for midwives remained high, notwithstanding the modern facilities available to expectant women after the opening of Flint-Goodridge Hospital. The large number of untrained nurses existed in part because of the absence of a nursing training school in the city. In 1938 Dillard University started a nursing program that eventually trained hundreds of African American women during the Jim Crow period.[30]

The steady rise in the number of black professionals did not extend to the field of law. Rather, the number of black attorneys in the city actually decreased between 1920 and 1950. Law, unlike other fields, brought black professionals into direct contact with whites and, therefore, with the proscriptions related to race. They were unable to retreat into a segregated environment to serve the black community effectively. Rene Metoyer, Frank Smith, and J. Madison Vance managed to maintain an active practice during the early Jim Crow period but often relied on other skills and jobs to supplement their income from legal fees. Smith, for example, was a stenographer and enjoyed a considerable reputation for his expertise. In 1925, when Alexander P. Tureaud graduated from Howard University Law School and later decided to return to his native city to practice, it marked a significant event in New Orleans black community development. Although Tureaud graduated from Howard University before Charles H. Houston became dean and transformed it into a top law school for civil rights law, Tureaud's law school connections eventually helped bring black New Orleans within the orbit of the NAACP-sponsored legal challenge to Jim Crow.[31]

The African American community and its individual members suffered directly because of segregation and discrimination, but the teaching profession benefited. Patterns of discrimination in the larger society probably forced individuals to become educators rather than lawyers or other types of professionals. Teachers dominated the professional class in black New Orleans, and the list of outstanding educators was extensive. The number of black teachers grew substantially throughout the period and reflected the expanding range of educational opportunities. In addition, in the early twentieth century the Colored Education Alliance and the black commu-

Table 6.2. Professional and Technical Workers, 1950

	MALES	FEMALES
Accountants and auditors	9	2
Actresses, dancers, entertainers	—	15
Architects	2	—
Artists and art teachers	6	8
Authors, editors, reporters	13	2
Chemists	4	3
Clergy	251	—
College presidents, professors, instructors	28	12
Dentists	16	—
Designers and draftsmen	2	1
Dietitians	—	22
Engineers	4	—
Lawyers and judges	3	—
Librarians	—	12
Musicians and music teachers	125	58
Natural scientists	7	—
Nurses	—	156
Pharmacists	20	—
Physicians and surgeons	48	2
Social scientists	5	3
Social welfare and recreation workers	17	63
Surveyors	1	—
Teachers	276	830
Technicians, medical and dental	175	17

Source: U.S. Department of Commerce, *United States Census of Population: 1950, Detailed Characteristics, Louisiana.*

nity led a successful campaign to remove the remaining white teachers from black schools. Although whites aggressively enforced the color line in most facets of city life, school officials initially proved unwilling to extend it to education, with the total removal of white teachers from black schools. Eventually, both black and white citizens opposed this seemingly contradictory position. School officials often defended the practice to both blacks and whites with the assertion that they could not find enough qualified black teachers. Rev. Henderson Dunn and other black leaders had a different view. They charged that the practice persisted because white teachers supported and participated in the effort to keep blacks in their "place." They also noted that it afforded additional employment opportunities for white teachers at the expense of blacks. Rather than end the practice, school officials on two occasions attempted to expand it. In 1906 two school board members tried to replace all of the black teachers with white teachers, but the full board voted against the measure. In 1910, however, only vocal protests from the black community convinced the school board to abandon its plan to staff an annex to a black school with white teachers.[32]

Between 1910 and 1916 African Americans in the city, convinced that because of their racial views white teachers could not provide black children with a quality education, accelerated their efforts to obtain an all-black teaching corps. The steady influx of qualified black teachers such as Lucian Alexis, John Hoffman, Lucille Hutton, George Longe, O.C.W. Taylor, and Fannie C. Williams undermined the board's claim that there was an insufficient supply of black applicants. In 1913 the board voted to remove white teachers from McDonogh No. 6 and McDonogh No. 32. And in 1915 and 1916 school board members voted to remove them from the remaining two schools that had white teachers: Lawton Elementary School and McCarthy Elementary School. Many African Americans shared the opinion that "the establishment of a completely colored division of the New Orleans Public School was . . . an educational triumph for the Negro race."[33] Although many in the black community viewed it as an educational triumph, it was not necessarily an economic one. For no class of black professionals in the city labored as close to economic subsistence as schoolteachers. Salaries for black and white teachers remained inadequate throughout the period, but racial discrimination made the situation much worse for African Americans, for school officials often paid them 50 percent less than white teachers. Some teachers pursued two careers in an attempt to supplement their meager income. Two editors for the *Louisiana Weekly* were teachers, Mayme O. Brown and O.C.W. Taylor. Another teacher, Edward Spriggens, served as the newspaper's society editor for several years.

If discrimination forced many talented African Americans to choose education as a career, the South's racial patterns kept others from obtaining positions in other areas of public employment. And when they secured city jobs, they did so as laborers. In 1920, for example, African Americans held

779 of the 1,431 labor jobs with the city and 821 of 1,870 in 1930. In 1909 city officials stopped employing African Americans as policemen, closing another avenue of employment because of race. And with the exception of the postal service, public service jobs with the federal government proved almost as elusive as those with the city and state; only 6 African Americans held federal public service jobs in 1920 and 18 did in 1930. The dearth of employment opportunities in the public sector was especially damaging to black community development because most of the positions did not require training or formal education above the high school level (table 6.3).[34]

In the building trades, unlike the public sector, black New Orleanians maintained a presence that had been gained as early as the antebellum period. Black Creoles held many of the skilled positions. Again, however, patterns of discrimination probably forced many third- and fourth-generation blacks to pursue the trade of their fathers rather than enter the professional class. In the main African Americans entered the skilled trades after a period of apprenticeship with relatives or friends. Many of them, such as George Allain and Albert Duncan, established their own businesses and secured jobs from black businesses, organizations, and individuals. Allain built the rectory of Holy Ghost Church. Although evidence is not extensive, it appears that black leaders and professionals made a concerted and consistent effort to use black skilled workers (table 6.4).[35]

The commitment to racial solidarity that brought business to some

Table 6.3. Selected List of Sales and Clerical Workers, 1950

	MALES	FEMALES
Bookkeepers	18	37
Cashiers	—	58
Insurance agents and brokers	224	125
Mail carriers	447	—
Real estate agents and brokers	9	—
Salesmen and sales clerks		
Manufacturing	23	—
Retail trade	190	274
Wholesale trade	26	—
Stenographers, typists, secretaries	—	205
Telephone operators	—	17

Source: *United States Census of Population: 1950, Detailed Characteristics, Louisiana.*

Table 6.4. Selected Black and White Male Skilled Workers, 1950

	BLACK	WHITE
Bakers	216	482
Boilermakers	14	274
Cabinetmakers	61	453
Carpenters	1,110	3,447
Compositors and typesetters	20	581
Cranemen, hoistmen, construction machine operator	103	672
Electricians	19	1,333
Linemen and servicemen (telephone, telegraph, power)	13	973
Locomotive engineers	3	253
Locomotive firemen	29	180
Machinists and job setters	35	1,310
Masons, tile setters, stone cutters	241	337
Airplane mechanics and repairmen	2	127
Automobile mechanics and repairmen	463	2,057
Radio and television repairmen	45	302
Painters (construction), paperhangers, glaziers	560	1,908
Plasterers and cement finishers	496	76
Plumbers and pipe fitters	57	1,230
Printing craftsmen	6	288
Stationary engineers	40	815
Structural metal workers	19	311
Tailors and furriers	41	163
Tinsmiths, coppersmiths, sheet metal workers	21	561
Toolmakers	1	40

Source: United States Census of Population: 1950, Detailed Characteristics, Louisiana.

black workers in the building trades had little effect on African American women in the city. If black men faced employment restrictions because of race, black women endured the double discrimination of race and gender. Nonetheless, black women managed to record some gains in the labor market in addition to the progress achieved in professional and technical fields such as teaching and nursing. Between 1920 and 1950 the number of black clerical and sales workers increased from 314 to 1,080. They secured employment as cashiers, secretaries, and sales clerks. Seeking to expand their range of economic opportunities, some women entered nontraditional fields and worked as machine operators, bookkeepers, and insurance agents. The ability of some to rise above society's imposed barriers because of race and gender held out a ray of hope for the daughters of the tens of thousands of black women who toiled as domestics and cooks. By 1950 black women in New Orleans had gained entrance into most of the professional and technical categories listed in that year's census. Nonetheless, there were still no black female lawyers, dentists, architects, or engineers (table 6.5).[36]

Black employment and economic gains occurred largely because of the initiatives of the black community, individuals, and leaders. Factors external to the black community also aided the rise in the economic level of blacks. More public money for education and the continued commitment to black higher education by several religious denominations helped black economic advancement. Black leaders were not unmindful of these efforts and, of course, encouraged them. In addition, they recognized the value of labor solidarity as another way to promote economic progress. Notwithstanding the onset of Jim Crow in the waning years of the nineteenth century, some black New Orleanians attempted to keep alive a tradition of unionism that first flourished during Reconstruction. In the 1870s, for example, black union leaders had organized the Longshoremen Protective Union Benevolent Association and the Screwmen's Benevolent Association No. 1. Both groups attempted to work with related white waterfront union workers and other unions to improve wages and working conditions

Table 6.5. Black and White Female Workers, 1950

	BLACK	WHITE
Professional and technical	1,281	8,399
Managers, officials, proprietors	504	3,261
Clerical and kindred workers	639	22,770
Sales workers	442	7,272
Craftsmen, foremen, kindred work	180	801
Operatives and kindred workers	4,366	6,008
Private household workers	11,013	619
Service workers (excluding private households)	6,574	4,924

Source: *United States Census of Population: 1950, Detailed Characteristics, Louisiana.*

and participated in the New Orleans general strike of 1892. Over twenty thousand black and white workers participated in the three-day strike that caused widespread disruption in the city's economy. The strike improved the interest of labor slightly; union leaders won a few small concessions but failed to achieve their two most important goals of establishing a closed shop and gaining wider recognition. Two years later the fragile alliance between black and white dockworkers suffered irreparable harm when an agreement that placed a hiring limit on the number of black screwmen who could work at any one time. The agreement eventually unraveled when foreign ship companies started employing black screwmen in excess of the agreement and at 50 percent of the prevailing wage. White screwmen and longshoremen went on strike over the issue, and violence quickly ensued. A federal court order ended the strike but failed to end the growing friction between black and white dockworkers.[37]

Labor solidarity failed to take hold in the 1920s and 1930s as well. A strike by dockworkers in 1923 shattered the last vestiges of black-white labor solidarity and signaled the death knell for progressive unionism on the waterfront. Shipping officials used black and white nonunion workers and a court injunction against picketing to break the strike and the unions. After the strike nonunion labor handled 70 percent of the port's cargo. The failure of the 1923 strike demonstrated two fundamental problems that plagued unionism in New Orleans during the Jim Crow era. First, the presence of a substantial number of unemployed or underemployed workers, many of them African American workers, gave employers a source of laborers in the event of a strike. Second, attempts at labor solidarity usually ruptured under the powerful weight of racial discrimination and hostilities. And even the involvement of national union leaders failed to produce different results. In 1937 the International Longshoremen's and Warehousemen's Unions (ILWU), an affiliate of the Congress of Industrial Organizations (CIO), attempted to rekindle the embers of worker solidarity that had once existed on the waterfront. ILWU officials chose Bob Robertson, a veteran organizer, to develop the union in New Orleans. When he arrived, he found thousands of workers disenchanted because of, in his view, widespread anti-union sentiment, racial tension, and ineffective American Federation of Labor leadership.[38] Many workers considered Robertson and the ILWU a welcome alternative to their present plight. Indeed, before the arrival of the CIO affiliated ILWU, the *Louisiana Weekly* recognized the possible benefits to African Americans if the

CIO established a presence in New Orleans. "More and more Negroes are becoming interested in the CIO," an editorial maintained, because of "its fairness toward Negro workers."[39]

When the ILWU arrived, Willie Dorsey, a black longshoreman with twenty years of experience on the docks, became an enthusiastic and fearless organizer. ILWU leaders needed a local person to win the support of the dockworkers, and Dorsey was not only fearless and committed to unionism but also a powerful speaker who had the respect of most black longshoremen. Dorsey soon had an opportunity to display his oratorical skills at an outdoor meeting. Waterfront workers, Dorsey told the crowd, "were burdened with heavy loads, long hours, and short pay." He vowed that conditions would improve if workers followed his lead into the ranks of the ILWU.[40] Dorsey, Robertson, and several other organizers disseminated the union message throughout the winter of 1937–38. And by the spring of 1938 they had secured enough signatures to petition the National Labor Relations Board (NLRB) to hold a union representation election. NLRB officials convened a hearing on 20 June 1938 to gather information on the request. One individual testified that fear of retaliation from the International Longshoremen Association (ILA), an American Federation of Labor affiliate, prevented ILWU members and supporters from openly aligning with the new union.[41]

Intimidation by the ILA represented only part of the problem encountered by the ILWU in trying to organize dockworkers. White business leaders and politicians opposed them because of their stance against racial discrimination and alleged connection to communism. One of those charges was sufficient enough to elicit white anger, but identification with two of them ensured some type of organized effort to discredit and defeat the ILWU. Four days after the NLRB hearing, police raided the CIO headquarters and arrested eighty-four people, including six women office workers. On the following day policemen beat Robertson and later conducted a second raid on the CIO office. In July 1938 the state legislature joined in the persecution when it adopted a resolution condemning the activities of the CIO.[42] The resolution revealed that state lawmakers thought more was at stake than labor-management relations on the waterfront. The issue, as the resolution made clear, was the maintenance of white supremacy. Using inflammatory language and appealing to advocates of white supremacy, the Louisiana legislative body declared that "one of the greatest dangers that is threatening the people of this state is that the insidious propaganda disseminated by these imported alien radicals has been directed to the organization of the Negroes of this state and it has unfortunately taken root and unless drastic steps are taken at once, it will spread to the rural parts of the state and white supremacy will be endangered."[43]

As the attacks mounted against them, union organizers became more cautious but continued their work as they prepared for the decisive representation election scheduled for 14 October 1938. Dorsey and Robertson remained confident amid reports that their organizers had registered or received commitments from 3,000 workers. Harry Bridges, the ILWU national president, predicted that his union would win with at least 80 percent of the vote. Bridges, Dorsey, Robertson, and the ILWU suffered a resounding defeat; the ILA received 2,701 votes and the ILWU a mere 874. Amid the disarray of defeat, ILWU officials groped for answers. Quite possibly, the ILWU lost the election because of electoral corruption. According to several individuals, large sums of money had changed hands on the day before the election. One ILWU organizer charged that the AFL and ILA spent over $100,000 to ensure victory.[44]

The failure of black longshoremen to win an increase in wages through union activities affected their standards of living. The majority of the city's African American population lived at or below the economic margin. It is difficult to arrive at an accurate assessment of the wealth of black New Orleanians during the Jim Crow period. Employment and occupational data, however, indicate that African Americans worked in the less-remunerative jobs, and their material wealth lagged behind that of whites. Business ownership and an increase in black professionals helped to reduce but not eliminate the income disparity between the races. The effort by community leaders and individuals to expand black economic opportunity had a direct impact on material wealth and living standards. Similar to the rationale for improved schools, African Americans knew their fight to gain full equality would produce concrete benefits. Each day they encountered the consequences of living in a society that discriminated and excluded some of its members because of race. Their neighborhoods and housing often reflected their marginal position in the New Orleans social order.

An examination of the housing stock of African Americans during the middle of the period provides some indication of their economic position in New Orleans. In 1930, 4,563 black New Orleanians owned their homes. Thirteen of the homes had a value of more than $20,000, and 504 had a value of $5,000 to $7,499. The vast majority of the homes had a value of less than $5,000. In 1940, 4,494, or approximately 11 percent, of the housing units occupied by African Americans were owner-occupied structures. On the other hand, 30 percent of the houses occupied by whites were owner-occupied buildings.[45] African Americans not only owned a smaller percentage of the housing units they occupied compared to white citizens; their houses were often substandard buildings in need of major repairs. The 1940 census provided information on the physical condition and rental value of the more than 137,000 housing units in the city. Thirty-eight percent of the houses occupied by African Americans rented for $9, while only 8 percent of white renters paid so little. Another 36 percent of the 41,295 units in which African Americans resided had a rental value of $10 to $14. That number contrasted sharply with the 17 percent figure for whites in the same rental range. The ability to pay a monthly rent of $25 or more probably indicated some level of middle-class status. Only 2.6 percent of blacks paid a rent that high, compared to 40 percent of white renters. The physical condition of the housing units usually correlated with the rental value. Low rent, in other words, usually meant substandard houses. Throughout the Jim Crow period the efforts to gain better housing and improved neighborhoods remained a key component of community development and individual initiative. And attempts by white leaders and citizens to enact laws designed to further reduce the number of quality housing units available to African Americans led to one of the early challenges to Jim Crow policies.[46]

7

Jim Crow Attacked

By the third decade of the twentieth century the political, social, and economic benefits of being white in America were substantial, and white leaders and citizens in New Orleans were determined to extend them even more. Unlike some cities with a large black population, African Americans continued to live in most New Orleans neighborhoods, much to the consternation of white citizens. Indeed, these white citizens attempted to emulate their southern and northern counterparts by enacting a residential segregation ordinance to prevent African Americans from moving into certain areas of the city. The effort to exclude blacks from residing in sections of the city gained momentum when a 1924 legislative act granted cities with a population of twenty-five thousand or more the right to enact a housing segregation ordinance. On 9 September 1924 the New Orleans Commission Council introduced an ordinance mandating residential segregation. Without much editorial comment the *New Orleans Times-Picayune,* the city's leading white daily paper, hailed the proposed regulation as a means to "protect white neighborhoods." New Orleans's black citizens, however, viewed the proposal as an additional violation of their civil rights and an attempt to hinder their personal and economic advancement. One week later, on 16 September, the Commission Council unanimously adopted the segregation ordinance. A large audience joyously applauded the council's action, secure in the knowledge that the mayor would sign it into law. Buoyed by the euphoric crowd, Mrs. L. E. Stephens rose and thanked the council for passing the ordinance and stated, "You may be sure that not only myself but every other mother of white children in New Orleans sincerely appreciates the restriction that will prevent Negro children coming into our communities and mixing with our children." Two days following that brief statement of allegiance to the solid South, the reform mayor Andrew J. McShane signed the ordinance into law.[1]

The new ordinance represented not only a statement of law but a race philosophy as well. In part it decreed that the measure was needed in the interest of "public peace and welfare." In its wording the ordinance appeared fair and impartial because it prohibited construction of houses for African Americans in areas designated white neighborhoods and construction of houses for whites in areas designated black neighborhoods. The adherence to democracy was present, however, for the law allowed exceptions "on the written consent of a majority of the persons of the opposite race inhabiting such community or portions of the city to be affected." In all the ordinance contained several sections. Section 4 stated that each seven-day period an individual maintained a home in violation of section 2 "shall be deemed to be a separate and distinct offense." In other words, a person living in a house for twenty-eight days in contravention of the segregation ordinance could be cited for four different crimes. Section 6 outlined the penalty for each violation, a maximum fine of twenty-five dollars and/or a maximum jail term of thirty days.[2] Interestingly, and this was understood by African Americans in New Orleans and throughout the South, New Orleans passed the ordinance despite the 1917 United States Supreme Court ruling in *Buchanan v. Warley* that ruled residential segregation unconstitutional. The ordinance was a clear indication of a commitment to rigid racial segregation and the continued belief that southern race relations should be left to white southerners to define.

Often officials passed laws that largely went without enforcement, but such was not the case with the New Orleans residential segregation ordinance. After its passage white officials and citizens wasted little time in attempting to implement the new law. On 18 September whites placed a sign in the 2700 and 2800 blocks of Louisiana Avenue designating the two-block area "for white people." Louisiana Avenue was a beautiful, tree-lined street that contained some of the better homes in the city. Moreover, African Americans already owned three double houses in the 2700 and 2800 blocks of Louisiana Avenue. During the spring of 1925 city attorney T. Semmes Walmsley vowed that his office would vigorously prosecute all segregation cases. To accomplish his mission, Walmsley placed an assistant attorney in charge of all segregation cases. When Anna Beck established her residence in a supposedly white neighborhood at 3428 Milan Street, in the uptown section of New Orleans, she became the first person convicted under the segregation ordinance. The judge fined her fifty dollars or sixty days in jail. The degree of arrests and harassment reached such proportions that local NAACP leaders James Gayle, Deborah Guidry, and George Lucas joined other leaders such as Joseph Hardin in seeking some type of redress from city officials.[3]

Hardin and Lucas helped spearhead the drafting of a lengthy petition protesting the "drastic, harsh and unjust" way in which the police department and city courts enforced the segregation ordinance. They were also part of a delegation of black leaders who presented the document to the New Orleans Association of Commerce in October 1925. In the carefully worded petition, African Americans stressed that the segregation ordinance was having a negative effect on black homeowners. They explained that some homeowners who depended on the rent from one side of an owner-occupied double could not keep tenants because the police scared them away with either arrest or threats of arrest. The petitioners asserted that "under the methods in enforcing the present segregation law, we are doubtful of the safety of the investment of homes for our people, as it is an easy matter to declare any part of the city a white community or it is an easy matter to turn any part of the city a white community by forcing out a sufficient number of our people from that community."[4]

On 9 November 1925, as a result of the conference with members of the Association of Commerce, Hardin and several black leaders managed to obtain a meeting with city attorney Walmsley, commissioner of finance Arthur J. O'Keefe, superintendent of police Thomas Healy, and three representatives from the Association of Commerce. Representatives from several of the homestead associations also attended the meeting, though only after intense pressure. The homestead representatives stated that they knew of many instances in which police had forced tenants out of double houses and as a result the property remained vacant. The homestead representatives were interested in protecting their investments. Their logic was simple: if African Americans could not meet their mortgage payments, the homesteads would risk losing their investments. The emphasis on the economic consequences of the residential segregation ordinance, however, was exactly what black leaders wanted.[5] And indeed, several whites in attendance at the meeting stated that they were in favor of a segregation ordinance but conceded that African Americans suffered unfair economic persecution. Hardin told the participants that the ordinance was "undemocratic, unnecessary and unfair" and maintained that "there has never been a case where Negroes have tried to force themselves upon such sections as Rosa Parks or Audubon Park. They do want to move out of districts unpaved and unimproved and enjoy facilities the same as any other people."[6] There is no evidence that city officials voluntarily made changes in the enforcement of the ordinance. In February 1926 officials of the Land Development Company sought an injunction to restrain the city from harassing African Americans who resided at 2328 and 2330 Palmer Avenue. According to Land Development Company officials, African Americans had occupied the 2300 block of Palmer Avenue for over twenty years.

To remedy the persistent harassment by policemen and city officials, African Americans sought an injunction from the state supreme court. The state's high court granted the injunction, which stopped the city from prosecuting any new or existing residential segregation cases until the United States Supreme Court heard the appeal of Benjamin Harmon.[7] As quickly as city officials began to implement the segregation ordinance, African Americans turned to the courts to have the ordinance declared unconstitutional. Under the leadership of George Lucas and the local chapter of the National Association for the Advancement of Colored People, African Americans prepared for a legal struggle. An opportunity arose to test the legality of the ordinance when Joseph Tyler received a preliminary injunction barring Benjamin Harmon, a black homeowner, from converting a single cottage located at 321 Audubon Street into a double house in which he intended to rent one side to African Americans. When the case of *Tyler v. Harmon* went to Judge Cage of civil district court, he favored the ordinance as "just and proper, based on traditions and beliefs and forming a part of the police power which each state should be entitled to exercise." But Judge Cage transcended the prejudices of the community. "I cannot find that the ordinance in question differs from the similar Kentucky ordinance on which an opinion was handed down reversing the decision of the Kentucky court of appeals, and I am forced to bow to that decision and hold the ordinance a violation of the Fourteenth Amendment," Cage wrote in his opinion. Comfortable with the social milieu in which he lived, Judge Cage offered whites some encouragement: "I hope this case will be carried through the proper channel to the Supreme Court and . . . local conditions will be recognized and the ordinance upheld."[8]

The temporary standard-bearers for their race, Tyler and Harmon then took their fight to the Louisiana Supreme Court. After hearing arguments in the case, the court ruled in favor of the plaintiff, Joseph Tyler, justifying, at least temporarily, the belief that the courts would continue to allow white southerners to define race relations. In summary the court ruled that contrary to Judge Cage's opinion, the residential segregation ordinance was not in violation of the Fourteenth Amendment. According to Chief Justice Charles A. O'Niell, who wrote most of the decision, "There is nothing in either the Fourteenth Amendment or the Acts of Congress suggestive of social equality between the white race and the colored race, or forbidding the states to discourage amalgamation or social intercourse between the white and colored race."[9] Justice O'Niell further maintained that the New Orleans segregation ordinance differed from the Louisville, Kentucky, ordinance argued in *Buchanan v. Warley*. The Louisville ordinance forbade whites from selling property located in a white neighborhood to blacks and forbade blacks from selling property located in a black neighborhood to whites. In contrast, the New Orleans ordinance did not prohibit the selling of property by blacks to whites or whites to blacks. O'Niell held that "the ordinance merely forbid[s] the purchaser in either case to carry out his intentions, without the consent of a majority of the citizens of the other race residing in the neighborhood. To say that such a law takes away the freedom of contract would be the same as to say that the so-called zoning ordinances . . . take away the freedom of contract because they forbid an owner of property in such districts to sell it to a grocer who is willing and ready to buy it only on condition that he may use it for his grocery store." The segregation ordinance, in the judge's opinion, was another kind of zoning ordinance.[10]

Two days after the state supreme court ruled, the *New Orleans Times-Picayune* printed an article lauding the court's decision. The editorial advanced the argument that if African Americans moved into white neighborhoods, property values would decline. Reflecting on the many residential segregation struggles occurring in northern cities such as Chicago, Detroit, and New York, the editorial writer piously remarked "that residential districts in Northern cities have been broken by racial invasions that provoked racial bitterness and enmity in degrees of intensity rarely developed in the South."[11] Following the court's ruling, African Americans continued the fund-raising campaign in an effort to secure enough money for an appeal to the United States Supreme Court. Black benevolent, social, and fraternal organizations, as well as individuals, contributed over ten thousand dollars to the segregation case. African American leaders retained two local attorneys, Loys Charbonnet and Frank Smith, to litigate the segregation suit. Charbonnet and Smith received assistance from the national office of the NAACP. Because both attorneys had worked on the segregation suit from its inception, Lucas and other African American leaders did not hesitate to secure their services for the important appeal to the Supreme Court. Charbonnet traveled to Washington, D.C., in April 1926 and filed his brief with the Court. Because of the 1917 Supreme Court decision in *Buchanan v. Warley*, African Americans in New Orleans were cautiously optimistic that the Court would void the segregation ordinance. But the scheduled summer recess by the Supreme Court justices postponed the case until the following spring. Meanwhile, some whites in the city elected to take the issue of residential segregation to the streets in the form of violence.[12]

On 30 October 1926 a bomb exploded near Lincoln Theater, located at Howard and Louisiana Avenues. The black-patronized theater did not suffer any damage. Two nights later someone placed an explosive device on the steps of the Louisiana Avenue home of Henry E. Braden. Braden, an insurance executive, owned one of the few black hotels in New Orleans. The explosion at the Braden home, which was valued at over twenty thousand dollars, shattered all of the windows and tore a huge hole in the front steps. Not coincidentally, as the *Louisiana Weekly* observed, "two explosions have recently occurred on Louisiana Avenue in the section where the bitter segregation fight was begun."[13] Within ten days of the bombing of Braden's house, two more bombs exploded in black neighborhoods in the uptown area of New Orleans, on Eight Street near Carondelet Street and at 325 Saratoga Street. The explosions caused little damage but heightened the fears of black New Orleanians about their safety. Their concern intensified when another explosion rocked Braden's home on 13 November 1926. Witnesses to the bombing stated they saw five white men throw the bomb from a cruising Essex automobile. Police officials vowed to investigate and promised to place officers in the areas. Responding to the latest bombing, African Americans held several meetings to formulate some type of protest. Public demonstrations did not occur, but a *Louisiana Weekly* editorial expressed the frustration and concern of many African Americans: "We want to feel safe and secure in this city. There must be a stop put to these kinds of outrages."[14]

Except for a few cases of police harassment of black tenants, the residential segregation issue remained dormant until attorneys for Tyler and Harmon prepared to carry their respective arguments to the Supreme Court in March 1927. Francis P. Burns, first assistant city attorney, assisted Tyler's lawyer, Winn W. Wright, and argued the case before the high court. Charbonnet and Smith, along with legal counsel from the NAACP, also traveled to the nation's capital to present their case for Harmon.[15] On 14 March 1927 the Supreme Court declared, without a written opinion, that New Orleans residential segregation ordinance was unconstitutional. The Court based its ruling on the *Buchanan v. Warley* decision reached in 1917. African Americans in New Orleans were understandably pleased; they had achieved an important victory with widespread community support. But just as significant, the victory suggested that relief from oppressive local discrimination could be secured through the federal judicial system and that southern race relations were not the sole purview of southern whites. One day after the Supreme Court rendered its decision, articles appeared in the white press lamenting the Court's ruling. An editorial in the *Times-Picayune* claimed, "In the public interest and for the welfare of both races, we believe that segregation ordinances along the lines of New Orleans measure and designed as this one is to give equal protection to both races, eventually will win judicial sanction."[16]

The African American community had a different view of its victory and the future, best expressed in a *Louisiana Weekly* editorial: "The United States Supreme Court this week handed down a decision to the effect that the Segregation Ordinance recently passed in the city was unconstitutional. To many this might seem just what the Supreme Court should have done, in the light of the precedent established by the Louisville decision of some few years ago. That might be true. But the question we are asking is, would the Supreme Court have acted in any manner without the effort that was put forward by the citizens of New Orleans? Let us determine that we shall contend with every legal and right effort for those things that should be ours and are denied us."[17] And the things that were denied them because of their race were many, including political influence because of a lack of suffrage. The entire residential segregation fight would probably not have occurred but for the absence of suffrage.

The desire for suffrage and meaningful political participation thus remained a constant goal of black leaders during the Jim Crow period. New Orleans's black leaders shared the view held by Du Bois and other national leaders: "We will not be satisfied to take one jot or tittle less than our full manhood rights. We claim for ourselves every single right that belongs to a freeborn American, political, civil, and social; and until we get these we will never cease to protest and assail the ears of America."[18] With less eloquence but with the same degree of determination and insight, the local black newspaper bluntly informed African Americans that until "we have some political power, we are utterly helpless."[19] Most African Americans understood this, however, and viewed politics as essential for community development and race uplift. How to transform that goal into reality presented the real problem for black leaders such as Walter Cohen, Deborah Guidry, Joseph Hardin, and George Lucas, for they could not summon the assistance of a benevolent federal government or the support of influential whites. Disfranchisement legislation and the use of white primaries still effectively limited black voter registration.[20]

In 1921 the number of black registered voters in New Orleans had been reduced to 802 and was still less than 5,000 when the United States concluded its epic struggle to make the world safe, again, for democracy. The experience of Robert Perry in his attempts to register to vote reveals the reason for the decline and the difficulties African Americans encountered in their attempts to obtain suffrage. Perry, an educator, high school principal, and active member of the Louisiana Education Association, recalled that he attempted to register sixteen times without success before he gained the franchise. Typically, he recalled, the white registrar stated that he had not successfully interpreted parts of the state constitution but always failed to explain to him what was wrong with the response. On several occasions while Perry stood waiting to register or after being rejected, he observed the ease with which white citizens registered to vote. Perry, a veteran of World War I and a scout leader, eventually registered because of the intervention of the executive director of the Boy Scouts. Few African Americans benefited from similar white assistance, and political participation depended on voter registration.[21] But as the experience of Robert Perry demonstrates, suffrage laws and white vigilance kept the number of black voters to a minimum. And those like Perry who managed to acquire suffrage could only participate as a Republican. The musing of Frederick Douglass that "the Republican Party was the ship and all else the sea" still held sway in black New Orleans and throughout the South during the Jim Crow period, despite the movement of northern blacks away from the party of Lincoln that occurred in the 1930s. The continued loyalty of black southerners existed in part because they had little choice. The Democratic Party in the South was still a "white man's" party, and the Democrats controlled local and state government. The only political "home" available to African Americans was the Republican Party, though it was devoid of real power in southern politics.[22]

Walter L. Cohen headed black Republicanism in New Orleans until his death in 1930. Cohen was born in New Orleans on 22 January 1860 to free parents, Amelia and Bernard Cohen. His parents, both Catholics, reared him in their faith and sent him to parochial schools. As a young boy, Cohen witnessed the first efforts by African Americans in politics and while still in his teens became involved in Republican politics. He received his early political education from P.B.S. Pinchback of New Orleans and Henry Demas of St. John Parish, two of Louisiana's most successful Reconstruction politicians. Cohen never won elective office, but his involvement in party affairs enabled him to gain several appointive positions, the first from President William McKinley. He retained the position of registrar of lands during the administrations of McKinley and Theodore Roosevelt.[23] And after Warren Harding succeeded Woodrow Wilson as president in 1921, Harding appointed Cohen to the prominent position of comptroller of customs for the Port of New Orleans. Southern senators, however, effectively blocked the nomination during Harding's term in office. In March 1924, after Calvin Coolidge had assumed office following the death of Harding, Cohen finally gained confirmation. His position was almost immediately challenged the next year, when federal officials accused Cohen of providing assistance to whiskey smugglers entering the Port of New Orleans. Throughout his indictment and trial Cohen maintained his innocence, and a federal jury eventually exonerated him of all charges. Cohen and his many supporters claimed that the indictment and trial had been racially motivated. The *Louisiana Weekly* stated that view forcefully and maintained that "Mr. Cohen has made enemies. Any man makes enemies when he enters politics. Any black man makes the greatest number of enemies possible when he enters politics for that has been declared a forbidden field for black folk." And statements by the chief prosecutor in the case, assistant U.S. attorney general Arthur N. Sager, did little to change the view held by many African Americans that race was a factor in the case. Two months after the trial ended, Sager told a group of Republicans meeting at the Roosevelt Hotel in New Orleans that the "leadership of the party should be confined to white men exclusively."[24]

Cohen and other local black Republicans — James Gayle, Samuel Green, Joseph Hardin, and George Lucas, for example — withstood several challenges to active African American participation in the party. In the 1920s Hardin increased his involvement with party affairs and served as an alternate delegate to the 1924 and 1928 Republican conventions. And from 1932 to 1952 he served as an at-large delegate to the Republican conventions. Ironically, the only political appointment he received came from Democratic presidents Franklin D. Roosevelt and Harry S. Truman. Hardin held the post of consul for Liberia from 1940 to 1953. James Gayle, a resident of the Seventeenth Ward, was a member of the Republican State Central Committee for several years. Cohen, Gayle, and Hardin knew the limitations of their party as a vehicle for full equality but also realized that through their efforts African Americans remained involved in southern politics. To do so, however, was a constant challenge.[25] For just as it was true that not all Democrats were antiblack, it was equally true that not all Republicans supported full citizenship for African Americans. Black Republicans faced recurring attempts by white Republicans to exclude them from leadership within the party. The so-called lily-white movement started in the nineteenth century and gathered momentum in the twentieth.

Republican leaders, in an effort to attract more southern whites, often flirted with the idea of creating a southern wing of the party devoid of black participation. Each of the Republican presidents from McKinley to Hoover tried to increase the party's strength among southern whites. Their efforts failed to attract many whites but did succeed in reducing the influence of African Americans. The failure of Republican leaders to gain white support at times tempered the drive for complete white domination within the party. Some Republican Party leaders thought it impractical to alienate the growing black vote in the North without the prospect of gaining more white votes in the South. Thus, throughout the period national Republican leaders attempted to placate two opposing positions: the demands of white southerners to control the party and the demands of African Americans for a share in party leadership.[26] In the 1920s, under the leadership of Cohen, black Republicans in New Orleans and throughout the state maintained an uneasy alliance with whites called the "Black and Tan" movement. Basically, it represented an attempt by both blacks and whites to conduct party politics without regard to race. Although noble in intent, in the race-conscious atmosphere of the South, whenever blacks and whites interacted in any capacity, the race issue usually came to the fore. And the Republican ascendancy of the 1920s increased the political spoils and the benefits of party control. In 1926 the lily-white issue surfaced once again. A new political group, the Pelican Republican Club, organized that summer. According to its leaders, they planned to promote and achieve "white supremacy in politics." The Pelican Republican Club supported the holding of a primary election to select a candidate for that year's congressional race and endorsed William C. Harder against the old-line Republican candidate Gus Oertling.[27]

Cohen, Gayle, and Hardin and other black Republicans supported Oertling, not because they thought he would eventually win in the general election but because his candidacy exemplified the continued existence of an interracial Republican Party. A win by Harder, many black Republican leaders believed, would provide momentum for the persistent threat of white control of the local Republican Party. In the primary election held in September 1926, the Pelican Republican Club candidate lost. Many African Americans hoped that the election result represented the "final settlement" of the lily-white movement in New Orleans. A final settlement proved elusive, however, and efforts to eliminate or diminish the involvement of African Americans in the party continued. Emile Kuntz, a white Republican who had been a supporter of Cohen and the Black and Tan alliance, joined the opposition. With Cohen's support Kuntz had gained a seat on the Republican National Committee and appointment as collector of customs in New Orleans. Kuntz's break with Cohen posed a greater threat to African American leadership in the party, for unlike the Pelican Republican Club, Kuntz's National Republican Club had ties to the National Republican Party.[28] In October 1927 the split between Cohen and Kuntz surfaced once again. The Republican State Central Committee met in New Orleans to certify candidates for the January 1928 primary election for delegates to the national convention. Kuntz and Cohen supported opposing candidates in each of the city's seventeen wards. Cohen unsuccessfully challenged the party affiliation and residence of three of the men Kuntz supported. Kuntz denied accusations that his position represented an attempt to exclude African Americans from the party. Cohen and many local black leaders remained unconvinced and worked to ensure success in the election scheduled for January. In the thirteen wards in which the Cohen candidates faced opposition, they emerged victorious. Cohen easily retained his committee seat from the Seventh Ward. For Kuntz and other white Republicans, however, the election did not settle the issue.[29]

Kuntz first asked the Republican State Central Committee to invalidate the election results. After several debates, motions, and votes by committee members, the Central Committee allowed the primary results to stand. Kuntz responded by establishing a separate Republican committee. The new group met in Alexandria, a city in central Louisiana that had effectively eliminated all except a few black voters. Black Republicans did not attend the meeting, and Cohen disclaimed any prior knowledge of it. Despite the absence of African Americans at the meeting in Alexandria, the Kuntz group added two African Americans, Henry Braden and Victor Collins, to the state committee. When the two men learned of their selection, they declined to serve. Both realized that their presence on the committee would buttress Kuntz's chances of defeating Cohen. Unable to gain the cooperation of Braden and Collins, Kuntz approached several other prominent African Americans; they all refused his offers. Eventually, he managed to persuade Rev. James Bingaman to align with his group. At the Republican National Convention in Kansas City, the Cohen faction suffered defeat. The credentials committee voted to seat most of the Kuntz faction. Cohen managed to retain his seat, but that did little to assuage his group's disappointment. They assembled after the vote to assess their options. They considered appealing the decision to the full convention but rejected the effort as futile. A group of black Republicans from Texas had earlier lost a similar challenge.[30]

When the Cohen forces leveled the charge against Kuntz that he supported lily-white-ism, he again denied the charges and pointed to the presence of a few African Americans among his group. Kuntz told the truth, for his delegation included Reverend Bingaman, pastor of the First African Baptist Church, one of the largest black churches in the city. Bingaman's association with Kuntz produced bitter attacks against him from the black community. In a scathing editorial the *Louisiana Weekly* maintained that Bingaman had been the only prominent black "so degraded as to be induced by the Kuntz crowd of Lily Whites to stand sponsor for their nefarious program and accept an appointment on their delegation to Kansas City."[31] Shortly after Bingaman returned to New Orleans from the convention, members of his congregation attempted to force him to resign. In addition, several organizations vowed to sever all ties with First African

Baptist as long as Bingaman remained its pastor. He managed to prevent the initial efforts to remove him. A subsequent decrease in attendance and church collections, however, sealed his fate. Bingaman thought that a public apology would silence his vocal detractors and "admitted that he had made a grave mistake . . . [that was] costly to his church and reputation." His apology fell on unsympathetic ears; a dejected Bingaman tendered his resignation effective 31 October 1928. As the Bingaman incident reveals, black New Orleanians, despite the limitations of the Republican Party and the suppression of black suffrage, considered political involvement and group unity important components of black community development.[32]

Activity within the Republican Party, of course, had no influence on crucial local issues important to the black community. Whites in New Orleans were as solidly Democratic as blacks were Republican, and the Democrats controlled local and state politics. But much like the shared sense of community brought about by racism and discrimination, involvement in Republican politics provided another cohesive element in the development of the black community. After the United States Supreme Court struck down the "grandfather clause" in 1915, Louisiana's white leaders searched for an alternative that would "include the poor illiterate white voter and exclude the Negro voter." The device they used was an "understanding clause" contained in Article 8 of the 1921 state constitution.[33] The law required that prospective voters had to demonstrate an interpretive knowledge of both the federal and state constitutions. Literacy and the payment of a poll tax remained as additional prerequisites for registration. Nearly 16 percent of the black population ten years and over remained illiterate, but that figure did not account for the small number of black registered voters. Other factors besides illiteracy accounted for the minuscule number of black voters — 1,803 out of a total registration of 100,256 in 1929, for example. The registrar of voters possessed the authority to deny registration to any individual or group. Only against African Americans was he expected and allowed to use his office to prevent persons from registering. "Anybody can step in the office and see hundreds of white men and women register without a word being said about the constitution," a black news editor charged. African Americans, however, were "required to meet the whims of an examiner."[34]

On Tuesday night, 29 October 1929, African Americans from throughout the city traveled to Gravier and Saratoga Streets to attend what they considered an important meeting. George Labat, serving as chairman, called the meeting to order and introduced the featured speaker, Walter L. Cohen. The purpose of the meeting, according to Cohen, was to gain support for a legal "test case to determine whether the present system of registration in Louisiana demanding that Negroes be able to interpret sections of the state constitution, is not unconstitutional." The group adopted a resolution that detailed some of the discriminatory practices of the registrar and stressed that "without the ballot our race will always be lynched; burdened with taxation without representation; receive no justice in the courts; segregated and deprived of our rights and privileges." Labat appointed four committees, which had as their main function the coordination of a drive to raise at least twenty-five thousand dollars. "By the middle of January," Labat declared as the meeting ended, "we'll go to court." Labat's assessment was overly optimistic.[35]

Two years passed before Labat and the black community transformed the enthusiasm and heady expectations of that initial meeting into a direct assault on the discriminating registration process. Problems in raising the projected twenty-five to thirty thousand dollars accounted for part of the delay. Those involved in the effort were convinced that the United States Supreme Court would eventually decide the case and wanted sufficient funds to see the case to a conclusion. To secure additional funds, the committee attempted to hold a statewide meeting in Baton Rouge. The plan remained fruitless because of a lack of interest or boldness by African Americans outside the New Orleans area. Undaunted by the lack of support from their neighbors, the committee continued to solicit funds from New Orleans's black community. Many social and pleasure clubs donated money. The San Jacinto Social and Pleasure Club, for example, pledged twelve hundred dollars to the effort. When the committee had collected the funds, they turned the money over to the NAACP. And fund-raising efforts continued despite the worsening financial conditions brought about by the onset of the Great Depression. In addition to difficulties with fund-raising, the deaths of Walter L. Cohen, George Lucas, and Arnold Moss claimed three of the black community's most dedicated and respected leaders. Conflicts within the group also added to the delay. In the residential segregation case black leaders had retained a white and a black attorney. They decided in the voter registration case, however, to hire the white law firm of Guion and Upton. Alexander P. Tureaud disagreed with the selection and thought the case should have been given to African American attorneys. The last delay occurred in July 1931 at the request of the national office of the NAACP.[36]

Confident that they would raise the necessary funds to litigate the case, the committee then turned to the question of securing a plaintiff. The members chose Antoine M. Trudeau, general manager of Safety Insurance Company and second vice president of the Seventh Ward Civic League. To start the suit, Trudeau told the city's registrar that he could not interpret a clause of the constitution. On this basis he failed to get his registration papers. All the pieces were then in place. On 6 October 1931 the registration committee filed its suit in the federal district court of Judge Wayne Borah and named registrar Charles Barnes as defendant. Henry W. Robinson served as counsel for the plaintiff, and Hugh Wilkinson represented Barnes. Trudeau based his suit on the argument that the interpretation clause violated the Fifteenth Amendment and prevented African Americans from registering. In his arguments to the court Robinson pointed out that in 1930 there were only 2,279 black registered voters. In the suit Trudeau sought five thousand dollars in damages.[37] And midway through the January 1932 trial, Judge Borah halted the proceedings to consider whether or not the trial should be heard by a three-judge panel. Borah eventually ruled that he did have jurisdiction and continued the court proceedings.

When the trial resumed, the attorney for the defendant argued "that the suit should have been filed first in the civil district court without cost." Wilkinson further maintained that the suit should have originated in civil district court before a twelve-member jury and stated the suit was premature, impertinent, and vague and had "no course of action." The "understanding clause," Wilkinson maintained, was valid, and his client was only performing his duties as an employee of the state. Judge Borah agreed with Wilkinson and ruled in favor of the defendant. In his opinion Trudeau had failed to demonstrate that the understanding clause contained in Article 8, section 1, of the 1921 state constitution discriminated against African Americans. Trudeau had based his suit on the United States Supreme Court decisions *Guinn and Beal v. United States* and *Myers v. Anderson*. According to Judge Borah, those two cases were "closely distinguishable from the case at bar, in that the state laws therein involved were openly and on their face discriminatory, and were held to be unconstitutional, not on account of their provisions as to educational qualifications, but on account of the presence therein of so-called grandfather clause; that is clauses which make the right to vote dependent on conditions existing at a date prior to the adoption of the Fifteenth Amendment." Borah noted that in the *Guinn* case the Supreme Court recognized the validity of literacy tests as a prerequisite for suffrage. In the *Myers* case the Court had ruled that property qualifications did not violate the Fifteenth Amendment. "Applying this language to the educational test," Borah reasoned, "it would seem to completely answer all of the plaintiffs' contentions in this case."[38]

After Judge Borah's decision, the registration committee appealed the case to the United States Fifth Circuit Court of Appeal and the United States Supreme Court. The arguments in the case were the same, and unfortunately for the cause of black suffrage, the result also remained the same. Judges Bryan, Foster, and Hutchinson ruled for the defendant. The appeals court ruled that Article 8, section 1, applied to all voters and did not deny any citizen equal protection of the law. "It lays down but one test, that of intelligence, which applied uniformly and without discrimination to voters of any race and color." Trudeau sought a rehearing from the appeals court but was denied. Money and options, but not enthusiasm, were running out. The last ray of hope was the U.S. Supreme Court. In the two preceding trials both courts had ruled that Trudeau should have sought relief through civil district court. In his plea to the Supreme Court, Trudeau attempted to prove that if he had used the civil district court, "he could never expect a local jury of white voters to give him relief against a law of their own making and enforcement." On 9 October 1933 the Supreme Court rejected that argument and refused to "pass on the validity" of Trudeau's registration case. That November the Supreme Court again declined to hear the registration case.[39]

"The refusal of the United States Supreme Court," began an editorial in the *Louisiana Weekly*, "to hear the plea of Mr. Antoine M. Trudeau in his fight for citizenship rights is a distinct cause for regret . . . to Negroes throughout the State of Louisiana and the Southland."[40] It was a "cause for regret" but not for surrender. The cooperative effort that went into the Trudeau case demonstrated that the same spirit of protest, as opposed to accommodation, that had helped propel the *Plessy v. Ferguson* case to the Supreme Court in the 1890s, while sometimes dimmed, still flickered for most African Americans in New Orleans. The courts' strong support of Louisiana's registration law failed to dampen the commitment by African

Americans to exhaust all legal remedies in an effort to win the case. In the midst of the Great Depression, with thousands of African Americans in the city unemployed, why did the black community continue to fight? Had the entire effort been in vain, a waste of scarce community resources? African Americans only had to look at their schools, neighborhoods, places of employment, city government, and the daily press to know that the fight for suffrage, which meant improvements in many areas of their lives, had not been in vain. They knew that national political participation was a right worth obtaining. And they knew that it was a right linked to personal safety and justice before the law as much as to suffrage and civic engagement.

The black freedom struggle always involved more than resistance and responses to disfranchisement, racial segregation, and civic and economic exclusion. Often the struggle centered on ways to prevent or reduce white-on-black violence, including violence committed by law enforcement officers. The great majority of the violence was political and had been used to underpin slavery and the racial oppression that followed slavery's end. Political violence, then, for most black southerners was more American than democracy. This was especially the case for the millions of them who lived in the rural South or the small towns that dotted the southern landscape. In those areas quasi-economic independence was not a shield against violence and could just as easily be the cause of it. Moving to urban areas in the South and out of the South was one response to rural violence. New Orleans, for example, saw its African American population increase throughout the Jim Crow period. And increased economic opportunities were not the only reason for the city's attraction to rural African Americans. In each succeeding decade of the twentieth century, African Americans who moved to urban areas could expect less risk of becoming victims of white violence. They did, in fact, experience a decline in white violence. They did not experience its elimination.

African American women had to contend with the additional threat of sexual violence. Protecting African American women usually fell to individuals and family members. Nevertheless, protecting African American women from sexual violence was seen as a community responsibility, as were efforts to obtain justice for those unfortunate females who had suffered from it. One such victim was Hattie McCray. In February 1930 McCray, only fourteen years old, was killed by Charles Guerand, a New Orleans policeman who was not on duty or in uniform. McCray was killed by two bullets, one to her head and the other to her abdomen. Two bullets fired into the body of a mere fourteen-year-old child. What crime had she committed? How did Guerand explain his actions? McCray, who worked at the restaurant where she was killed, had been murdered because she had resisted Guerand's sexual advances. A police investigation, newspaper accounts, and trial testimony eventually revealed that on several occasions Guerand had made sexual advances toward McCray before killing her on 10 February. According to Guerand, he killed Hattie McCray in self-defense after she threatened him with a knife. The murder of McCray was a painful reminder to the black community of the vulnerability of African Americans in general and African American women in particular. As a result, the African American community did more than mourn the loss of a young life.[41]

Outrage over McCray's murder touched the entire African American community, most of all perhaps by its female members. Althea Hart articulated the thoughts and feelings of many in a letter to the national office of the NAACP. Her letter, written to W.E.B. Du Bois, stressed that "it was high time something be done to protect our people. Far too many of our people have suffered the same injustices as this girl." Hart believed, as did others, that the African American community could not 'just look on while such injustices are done our race." She expressed confidence that the NAACP would pursue the case, although she was less confident that justice would prevail. Guerand, she pointed out, "claims it was self-defense. But you know better. A lie for a white man is better than the truth for a black man." In her closing sentence she expressed her understanding of the collectivist ethos that existed along with individualism within the African American community. "I do not know the girl but I know she is a member of our race and that is sufficient." It was also sufficient for the staff at the NAACP's national office and for leaders of the association's New Orleans branch.[42]

It is doubtful that Althea Hart had more than a cursory knowledge of the workings of the staff at the NAACP national office and may have been surprised to receive a prompt and encouraging response. Her letter to Du Bois was sent to Walter White, at the time the acting secretary. White assured her, after the obligatory if "facts are found to be as given in these clippings" statement, "that it is a case in which something ought to be done." He promised to confer with the local branch and, as if to emphasize that the local branch leadership had the capacity and commitment to actually get something done, added that branch president George Lucas "is a member of our National Board of Directors and is an uncompromising fighter against such injustices as this one." Although not expressed in his letter to Hart, White knew that racial and gender justice had eluded many uncompromising fighters. And he also knew that rough justice continued to exist in both the rural and urban South. He knew it from personal experience when as a young boy he and his family were threatened with possible white violence during the 1906 Atlanta race riot. He knew it, too, from his work investigating lynchings as an NAACP staff member. White's letter to Lucas informing him of his communications with Hart reflected this personal knowledge. "I am sure the New Orleans Branch will do everything it can to try to get this policeman punished," he stated.[43]

By the time the NAACP's national office received Hart's letter regarding the murder of young Hattie McCray, news of the incident had circulated widely within the black and white communities. African Americans throughout the city were as upset as Hart and were equally passionate in demanding justice. "No matter how one looks at this dastardly deed," stated a *Louisiana Weekly* editorial, "one cannot but say that a coward and a man of low morals . . . violated that trust imposed in him and took that which no man can restore—life itself." Expressing a desire to allow the "law to take its course in this case," the editor conceded that this strategy might not produce justice. Devoid of political power and with little ability to influence directly decisions made by law enforcement officials, including the city attorney, African American leaders such as Guidry and Lucas and concerned members of the black community such as Althea Hart knew that in the McCray case they would again need to call on the commitment and resources of the black community. The cost to obtain justice for African American victims was often high, expressed in money, time, and possible white backlash. The cost of doing nothing was higher still; it meant the continuation of acts such as the harassment and murder of Hattie McCray.[44]

It was nevertheless fortunate that the white South's focus on race, or more accurately racial oppression, never created an environment in which any and all levels of violence against African Americans were considered broadly acceptable. Charles Guerand's action represented a level and type of violence that the majority of whites in New Orleans condemned. Many white public officials and opinion leaders denounced the murder and demanded justice in the case. The superintendent of police, for instance, dismissed Guerand from the police force within hours of the incident. More important, police arrested Guerand on the same day as the shooting. He initially faced the charge of shooting and wounding, but that charge was later changed to murder after McCray died from her wounds. In less than twenty-four hours Guerand was fired, arrested, and charged with murder. In addition, public opinion was, at least for a time, decidedly against him. Justice appeared to be moving in the right direction, but caution, at least within the African American community, remained. African Americans were unsure about several questions. Once Guerand was arrested and charged, would the city attorney's office prosecute the case against him with vigor? Would an all-white jury convict him? And if convicted, would Guerand eventually gain his freedom on appeal?

Faced with such questions, African Americans responded with a campaign to assist the scales of justice. The local NAACP branch, the Federation of Civic Leagues, and the *Louisiana Weekly* led a campaign to raise sufficient funds to hire a private attorney to assist the city attorney's office in its prosecution of Guerand. For the local NAACP involvement in issues such as the McCray case was a major part of the branch's program and one of the reasons for its existence. For the Federation of Civic Leagues, however, direct involvement and leadership in police brutality or white violence cases took the organization far from its usual program activities. And the Hattie McCray case moved the *Louisiana Weekly* away from its customary activities of information and advocacy. Nonetheless, the three organizations worked together to lead a successful fund-raising campaign that enabled the African American community to secure the services of a white private attorney, Chandler C. Luzenberg Sr., to help with the prosecution of the case.[45]

African Americans had no reason either to lament the pace of the judicial proceedings or to denounce the outcome of the first trial. On 4 April 1930 a jury convicted Guerand of murder. The sentence carried with it the death penalty. The *Times-Picayune* considered it a "just verdict" and noted that "if the circumstances in this case had been reversed—had the slayer been a negro and his 14-year-old victim a white girl—the crime would have aroused a storm of indignation throughout the community." The trial's outcome represented "a vindication of law and justice," the editor claimed.[46] But as contemporaries noted, the verdict represented something else as well. "The criminal court records of New Orleans," another white newspaper reported, "disclose no previous instance in which a capital verdict has been returned against a white man where the victim was of the opposite race."⁴⁷ The evidence against Guerand had been substantial, which included testimony for the prosecution by the owners of the restaurant where the murder occurred, by the police officer who questioned him at the scene, and by an assistant city attorney who interviewed him before and after his arrest. Given the state of race relations in New Orleans and throughout the South, it probably did take a degree of courage, as all the newspapers maintained, for the white jurors to return a verdict that included a sentence of death. And whites also used the verdict to validate their claims that African Americans could receive impartial justice in the South.

African Americans, on the other hand, placed a more nuanced interpretation on the verdict. Many of them shared the view expressed by the *Louisiana Weekly,* a view consistent with that of white opinion leaders, that "the Goddess of Justice rendered a just sentence . . . when the twelve stalwart white citizens . . . pronounced the supreme penalty for Charles Guerand." But many African Americans saw the verdict not as a validation that justice for them in the courts already existed but, rather, as a hopeful "forerunner of a better day in the courts for the colored group." ⁴⁸ George Lucas and other African American leaders were extremely pleased with the verdict but took seriously Guerand's attorney's vow to appeal the decision. "We intend to go to the court of last resort if necessary," Lucas pledged, "to hold our victory." Indeed, it proved to be necessary. Guerand's attorneys appealed his conviction and convinced the court that he was insane during the trial. He was held at a state psychiatric hospital, where he received treatment during his five-year stay. Guerand was eventually granted a new trial, allowed to plead guilty to manslaughter, and sentenced to only three years in prison. The final outcome of the killing of Hattie McCray was for the McCray family justice denied. For the New Orleans African American community it indicated that "the better day in the courts for the colored group" had not arrived.⁴⁹

Throughout the 1930s and 1940s activities that challenged Jim Crow policies took many forms and continued to cut across class lines. The work to achieve justice in the death of Hattie McCray addressed one type of discrimination, and efforts to equalize the salaries of black and white teachers represented another. The separate-and-unequal doctrine extended to teacher salaries as well as school facilities. In the midst of the 1900 campaign to reduce black education to the primary grades, for instance, the

Committee on Elementary Schools considered a proposal to make the salaries of black and white teachers equal. The plan never reached fruition, and the practice of paying black teachers less than white teachers became entrenched, despite the protests of black teachers and their supporters. In 1920, for example, a first-year white elementary schoolteacher earned $80 a month; a black teacher with the same qualifications received $70. The differential widened throughout a black teacher's career. A white teacher with six years of experience received $120 dollars a month and a black teacher $110. Given the low and often late salaries paid to black and white teachers, both groups had a right to complain, and many of them did so.[50] Black teachers throughout the South also suffered because of discriminatory salary scales. The salary "differentials amounted to a loss of approximately 10 million dollars to Negro teachers," according to one researcher. Through individual effort and eventually the coordinated assistance of the national and local NAACP, black teachers used the court system to challenge salary discrimination. The campaign started in Maryland in 1936 and resulted in a 1939 consent decree to equalize teachers' salaries in that state. The stirring of change in the distant state of Maryland had no immediate effect on the local school board in New Orleans. The salary schedule for the 1937–38 school year maintained past inequities.[51]

An editorial in the *Louisiana Weekly* placed the issue in a broader context and argued that more was at stake in this struggle than additional money for black teachers and warned that "if the Negro teachers employed by the Orleans Parish School Board accept without protest this most recent discrimination, we fear for children who enter their classrooms, so humble and lacking in dependence will they doubtless be due to the attitude of their instructors."[52] With assistance from several organizations—the league for Equal Rights and Justice, the Colored Educational Alliance, and the New Orleans NAACP—black teachers through the New Orleans League of Classroom Teachers and later the New Orleans Citizens' Committee for Equalizing Educational Opportunities attacked salary discrimination. Following what by then had become a traditional approach, in their petitions to the board the teachers first outlined their grievances and requested changes. They sent one such petition in January 1938 and another that July. Using statistical information published by the board, they pointed out that a first-year white teacher with a bachelor's degree received an annual salary of $1,000. On the other hand, a black teacher with a bachelor's degree had a starting salary of $909 a year. The disparity increased with the level of experience. By the eleventh year in the system a white teacher received $2,200 dollars annually, $760 dollars more than a black teacher of the same rank. "The added strain of financial worries," the teachers argued, "take from us energy which we strongly desire to use in rendering the highest degree of efficient service to our children." They expressed confidence in the willingness and ability of the school board to eliminate the inequities, a confidence rooted more in hope than tangible experience.[53]

But this time the teachers decided to do more than simply submit a petition and hope for a favorable response from the school board. Between the mailing of the first and second petitions, they hired a lawyer to pursue a court challenge. Unfortunately, their enthusiasm may have exceeded their judgment in the selection of an attorney. They first secured the services of a white attorney who "informed the teachers that they needed a plaintiff; and besides he had not had much experience in that type of law." Dismayed but not discouraged, the teachers next sought the aid of Thurgood Marshall, the attorney responsible for the salary equalization victories in Maryland. Marshall, a graduate of Howard University Law School, had joined the NAACP as a staff attorney in 1936. Marshall had visited New Orleans several times in the past and arrived in March 1939 to assist in the pay equalization fight. A meticulous organizer and strategist, Marshall informed the group "that certain steps should be taken before filing suit. The teachers should organize a special committee, raise money, and find suitable plaintiffs." Before returning to New York, Marshall selected the local black attorney Alexander P. Tureaud to help him in the case and assured the group that Tureaud would receive his steady assistance.[54]

The New Orleans Citizens' Committee for Equalizing Educational Opportunities, chaired by Donald Jones, a community activist, provided funds to fight the case. Forming an organization proved easy, but finding a plaintiff took more care because of the threat of reprisals by school officials. Officials in some southern communities had dismissed black teachers who had taken similar action. Unlike most black professionals and business owners in New Orleans, public schoolteachers worked at the pleasure and discretion of whites. Despite the possible loss of his position, Joseph McKelpin, a nontenured teacher at Ricard Elementary School, agreed to act as the plaintiff. But two years elapsed between Marshall's visit and definitive action by black teachers. The most plausible explanation for the delay was that the teachers believed or hoped school officials, being cognizant of successful challenges in other areas, would abolish salary discrimination without a court fight. They failed to realize that what may have started out as just another form of petty discrimination had become in New Orleans a means of holding down the cost of black education and, therefore, of subsidizing white education. Once on the back of the tiger, it was difficult for school officials to dismount without a push. The push came on 9 May 1941 in the form of a four-point petition presented by Tureaud on behalf of Joseph McKelpin. Tureaud's petition for the black teachers called for the board to abolish pay discrimination for all teachers and principals and sought positive action immediately.[55]

School officials, led by school board president Henry C. Schaumberg, assured Tureaud that the board would consider the petition. Tureaud seized the initiative, however, and filed suit in June 1941. Schaumberg then called a special meeting to consider what actions the board should take. One board member, George Treadwell, believed that Tureaud had filed the suit prematurely because the board had not yet refused to grant the requests presented in the petition. Yet neither Treadwell nor the other members proposed to eliminate or narrow the differential between the salaries of black and white teachers. Instead, they referred the suit to the city attorney, Howard Lenfant, and instructed him to litigate. On 7 July Lenfant filed a "Motion for Extension of Time to Plead," and the court granted his request. Faced with precedents recently established in other states, Lenfant had concluded that a strategy of delay and dismissal represented his best option. After receiving a delay, in September he next filed a motion of dismissal.[56] In addition to working on the case in New Orleans, Tureaud remained in constant communication with Marshall in New York. Tureaud asked Marshall when he "would like to argue the motion to dismiss." It was Tureaud's first important civil rights case, and he was concerned that the motion to dismiss might have legal merit. Marshall, who had more experience in the emerging field of civil rights law, considered the dismissal motion "completely without foundation" and assured Tureaud that any points Lenfant could raise had been attempted and lost in other salary equalization cases. Meanwhile, the case, assigned to Judge Wayne Borah, remained dormant for several months. Tureaud called the judge's clerk several times hoping to hear encouraging news, only to learn that Borah had still not reached a decision.[57]

Dismayed over what he considered the judge's inordinate delay in reaching a decision, Marshall proposed that he and Tureaud meet with

Borah in hopes of expediting the matter. Before the meeting took place, Borah threw out the motion to dismiss and later scheduled a trial for August 1942. The prospect of a trial and almost certain defeat led school board officials to attempt a settlement. August J. Tete, who became superintendent in January 1942 after Nicholas Bauer resigned, presented Tureaud with a proposal. Tete offered what he considered a "better proposition" because his plan would eliminate not only the differential between white and black teachers but that between degreed and non-degreed teachers as well. According to Tureaud's figures, about 30 percent of the black teachers did not possess at least a bachelor's degree; under Tete's plan they would also receive a salary increase. Tete requested five years to implement the plan. Black teachers would receive 20 percent of the differential in salaries each year until they were earning the same as white teachers. Tureaud lacked the authority to accept or reject the offer and forwarded Tete's plan to Marshall. Thurgood Marshall made his views clear: "I think the plan submitted by the school board stinks," he declared and outlined his reasons. "In the first place five years is too long. In the second place, there are too many catches. And in the third place, I'm sure that our teachers are opposed to it."[58]

Rebuffed, Tete changed his approach and asked Marshall and Tureaud to suggest "terms" they could accept. Neither Tete nor the school board envisioned equalizing the salaries in one step. Tureaud also endorsed the concept of gradual equalization. "I still believe," Tureaud wrote, "that we could with some propriety fix at least a maximum time we would grant them, and leave the details of the plan to be worked out after they have indicated their acceptance of any suggested plan." Why did Tureaud give tacit support to a compromise that clearly favored the school board? Unsubstantiated charges would later surface that Tureaud had received a bribe from school officials for his endorsement of a compromise. Tureaud was a man of impeccable integrity and often labored without compensation in the black struggle for civil rights. A bribe was definitely not the reason. He supported a compromise for the same reason black teachers eventually accepted one—litigation was costly, sometimes lengthy, and its outcome uncertain. Although Marshall refused to propose terms to school officials because "the pressure at the present time is on the school board, and not on us," he, too, soon supported a compromise.[59]

"Unless they propose a plan that is satisfactory to us, they will have to go to trial in August; and this they do not want to do," Marshall wrote in

July 1942. Marshall's instincts proved correct. In August school officials came forward with an offer satisfactory to black teachers and to Judge Borah. The opposing sides agreed to a two-year equalization plan. The board promised to reduce the differential by 50 percent in September 1942 and the remainder in September 1943. Black teachers were understandably happy, but Judge Borah's ruling contained a broader implication for the entire black community. In making his decision, Borah had partially resurrected the principles of the Fourteenth Amendment, principles that for African Americans had at one time held such promise and hope. Borah stated that the differentials in white and black salaries were "in violation of the equal protection clause of the Fourteenth Amendment of the Constitution of the United States." The *Louisiana Weekly,* also well aware of the implication of this statement, placed the issue in the larger context of community development and black liberation: "The teachers won equal pay. Why shouldn't equal facilities for Negro children be the next step?"[60]

America's entry into World War II did not produce, as it had during World War I, a cessation of protest activities against racial discrimination. The "Double-V" campaign — victory against the Axis abroad and Jim Crow at home — served notice that African Americans wanted change. Indeed, during the war the NAACP successfully litigated the important voting rights case *Smith v. Allwright*. In 1944 the U.S. Supreme Court ruled that a political party could not exclude potential members because of race. The decision eventually contributed to increased black voter registration and participation in the late 1940s and 1950s, especially in the urban South.[61] But as the nation expanded its efforts to become the "arsenal of democracy" and the military need for soldiers grew as well, the war effort overshadowed the freedom aspirations of African Americans. They eventually donned military uniforms, and an even greater number participated in the booming war economy. The South once again experienced an exodus of dissatisfied or aspiring African Americans. New Orleans, too, would surrender its African American sons and daughters to eastern and western cities. Most stayed, however, and accepted both the opportunity and the challenge of residency in World War II–era New Orleans. To the many African American soldiers who eventually returned to the city from military service in Europe, Asia, or Africa, it appeared that not much had changed. The Jim Crow trains still brought them into the city, past hotels they could not enter, restaurants they could not dine in, and office buildings in which they could not work. There were few indications that significant change loomed over the horizon. Few of them had heard of the Swedish scholar Gunnar Myrdal or his team of investigators of race relations in America who in 1944 produced a book entitled *An American Dilemma*. And none of them could anticipate that President Harry Truman would take seriously NAACP executive director Walter White's stark and candid assessment of the harmful legacy for African Americans of seventy-five years of unequal opportunity and discrimination and form a committee that would produce the report "To Secure These Rights," a detailed and candid assessment of race relations in America and specific recommendations to end racial discrimination and exclusion.[62]

Not even Richard English, a New Orleans native, black army captain, and educator, knowledgeable and well read, could foresee more than glacial-like change. So, in 1945 English did not pass hotels, restaurants, and office buildings that he could not enter, choosing instead to remain in Germany. English taught at a United States military school for the children of soldiers stationed in Germany. He traveled extensively throughout Germany, making friends and collecting Nazi memorabilia. His family eventually joined him. Except for what he read in occasional letters from his mother, the harshness of Jim Crow seemed far away. While three English children—the youngest was born in Germany—learned the German language and sampled foreign foods, black children in New Orleans faced a different challenge. Many of them learned their language skills in crowded classrooms and from outdated books. In the 1946–47 school year, for example, several black elementary schools had a sixty-to-one pupil to teacher ratio. English eventually returned to his native city, but by that time the black community had accelerated its demands for full equality.[63]

In post–World War II New Orleans the fight against racial segregation and exclusion centered initially on education, remained confined to the federal courts, and depended on the cooperation and support of the entire black community. The involvement of Thurgood Marshall and the national NAACP office in the early teachers' salaries equalization suit signaled a new departure, and the local NAACP branch became facilitator and conduit for the next series of challenges to Jim Crow. The pace of the New Orleans branch's activities became linked to the protest rhythms of the black community and to similar protest activities throughout the South. Given the importance that African Americans had historically placed on education in gaining full equality in the United States, it is not surprising that black leaders mounted an attack on inequities in education. And the strategy to use the courts that New Orleans's black community adopted had originated with the national NAACP office chief lawyer Nathan Margold. To overturn the *Plessy* decision, Margold recommended that the NAACP challenge the "separate but equal" doctrine with a focus on elementary and secondary schools. Charles Houston liked the basic framework of the idea but thought it had little chance of success. As a result, he modified it to attack an "area where the whites were most vulnerable and least likely to respond with anger" — graduate and professional schools. Houston realized that the tactics he favored would make it a slow process, but he remained confident of ultimate victory. Houston also favored his approach because he wanted to use the sustained legal fight as a means to further politicize black communities for a direct challenge to Jim Crow.[64]

A petition submitted to schools officials in May 1946 by local black leaders charged that deficiencies in black schools existed because of racial discrimination. The lengthy petition listed eleven areas in which school officials discriminated against African Americans — the number of kindergarten, special education, and vocational classes; the number of visiting teachers; the number of gymnasiums; the use of city parks; teaching loads; the high school academic curriculum; the quality of school buildings; expenditures; and business education. Each section of the petition started with the phrase *discrimination in* and summarized the particular deficiency. More important, the petitioners contended that failure to remedy the problems represented "a violation of the Equal Protection Clause of the 14th Amendment of the Constitution." School board officials accepted the petition and met with Tureaud on 25 July 1946 to discuss it. The July meeting and subsequent attempts by Superintendent Lionel J. Bourgeois and school officials to improve black schools produced some positive results but fell well short of meeting either the demands or needs of the black community.[65] Of all the proposals the most promising idea to upgrade black education was a consolidation and conversion plan recommended by Bourgeois. He wanted to consolidate white schools with low enrollment and convert the schools no longer needed for whites for use by blacks.[66] White and black parents and leaders attacked the plan, though for different reasons. Representatives of McDonogh No. 16 reflected the attitudes of the white community and demonstrated their dissatisfaction with a petition signed by nearly eighteen hundred individuals opposed to Bourgeois's conversion plan. And white opponents to the plan were unmoved by the superintendent's claim "that the board has the humanitarian and legal obligation to provide school facilities for children regardless of race." Whites were not the only ones opposed to the plan. Tureaud and other leaders objected, too, if it meant assigning black students to substandard schools.[67]

In May 1948 over sixteen hundred African Americans gathered at the Booker T. Washington High School auditorium and heard the featured speaker, Thurgood Marshall, inform the crowd that "the issue is not for separate but equal facilities, the real fight is against segregated schools."[68] Marshall's presence in the city exemplified the close relationship that existed between local civil rights activists and national leaders. The national NAACP office provided New Orleans's black community with legal expertise, direction, and encouragement in its decades-old "real fight" for full equality in America. The Colored Educational Alliance, the New Orleans Federation of Civic Leagues, and other protest and community improvement organizations gradually surrendered much of the leadership of protest activities to the New Orleans Branch NAACP. For nearly a half-century those organizations had served the black community well. Using protest, petitions, and unwavering agitation, their efforts had produced improvements in the economic, social, and political lives of members of the black community. The transition from offering protests and petitions to seeking judicial redress occurred with only minor friction, animosity, or any noticeable splits within the community's black leadership, for the NAACP was an inclusive organization with members from throughout the city. In addition, the new strategy was more evolutionary than revolutionary, and the various ward and neighborhood organizations continued to shape and influence civil rights initiatives and activities. This was especially the case for neighborhoods and wards with dynamic leaders and organizations such as the Ninth Ward Civic and Improvement League. Black New Orleanians had used the federal courts in the past to eliminate discrimination. With ties to a national organization, the local NAACP branch had access to some of the best civil rights attorneys in the country, and a string of successes in the courts brought prestige and members into the fold.

Local NAACP leaders such as Daniel Byrd knew, however, that the members would remain in the fold only if the NAACP supplied aggressive leadership and steadily attacked segregation and discrimination. Daniel Byrd, a native of Arkansas, moved to New Orleans at age twenty-seven and quickly emerged as one of the city's leading civil rights activists. He joined the New Orleans Branch NAACP, helped to organize the state chapter, and later became president of the NAACP State Conferences of Branches. Byrd possessed enormous energy, intelligence, and courage and established the tone for an aggressive NAACP. At a school board meeting on 12 August 1949, for example, he expressed the mood of the new leadership. He questioned the board's decision to spend hundreds of thousands of dollars on improving white schools when black children still attended school part-time because of overcrowding. He wanted to know "if the members of the board realized that if a parent of a colored pupil living in the district of an overcrowded school took a child to a white school and asked for admission, that in accordance with the Fourteenth Amendment of the Constitution local discrimination statues would not apply." Noting the refusal of the school board to convert many of the underutilized white schools to black use because of white opposition, Byrd wanted it known that "if the school board reacts to pressure and antagonism, then we are ready, and ready now, to start our antagonism and pressure." Byrd reminded the school board members that talking with representatives of the NAACP was "not the same as talking to groups of black principals and teachers."[69]

Byrd, along with local and national black leaders, realized the difficulties associated with undertaking a legal assault on segregated elementary and secondary schools and proceeded cautiously to build support within the black community. In this regard the organizational structure of the NAACP became important. Unlike many of the other groups that had fought for improved schools, the NAACP held regular monthly meetings, had officials elected by the entire community, and had members. The monthly meetings provided a forum in which to discuss, for example, issues related to education. The NAACP kept the members informed about the activities of other communities and the proposals and strategies recommended by the NAACP national office. Moreover, the monthly meetings gave members and others in attendance from different neighborhoods an opportunity to articulate their views on a variety of issues related to community development and liberation. And the issue of using the federal courts to gain equal educational opportunities became a dominant one. They knew, for example, that southern states and school districts were substantially expanding their appropriations to black education in response to lawsuits. They also knew, as former Dillard University professor Horace Mann Bond stated, that "the development by Negroes of the strategy of an appeal to the Federal Courts, to gain equal school facilities, both elementary and higher, is the feature of this generation."[70]

By 1951 black leaders in New Orleans such as Byrd and Tureaud were part of that generation and had made the commitment to seek the total desegregation of schools. And Byrd, in talks with Marshall and Tureaud, stressed the need to provide the community with as much information as possible. Byrd wanted to ensure that African Americans throughout the city fully understood and supported the new initiative and would be willing to transform that support into a direct legal challenge to segregated schools. "Rather than start from scratch," Juliette Landphair has stated in her examination of the interplay between dynamic neighborhood leadership and the civil rights efforts of the NAACP, "Tureaud approached [Wilfred] Aubert and his fellow activists in the Ninth Ward Civic and Improvement League to test their willingness to challenge Jim Crow." They were willing and indicated it at a well-attended meeting in the Ninth Ward on 6 November 1951.[71] Six days later Tureaud presented another petition to the school board, as he and other African Americans had done for over three quarters of a century. Tureaud's petition again detailed the substantial inequalities in the educational opportunities available to blacks and whites. Declaring that his petition "represented the sentiments of the entire Negro citizenry," Tureaud demanded the integration of the New Orleans public schools. The president of the board, Dr. Clarence Scheps, thought Tureaud had raised "a very grave question" and promised to "study the petition and prepare an answer in due time." Two weeks later the board issued a unanimous response.[72] "After careful study of the petition," the resolution began, "the board is of the firm opinion that such a radical change of policy could not, at this time, serve the best interests of the system. The board believes, rather, that such a departure from tradition and custom, quite apart from the fact that such action by the board would be illegal, could result in chaos and confusion and further, quite possibly cause a very serious worsening of race relationships in the community as a whole."[73] The school board's statement did not come as a surprise to Tureaud; by the time he submitted the petition, he was formulating a desegregation strategy with NAACP attorneys Robert Carter and Thurgood Marshall.

Oliver Bush and several other parents, on behalf of their children and through their attorney Tureaud, filed suit against the Orleans Parish School Board. Bush, who was active in the parent-teacher association, participated in the court case, he later recalled, because he was "dissatisfied with what we were getting in our schools in comparison with the rest of the [white] schools. I gave it some thought. I felt that the good that would come out of it, even if I had to sacrifice my life, would far outreach the price that I would have to pay as an individual."[74] Bush and the other plaintiffs in the suit requested complete integration of the New Orleans public schools. At their next meeting the school board members ordered the superintendent, O. Perry Walker, to forward the suit to the state attorney general.[75] Three months earlier the U.S. Supreme Court had agreed to hear two similar cases that had originated in Kansas and South Carolina. In October and November 1952 the Supreme Court justices added three more cases—from Delaware, Virginia, and Washington, D.C.[76] The justices would use four of the cases, consolidated as *Brown v. Board of Education of Topeka, Kansas,* to rule on the continued legality of segregated elementary and secondary schools or, in a larger sense, on "whether the white people of the United States might continue to treat the black people as their subjects."[77] And on 17 May 1954 in a unanimous decision the nine members of the Supreme Court ruled "that in the field of public education the doctrine of 'separate but equal' has no place. Separate educational facilities are inherently unequal."[78] African Americans throughout the country were predictably pleased with the Court's decision. Tureaud called it "a very momentous decision and one which will go down in the annals of our American jurisprudence." Another local black attorney considered the decision a "victory for Negroes in particular, and Americans in general."[79] Both men believed the *Brown* decision would alter the social, educational, and political fabric of New Orleans.

After the *Brown* decision the Louisiana legislature became an active ally in the local school board's efforts to delay school integration as long as possible. One result of that alliance was the creation of the Joint Legislative Committee on Segregation, chaired by Senator William M. Rainach of Summerfield. The state's adherence to the strategy of "legislate and litigate" effectively prevented the desegregation of New Orleans public schools for six years. In 1954 the legislature passed several bills designed to keep schools segregated. Acts 555 and 556 served as the centerpiece of the legislative initiative. Act 555 prohibited local school systems from establishing desegregated schools. Failure to comply with the law would result in the loss of accreditation and funding. Act 556 established a pupil placement law designed to prevent desegregation. A proposed constitutional amendment also would allow the state to exercise its police power to operate segregated schools.[80] The Supreme Court's 31 May 1955 decision on implementation led to another flurry of activity. The Court's ruling that desegregation should proceed "with all deliberate speed" gave most white southerners reason for optimism, though their views varied. Some extreme segregationists saw it as a mandate to desegregate the schools gradually. The president of the Louisiana State Senate, Robert A. Ainsworth Jr. of New Orleans, recognized as much and "welcome[d] the order's mild tone which furnishes us an opportunity to examine local conditions and act accordingly to get our house in order." On the other hand, state representative John Garrett saw the decision as a victory for the segregationists. Garrett "firmly believe[d] the justices realized that they had made a mistake . . . and this was their easiest way out, putting it back on the local level." And Leander Perez, longtime political leader in Plaquemines Parish and a deeply committed racist, charged that the decree represented "a disgrace to the country." Tureaud also expressed some disappointment because he "expected the Supreme Court to put a time schedule beyond which local school boards may not delay in carrying out the decree."[81]

As the state used its resources to prevent desegregation, the black community attempted to counter with its own resources. On 22 and 23 May 1954 Daniel Byrd attended a NAACP meeting in Atlanta, Georgia, composed of representatives from the seventeen states and the District of Columbia that were still operating legally segregated school systems. When the meeting concluded, the participants issued a statement known as the "Atlanta Declaration." Although brief, only one page long, the document was substantial in its insistence that black leaders were determined to see *Brown* implemented. These leaders urged all Americans to support the *Brown* decision and took encouragement from "the pledges of support and compliance by governors, attorney generals, mayors, and education officials." They offered "to work with other law abiding citizens who are anxious to translate this decision into a program of action to eradicate racial segregation in public education as speedily as possible." They asked local black communities and NAACP branches "to petition their local school boards to abolish segregation without delay and to assist these agencies in working out ways and means of implementing the court's ruling." They expressed their commitment to "resist the use of any tactics contrived for the sole purpose of delaying desegregation." But the ninety-two conference participants were experienced civil rights activists; they realized that even as they met, vitriolic white opposition had crystallized.[82]

Over the next several years African Americans in New Orleans had to counter many tactics designed to prevent the desegregation of the schools. Even as they did so, New Orleans's black leaders pursued three objectives. First and foremost, they continued to litigate the Bush suit. The 1954 *Brown* decision and the 1955 implementation decree, coupled with the state legislative resistance, led to a costly and time-consuming legal battle. The school board refused to pursue any desegregation plan; black leaders had to sue to force compliance with the *Brown* decision. The second and third objectives were related to the first. At the local level African Americans needed to display enough militancy and aggressiveness to keep the desegregation effort going forward. African Americans responded by submitting petitions and filing applications for admission into white schools. They also raised money to help pay for the litigation. Finally, black leaders attempted to win support from members of the white community. This objective proved extremely difficult to achieve, especially getting the support of the business community. Indeed, as historian Adam Fairclough maintains, "the refusal of leading businessmen and professionals to prepare for integration played into the hands of the ultrasegregationists."[83] And for a time segregationist leaders guided and influenced school desegregation and race relations policies in New Orleans and throughout the state.

New Orleans's resistance to desegregation extended beyond the polemics of public officials such as William Rainach and John Garrett, the segregationist leader in the state House of Representatives. The rapid rise of white citizens' councils attested to the depth of segregationist sentiment. The initial Louisiana chapter was formed in Rainach's home parish of Claiborne in April 1955, and a second chapter was established in New Orleans in September under the leadership of Emmett Lee Irwin, Louis Porterie, and Jackson Ricau. The three council leaders were professionals—Dr. Irwin was a respected surgeon and former president of the Louisiana Medical Association, Porterie was a member of a prominent New Orleans family, and Ricau was a former public schoolteacher.[84] And spokesmen for the local council quickly made their presence and ideology known. Appearing at a 26 September 1955 school board meeting, Porterie produced a petition with nearly fifteen thousand signatures "requesting that the board not abandon segregation in the schools." Porterie assured the board that if necessary the council could have secured even more signatures.[85] Several months later, on 20 March 1956, over eight thousand whites attended a pro-segregationist rally at the Municipal Auditorium to protest Archbishop Joseph F. Rummel's support of integration. The council later sponsored a parade and rally at which over four thousand whites "gustily cheered what sounded to most like a call to re-fight the Civil War before submitting to integration." The Greater New Orleans Citizens' Council predicted it would enroll over fifty thousand members.[86]

In the main white New Orleanians opposed desegregation with the same force and conviction as their supposedly less cosmopolitan neighbors. But some antisegregation elements did exist within the white community, and their numbers increased, though only modestly, as the state exhausted its legislative and legal options. It is significant, however, that throughout most of the period no political figure in the city advocated compliance with the *Brown* decision. The moderates, to the extent that they mobilized, had to rely on businessmen and professionals rather than politicians. It was not that white moderates were feeble or insincere in their efforts; they were simply too few and too far outside the white mainstream's views on race relations. On the same day, for example, that approximately 400 people attended a meeting in favor of desegregation, 8,000 whites gathered in support of segregation. In September 1955 a group of white moderates and liberals presented the school board a petition signed by 179 individuals who supported school desegregation. Two weeks later, however, segregationist leaders submitted a petition with 14,962 signatures in support of continued school segregation.[87]

Anticipating and expecting little assistance from white racial moderates, African American leaders knew that the same force that started the fight against desegregation in the schools needed to sustain it throughout the crisis: the black community. When asked where the NAACP would get the money to litigate thousands of cases throughout the nation, Thurgood Marshall answered that it would come from the black community.[88] He spoke the truth, but maintaining that support involved considerable effort and constant engagement with the community. Arthur Chapital and Mildred Byrd, the vice president of the branch at the time of the *Brown* decision, were part of a tireless and aggressive NAACP leadership team that participated in hundreds of community meetings in the 1950s. In July 1954, for example, the branch held an "NAACP Victory" meeting at Greater Providence Baptist Church, where Chapital and Byrd discussed the recent Supreme Court decision and made appeals for continued support of the school integration case and the larger struggle for black equality. NAACP leaders rarely missed an opportunity to appear in at least one church service each week. Usually local leaders and members appeared on behalf of the NAACP. At other times national leaders participated as well. On 26 May 1957 NAACP executive secretary Roy Wilkins was the guest speaker at First African Baptist Church. And emblematic of the historic social justice role of the black church, in February 1958 St. John Institutional Mission Baptist Church hosted a mass meeting at which major league baseball star Jackie Robinson gave the keynote speech. Later that year the branch sponsored a program to recognize the fourth anniversary of the *Brown* decision. Those in attendance that Sunday learned of some of the "implications of the Supreme Court ruling" and the importance of voter registration. Surely they drew inspiration, resolve, and a collective identity from the several speakers. Perhaps sharing the music and songs — "The Star-Spangled Banner," "Lift Every Voice and Sing," "Deep in My Heart," and "Blest Be the Tie That Binds" — added to their resolve and sense of a shared community as well.[89]

The support gained from the community meetings, the persistence of NAACP leaders, and Louisiana Education Association officials sustained the push for school integration in New Orleans. The continued challenge to school segregation, however, brought out the worst in a number of whites in the city before many others allowed their "better angels" to influence their public positions. Chapital often opened branch mail that figuratively dripped with hatred. "You had better tell those Negro members of your damn association to back down, because if they don't they will be sorry," one writer stated. "If they don't stop trying to get into our schools, it will be too bad for them," he added.[90] Attorney Tureaud, like Chapital, was publicly identified with the school integration effort and received his share of profane and threatening phone calls and mail. According to Tureaud, "It was almost a daily or nightly experience for me to get threats at home, my family, and everybody else. They'd call the neighbors, who would tell me not to sleep home at night because my house was going to get bombed."[91] Tureaud, despite the threats, maintained his legal assault on white resistance to school integration, and in June 1959 he petitioned Judge J. Skelly Wright to compel school officials to devise a desegregation plan. In the following month Judge Wright ordered the board to "prepare, present and file . . . by March 1, 1960, an overall plan covering the complete desegregation of the public schools in this city."[92] When school officials failed to respond, Judge Wright issued his own plan in May, ordering the gradual desegregation of schools starting with the first grade when schools reopened for the 1960–61 school year.[93]

Wright's modest proposal immediately drew the ire of whites throughout the city. School officials only added to the unrest by mailing a survey to black and white parents of students in the school system to learn if parents wanted the schools closed or opened in the event that the court forced the school system to integrate. School officials distributed approximately 70,000 questionnaires, and parents returned 27,092 of them. Among those who responded 14,114 voted to keep the schools open, and 12,978 voted to close the schools rather than integrate. Less than a week after reviewing the results of the survey, Lloyd Rittner, president of the school board, stated he would disregard the survey. Rittner reached his conclusion because out of the 14,114 parents who voted to keep the schools open, 11,407 were black. Analyzing the vote in terms of race, 12,299 whites voted for closing, and only 2,707 wanted the schools to remain open. By contrast, blacks voted overwhelmingly to keep the schools open, 11,407 to 679. Considering the racial composition of the vote, Rittner felt confident in his stance "because whites are the people who support the system." The 1959–60 school year came to a close amid the possibility that the regular school vacation would greatly exceed the usual three months.[94]

The New Orleans Branch NAACP wasted little time in attacking the school board's position. Branch president Arthur Chapital wrote a letter to school board officials strongly denouncing their actions. Moreover, he questioned the propriety of elected officials openly advocating disrespect for the law. During this time, however, NAACP branch members did more than write letters. Under the direction of Chapital, they continued to hold meetings throughout the city to discuss the school integration crisis. The NAACP wanted to keep the black community informed about the integration effort and allay any fears that might exist within the black community. NAACP leaders had to convince black parents to send their six-year-old children to schools that did not want them, with teachers who most likely despised them and children who probably hated them. In the month of June 1960 the branch held more than ten meetings, often conducting two or three meetings on the same day in different parts of the city. On 6 June, for example, a meeting to "clarify the issues for the parents" was held at Law Street Baptist Church and at the Central Congregational Church. On 14 June the branch sponsored three meetings at the

Masonic Temple, Branch Bell Baptist Church, and Mount Zion Baptist Church. Branch leaders also held meetings at Shaw Temple Methodist Church, St. Augustine High School, St. John Institutional Missionary Baptist Church, and Carver-Desire Baptist Church. At the meetings NAACP representatives stressed the importance of the desegregation effort and reminded the parents that the court victory was not complete until African Americans began attending the schools of their choice.[95]

African Americans were for the most part sympathetic and supportive of the NAACP's struggle to integrate New Orleans public schools. Nonetheless, much to the chagrin of some NAACP leaders, black parents were not flocking to the school board office to register their children in white schools. It would have made little difference, for despite the objections of attorney Tureaud, school officials implemented a Pupil Placement Plan designed to restrict the number of black students entering previously all-white schools. In fact, of the 135 students who did apply for a transfer before the deadline, school officials only approved 5 (one would later withdraw). The courageous parents of six-year-old Ruby Bridges, Gail Etienne, Tessie Prevost, and Leona Tate agreed to submit their children to the ordeal of integrating New Orleans public schools.[96] The four girls would be the first African Americans to attend previously all-white schools since Reconstruction. And on 14 November 1960 armed federal marshals escorted the four students to the previously all-white William T. Frantz and McDonogh No. 19 Schools. After the students received their classroom assignments, white "mothers clad in slacks and pedal pushers arrived to take their children home." Shouting slogans such as "The South will rise again" and "Two, four, six, eight, we don't want to integrate," large crowds remained at the two desegregated schools for the entire day but dispersed without violence. On the second day hundreds of teenagers attempted to force their way past police to enter McDonogh No. 19. Police made arrests at both schools, and the police chief sent additional officers to the schools. Over the next several days mob action and interracial violence occurred throughout the city. New Orleans at last reaped, in lawlessness and negative national publicity, what six years of defiance and racist rhetoric had sown.[97]

With the legal battle for desegregated public schools finally entering the implementation phase, Chapital, Leontine Luke, and other black leaders started to concentrate on the task of ensuring that the four young students were not harmed physically or psychologically. Under the direction of Chapital and Luke, the NAACP coordinated a local and national campaign to obtain moral support for the students. In order to shield them and their parents as much as possible, the branch requested that all correspondence to the children be sent to Chapital at the NAACP office. The response to the NAACP's effort was impressive. Cards, letters, and small donations began arriving almost immediately. A typical letter arrived from Mrs. A. J. Shaw of Brookline, Massachusetts, who sent five dollars for "candy for the children." A parent-teacher association group from New York City sent a resolution indicating its support of integrated schools in New Orleans. Another letter was addressed to "Dear mothers and fathers — and to your four little girls." The writer shared her own sense of the burden of race: "I am white and the shame and stain of ugly racism hangs heavy in my heart. We feel pride in those tiny girls so bravely walking up those school steps and the parents who take them." A letter from Chester W. Hartman of Cambridge, Massachusetts, also epitomized the response the NAACP attempted to generate. Hartman thought the girls' "daily anguish must be so great that it was very important to try to offset this with some expression of friendliness." He therefore collected several thousand signatures, including that of noted economist John Kenneth Galbraith, on a "huge greeting card" and sent it to the four girls. Hartman pledged that he and a group of friends would also publicize the need to send additional letters of encouragement.[98]

As concerned writers such as Hartman feared, Ruby Bridges, Gail Etienne, Tessie Prevost, and Leona Tate did, indeed, experience "daily anguish." Bridges, for instance, later stated that she "knew little about the racial fears and hatred in Louisiana." Her first day at William T. Frantz exposed her to those racial fears with a clarity that a child of six found at times difficult to understand. "Many of the boys carried signs and said awful things," she later recalled. "But most of all I remember seeing a black doll in a coffin, which frightened me more than anything else." It took "a long time," she maintained, "to own the early part of my life." The girls relied on their families, their faith, and a caring black community to sustain them in their long and mostly lonely ordeal. Bridge's mother taught her "that God is always there to protect us."[99] That type of faith was necessary and needed because although school officials had finally implemented a partial integration plan, they attempted to prevent or delay complete school integration. As a result, throughout the 1960s black leaders maintained their fight to achieve equal educational opportunities for all children, with groups such as the NAACP Education Committee continuing to monitor the school system, assist parents in placing their children in the most beneficial environment, and pressure school officials to accelerate the integration of schools. Still, despite the efforts of black citizens, only 347 black students registered at integrated schools when the academic year began in 1963. In fact, school officials did not begin to meet the letter and spirit of *Brown v. Board of Education* until the late 1960s.[100]

8

Freedom Now

The attitudes and activities of African Americans in New Orleans and in other southern communities justified attorney Charles Houston's belief that a legal attack on segregated schools could also politicize black communities. It was not a coincidence that direct action protest activities occurred in the years following *Brown v. Board of Education*. The decision gave black leaders such as Martin Luther King and Bayard Rustin on the national level and Daniel Byrd and A. L. Davis on the local level something more tangible than appeals to morality to attack racial segregation and exclusion. Liberation strategies and activities employed in New Orleans mirrored this trend. In the 1960s black New Orleanians and their white allies grafted the strategy of nonviolent direct action to their decades-old legal challenge to wage an assault on racial segregation and exclusion. Many members of the black community shared the opinion expressed in a *Louisiana Weekly* editorial that the "nonviolent demonstrations are an appealing new strategy to gain first class citizenship."[1] At least as early as the 1930s, black leaders had advocated the use of direct action activities. The "Don't Buy Where You Can't Work" campaign during the Great Depression is just one example. The direct action tactics of the 1960s, however, even though they stressed nonviolence, represented a more aggressive and confrontational program designed to topple segregation immediately.

Throughout the Jim Crow period the New Orleans Branch NAACP led the black freedom struggle in the city. Beginning in the early 1960s, other organizations participated in important civil rights initiatives. In addition, the local NAACP's own youth council garnered increased autonomy and assumed a separate identity, making contributions to the struggle for civil rights distinct and apart from its parent branch. The participants in the prominent civil rights groups did compete against each other, but their actions did not undermine the overall objectives of gaining full equality and first-class citizenship. Indeed, evidence exists to support the view that at least on the local level the "friendly" competition that occasionally developed actually made each group more effective. The behavior of Arthur Chapital and the NAACP branch is but one example. Chapital assumed the presidency of the branch in 1951 and retained that office continuously until 31 December 1962. He recognized the possible threat that the new groups posed to the branch's leadership in the civil rights movement. He realized that how the branch responded to the burgeoning militancy of civil rights activists would help determine to what extent his organization would retain its leadership role. In a sharply worded letter to the NAACP executive secretary, Roy Wilkins, Chapital pointed out "that between 1956 and February 25, 1960, we have failed to accept our responsibilities to the NAACP and to the Negroes in Louisiana." He believed that the absence of sufficient NAACP-sponsored activities made possible the popularity of "Johnny come late organizations such as SCLC, CORE and local groups." To reverse the trend, he advocated that branches throughout the state should engage in "some things that are spectacular and consistent with our programs."[2]

National NAACP leaders shared Chapital's concern and responded in several ways. NAACP officials mailed letters to branches throughout the country stating their agreement with the strategy of direct action and specifically with sit-ins and demonstrations. In one letter to the various branches Gloster B. Current, director of branches, "urg[ed], encourag[ed], and sanction[ed] picketing and demonstrations."[3] And at the NAACP annual convention in June 1960 the delegates adopted a resolution supporting nonviolent direct action. One resolution stated in part that the demonstrations were "symptomatic of the growing impatience of Negro Americans with the injustices of segregation and the snail-like pace of desegregation." It further implored the "membership, officers, and executive committee of its various branches to assist these demonstrations to the fullest of their capabilities."[4] For several reasons the local branch did not become immediately involved in direct action demonstrations. Beginning in 1956, the state legislature and attorney general had waged a campaign to close NAACP branches throughout the state and finally forced the New

Orleans branch to suspend its operations in October 1959, and the executive committee did not hold another official meeting until the following March. As a result, in the spring and summer of 1960 Chapital and other branch leaders devoted much of their efforts to reorganizing the branch, contacting former members, and recruiting new members. In addition, the legal battle to integrate the public schools had entered a climatic stage, furthering limiting the ability of branch leaders to assume leadership positions in direct action demonstrations.

The initial lack of direct action protest by the local NAACP branch, however, did not prevent the involvement of other individuals and groups in these activities. In March 1960 students from Dillard University participated in an on-campus demonstration to protest racial segregation and received some support from the black community. The *Louisiana Weekly* believed the demonstrations were "an appealing new strategy to gain first class citizenship." And in a later editorial the newspaper reasoned that student demonstrations were also helpful because they gave students an opportunity to develop leadership qualities and exposed them to the inequities of the judicial system. The editor concluded the piece with the strong opinion that the demonstrations were the "best thing that ever happened to the South." A more measured but still supportive opinion came from a segment of the white community in response to student-led demonstrations in New Orleans and Baton Rouge. A WDSU editorial, broadcast on both its television and radio stations in the New Orleans area, noted that Louisiana had experienced "its first wave of demonstrations" but saw "no reason to get excited or alarmed about them." The editorial noted, correctly, that "the demonstrations . . . have not caused any segregation barriers in this state to crumble, and there does not seem to be much chance that they will have any such effect in the near future." It cautioned political and educational leaders at the city and state levels not to overreact and "to accept calmly the right of these students to make their opinions known as long as they do it peacefully." In the view of the editorial the students were "simply engaging in the old American custom of blowing off steam." Concerned that the "blowing off steam" comment might be misinterpreted, the editors added: "We don't mean to belittle these students. We believe they're sincere in what they're doing. And we believe they have shown that the feeling among Southern Negroes against segregation is more widespread than some officials like to admit."[5]

That feeling was definitely more than the mayor of New Orleans, deLesseps Story "Chep" Morrison, was willing to admit. Less than two weeks after the WDSU editorial, Morrison had an opportunity to state his opinion on race relations and the existing patterns of segregation in the city. In a letter to Chapital, though not directly related to the student demonstrations, Morrison indicated his steadfast commitment to the racial status quo. According to the mayor, New Orleans had "good race relations," and white city leaders had worked to "create and maintain a climate for the realization of greater economic opportunity" for African Americans. These conditions, he asserted, had developed "within the framework of existing State laws and customs." Morrison believed that efforts to change segregation laws by groups such as the New Orleans Branch NAACP did "a dis-service to the community in general and to the well being of the Negro population in particular."[6] The mayor's vision for African Americans and race relations in New Orleans looked back rather than forward, an embrace of the racial thinking that had existed for a brief moment during the post-Reconstruction period, when some whites supported limited black advancement within the context of rigid racial segregation and white economic and political control. It was consistent, then, for Morrison to court the still small but growing black vote yet at the same time to work mightily to retain segregation.

As they had expressed for nearly a century, however, African Americans wanted to decide for themselves what was in the best interest of the black community. Perhaps encouraged by the support for demonstrations by the black community and some support from the white community, the Consumers League of Greater New Orleans, a newly formed group, held a mass meeting in April to coordinate plans to protest the lack of job opportunities for African Americans at retail stores in the Dryades Street area. Most stores located there were owned by whites, while the great majority of customers were African Americans, and these stores only employed African Americans as janitors and stock clerks. Over twelve hundred people attended the meeting at New Zion Baptist Church and applauded Dr. Raymond Floyd's announcement that the Consumers League would begin picketing the Dryades Street area stores that refused to hire African Americans above the menial level. These demonstrations focused on expanding employment opportunities. Floyd, who was president of the Consumers League, asked African Americans to refrain from shopping at the stores scheduled for picketing.[7]

Two weeks after the start of the boycott and picketing, Dryades Street area store owners experienced a drop in revenues and profits. The reduction in customers and decline in profits influenced several of them to agree to hire African American sales clerks. By 7 May 1960 only one store still refused to hire African Americans. The rapid pace of change in hiring practices made the boycott organizers cautiously optimistic about the potential benefits of direct action. Their caution appeared justified, for on closer examination their easy victory was misleading. They had won concessions from store owners who were almost totally dependent on the black community for their profits. The concessions they made, the hiring of black clerks, did not disturb the racial social order because black clerks serviced black customers within a segregated environment. The distance between the downtown area of the city and Dryades Street could be traveled by car in less than ten minutes. But the pattern of race relations that existed in the two areas stood light-years apart. African Americans could not obtain meaningful employment at any of the downtown stores. In addition, some public and most private buildings had separate facilities for the two races. The Dryades Street area demonstration failed to solve the core problems: lack of meaningful job opportunities and discriminatory practices throughout the city. Then, too, Chapital wondered if the Consumers League would weaken the branch's effectiveness in the civil rights fight. "Even though you are doing a swell job under the title of the Consumers League," Chapital wrote the league's president, Raymond Floyd, and its secretary, Rev. Avery Alexander, "you both are aware of the singular position that the NAACP holds in this community." During the spring and summer months of 1960 civil rights groups in the city continued to meet, talk, and plan.[8]

Despite the limitations of the Dryades Street campaign and the concerns of NAACP leaders, the protest provided more African Americans in New Orleans an opportunity to become involved in direct action demonstrations. Oretha Castle and many other student activists, for example, received their first exposure to protest activities during the Dryades Street demonstrations. Castle was born in Oakland, Tennessee, and with her family moved to New Orleans in 1947. She enrolled in Southern University in New Orleans in 1959 and, along with other young students from New Orleans's area colleges, would infuse the black freedom struggle with a degree of dedication and a sense of urgency that helped to end legal segregation and exclusion. Veteran civil rights activists viewed the boycott as another small battle in the century-long struggle for equality and justice in

New Orleans. Oretha Castle and other newcomers, however, saw it as the dawn of a new day. During the two weeks Castle participated in the boycott, she became acquainted with other student activists. One of them, Rudolph "Rudy" Lombard, became a trusted friend. In July, Castle and Lombard became charter members of the New Orleans chapter of the Congress of Racial Equality (CORE). The new group, composed of students from several of the city's black and white colleges, maintained an active presence in New Orleans throughout the early 1960s. Castle emerged as one of its leaders, and her activities over the next several years indicated that the next generation of black leadership rested in capable hands.[9] Castle's protest activities and leadership represented both continuity with and change from earlier work by black female leaders in New Orleans. She combined the confrontational, direct action protest activities practiced by members of her generation with the willingness to negotiate to produce change so artfully used by members of past generations. Moreover, Castle worked well with other organizations in the city, thus continuing the tradition of cooperation exemplified by the public career of female leaders such as Fannie C. Williams and Deborah Guidry.

The presence of CORE, the work of activist leaders such as Castle and Lombard, and the growing commitment of African Americans to direct action placed additional pressure on the older civil rights groups, most notably the NAACP. Litigation, negotiation, and compromise had served the New Orleans black community and groups such as the NAACP well in the past. They remained committed to those tactics during the initial desegregation struggle of 1960, with one added feature. If compromise failed, NAACP branch president Arthur Chapital and his organization were more than willing to use the strategy of direct action. On 12 August 1960, for instance, Chapital wrote a letter to the managers of Woolworth, W. T. Grant, and Kress stores asking for a meeting to discuss the desegregation of lunch counters "before sit-ins are necessary."[10] In their reply Woolworth officials stated that they were glad the NAACP did not want sit-ins and agreed to meet with Chapital if the conferences included city officials. Kress and W. T. Grant officials issued a similar response. The absence of Mayor Morrison from the city prevented the group from holding the meeting. But before the local NAACP branch managed to initiate its version of the carrot-and-stick approach, on 9 September 1960 seven members of CORE staged a sit-in demonstration at the Woolworth department store. Police arrested all seven demonstrators. The following day several members of the newly reorganized NAACP Youth Council began picketing the same Woolworth store. The mayor reacted to the second demonstration by ordering the police to enforce the new state trespassing law.[11] He stated that the demonstrations "were not in the public interest of this community." According to Morrison, the demonstrations had been "initiated by a small group of misguided white and Negro students." Indicating how completely out of touch white leaders were with the changing sentiments of the black community, the police chief thought the protesters did not represent "the intelligent thinking Negroes or whites of the community."[12]

Just the opposite was true. The intelligent and thinking African Americans, such as Byrd, Castle, and Chapital, wanted equality and increasingly embraced direct action to achieve it. On 17 September 1960 Castle joined Rudy Lombard and Sydney Goldfinch in a demonstration at McCrory's department store. They received the typical response of hostility and arrest. They also received another emerging response: the commitment by the black community to support the students. Various African American organizations pledged financial support to assist with the legal fees for those arrested. Meanwhile, NAACP officials continued their negotiating effort with Woolworth, Kress, and Grant. The talks remained unproductive, prompting the New Orleans Branch NAACP Executive Committee to vote to cease negotiating with store officials. At the same October meeting Executive Committee members asked attorney Tureaud to file suit to have the legislative acts outlawing picketing and sit-ins declared unconstitutional. Although Tureaud was philosophically opposed to sit-ins and direct action tactics, perhaps it was painful for him to refuse a request by the local NAACP branch, but refuse he did. He did so, according to two recent biographers, because direct action protests "increased the burden of civil rights lawyers already overwhelmed and overworked." But as they also pointed out, Tureaud had mentored a younger group of African American attorneys, including Robert Collins, Lolis Elie, Norman Francis, and Ernest Nathan "Dutch" Morial, who were capable and willing to join the multiple fronts in the escalating civil rights struggle in New Orleans.[13]

In November 1960 attention shifted to the desegregation of schools. As a result, for the next two years black leaders did not devote all their protest efforts to direct action. Some activities continued, mainly through the efforts of CORE, but no significant widespread change in race relations occurred. From 1961 to 1964 Castle served as chairwoman of New Orleans CORE. And during this period women provided the chapter with some of its most dynamic participants. Castle and other CORE members moved on several fronts. They picketed area stores, theaters, and public facilities to achieve desegregation. On one dramatic occasion they formed a human chain around Loew's theater in protest of the management's refusal to break the color line. The arrest of Castle and other protesters only intensified their resolve. Admittedly, however, arrest for protesters in New Orleans rarely entailed the same level of danger that it did for individuals in other parts of Louisiana and across the South. Nonetheless, the specter of violence remained as CORE members escalated their attacks against various manifestations of racial oppression.[14]

In addition to confrontational tactics, CORE sanctioned the use of the courts and cooperation with other groups in the effort to topple Jim Crow. Castle, for example, served as one of the plaintiffs in a suit to desegregate area supermarkets. She exhibited a sterner test of her leadership skills as a member of the Citizens Committee, a small group composed of leaders of several black protest organizations. Despite her presence as the youngest, and the only female, member of the committee, she gained the respect of the older members. Perhaps the best indication of her place among black leaders occurred on 30 September 1963, when she and several members of the Citizens Committee led the largest protest march in the history of New Orleans. The ten thousand marchers—led by Avery Alexander, Oretha Castle, Arthur Chapital, and Ernest Morial—hoped to deliver a clear message to the city's white leadership that, one hundred years after the Emancipation Proclamation, segregation and racial inequality had to end. Yet it would take more than one massive march to move New Orleans closer to ending the system of racial privilege that had truly become for the great majority of whites in the city "a way of life."[15]

One of the thousands who marched on that historic day was Virginia Y. Collins, in her fourth decade of activism. The daughter of a Baptist preacher and a social activist mother, Collins inherited from her parents a commitment to fight for racial and social justice. From them she also inherited a fierce desire for personal growth. Her career choices, however, had reflected the limitations imposed on women: she was a teacher and a nurse. By the time she participated in the September 1963 march, she had involved herself in most of the important protest activities conducted by African Americans in the 1940s, 1950s, and 1960s. And more than most black activists, Collins worked with members of the city's small group of white moderates and liberals. In 1938 she had joined the Southern

Conference for Human Welfare and later worked with the Southern Conference Educational Fund. Her concern for improved black education stemmed in part from the frustrations she had experienced as a parent in her attempts to gain a quality education for her children.[16]

With the rise in the number of groups actively pursuing an end to discrimination, an umbrella-type organization such as the Citizens Committee served a useful purpose. The NAACP had four representatives on the committee; of the four, however, none were from the NAACP Youth Council. The omission of a Youth Council representative on the Citizens Committee eventually led to some dissension within the committee. Until the summer of 1963 the Youth Council had, with only slight and sporadic deviation, followed the tone and pace of the branch in the protest movement. Local NAACP Youth Council leaders Raphael Cassimere Jr. and Vallery Ferdinand III and senior advisor Llewelyn Soniat started to reassess the past accomplishments and future prospects of the civil rights protest movement and the policy of gradualism they suspected the Citizens Committee of pursuing. Furthermore, they believed some branch leaders seemed equally committed to peaceful negotiation and gradual improvement in civil rights. By 1963 the desegregation of Audubon Park, City Park, the Municipal Auditorium, public transit, and all city-owned recreational facilities through litigation or the threat of litigation initiated by the local NAACP branch demonstrated the branch's unwavering commitment to complete desegregation. And the admonishment of city officials by the judges hearing the desegregation case that "New Orleans here and now must adjust to the reality of having to operate desegregated public facilities" strongly suggested that in time legal segregation would end.[17]

But how many back doors, side windows, flights of stairs, colored-only signs, white-only ads, racial insults, brutal police tactics, discriminating employers, racist legislators, and other manifestations and reminders of Jim Crow would African Americans in New Orleans endure before Jim Crow became truly a stranger? On 25 July 1963 the NAACP Youth Council answered for many African Americans in the city that the wait for full equality would be too long without direct action. For two years, undaunted by resistance from some members of the black community, false accusations by rival groups, and some defections within their own ranks, NAACP Youth Council picketers remained on Canal Street until legal segregation came to an end. The desegregation victory they eventually helped win by demonstrating on Canal Street did not come easily. When the Youth Council started picketing stores located on Canal Street, some members of the Citizens Committee were incensed. They indicated their unequivocal opposition to the action taken by the Youth Council. They labeled Youth Council leaders glory seekers and raised the rhetorical question, "Where were they when the going was rough . . . when Canal Street picketers were being jailed?" According to a spokesman for the Citizens Committee, negotiations with white businessmen had led to a promise to hire seventy-five African Americans above the menial level. In fact, the spokesman stated, fifty-nine blacks had already been hired. Based on a survey conducted in July to verify the number of African Americans hired by downtown businesses above the menial level, Youth Council members found less cause for optimism than members of the Citizens Committee had. Yet the issue in the opinion of Youth Council president Raphael Cassimere rested in a larger context. The point was not to place a small number of African Americans in positions but to create a climate that enabled qualified black applicants to have the same chance of employment as qualified white applicants. And Cassimere summed up his group's position by declaring: "We are told that we have no experience in these matters. We answer that previous dealings in these matters have been almost nil and we can't do worse."[18] The NAACP Executive Committee apparently agreed and voted to support the actions of the Youth Council.

Instead of negotiations with downtown store owners as a group, the strategy that had been used by the committee, Youth Council members decided to negotiate with each owner or manager individually. They reasoned, correctly, that if an agreement could be reached with a few stores, the remaining boycotted stores would experience additional pressure to comply. Youth Council leaders appealed to the black community for support and asked African Americans to refrain from crossing the picket lines. They used the news media, circulars, and branch meetings to disseminate information to the community. At first the black community was slow to respond but finally succumbed to the persistence of the picketers. The individual merchants proved less pliable. Eventually, however, the desire to maintain profits soon began to triumph over racial prejudices. On 22 February 1964 the Youth Council reached an agreement with F. W. Woolworth. That represented the first significant breakthrough; within the next several weeks Grant's, Mayfair, Rubenstein, and Three Sisters reached agreements. By July 1964 the Youth Council had reached an accord with more than twenty-five downtown retail establishments, including Krauss department store, considered one of the "big five" because of its volume of business. Throughout the summer and fall the number of stores ending discriminatory practices continued to increase. Four of the big five stores still refused to capitulate: Holmes, Maison Blanche, Marks-Isaac, and Sears. Indeed, those four stores continued their discriminatory practices until after passage of the 1964 Civil Rights Act.[19]

The direct action campaign, although relatively successful, could not be used against businesses that did not sell consumer goods. When Title VII of the 1964 Civil Rights Act went into effect in July 1965, African Americans possessed a new weapon in the fight against discrimination. With almost religious zeal during the summer of 1965, Raphael Cassimere, the newly appointed NAACP Title VII coordinator, worked to ensure that area businesses complied with the new law's employment nondiscrimination requirement. Cassimere recruited and encouraged African Americans to apply for jobs that had traditionally been held by whites. Each day Cassimere, along with other NAACP workers, scanned the help wanted sections of the paper to ferret out discriminatory want ads. If their search produced any violators, Cassimere would dispatch a letter to the company demanding an end to "white only" ads. Under the watchful eye of activist leaders, some New Orleans employers attempted to comply with the recently enacted civil rights legislation and started to eliminate discriminatory practices in anticipation of the implementation date of the Civil Rights Act. In reply to Cassimere's inquiry concerning his company's hiring practices, an IBM branch manager maintained that "for quite some time now, our employment practices have embraced all the suggestions which you mentioned." The IBM official assured Cassimere that he "would be most happy to cooperate with your office in any way possible to further the cause of the equal employment program." Other employers were even more accommodating. A local bakery official, for example, wrote a letter detailing his efforts to expand the number of black employees and ended the letter by offering the "hope that the above courses of actions will meet with the approval of the NAACP."

That type of response was not universal; most employers did not express a willingness to cooperate with the NAACP. Attorneys representing the Eye, Ear, Nose, and Throat Hospital informed NAACP officials that enforcement responsibility for the Civil Rights Act rested with the federal government. In a similar vein executives for New Orleans Public Service refused to meet with members of the NAACP. This was also true for Godchaux's and several other department stores. Their refusal to meet with members of the NAACP, as they all stressed, did not mean they were refusing to comply with the Civil Rights Act. Nonetheless, the local NAACP office continued to receive complaints that detailed discrimination in hiring. Arthur Chapital, who served as branch executive director from 1964 to 1968, noted in his year-end report for 1968 that the branch had "received... many complaints regarding discrimination in employment and under-employment." According to Chapital's report, some of the complaints had been successfully handled by the NAACP branch, and others had been referred to the Equal Employment Opportunity Commission. The following year Chapital indicated approximately the same number of complaints. It was apparent that legislative fiat alone would not be sufficient to end racial discrimination.[20]

Another campaign to elevate African Americans to the status of full citizens involved voter registration and voter education. Until the passage of the Voting Rights Act of 1965, the registrar of voters hindered the effectiveness of black voter registration campaigns. In March 1960 New Orleans had 168,786 white voters and 34,981 black voters. African Americans constituted approximately 37 percent of the population but only 17.5 percent of the number of registered voters. Increased black voter registration continued to be a top priority for community leaders. And beginning in 1960 the NAACP's Voter Registration Committee and Youth Council expanded their efforts to educate and register voters. The Voter Education Committee chairman in 1960, Victor Lele, attempted to recruit a leader for each of the seventeen wards in the city. These people would have responsibility for recruiting individuals to serve in their particular ward. The registration committee usually met once a week to coordinate its activities. Churches and fraternal organizations assisted the registration drives by disseminating information to their members or allowing the committee to use their facilities. In addition, the registration chairman expected clergy leaders to preach the importance of the vote to their congregation. Many clergymen needed little prodding, for a number of ministers remained in the forefront of the struggle for civil rights.[21]

To advance the voter registration effort, activists such as Lele employed several tactics and welcomed new allies. They staged several mass meetings, for example, to dramatize the importance of voter registration. In January 1961 W. C. Patton, an NAACP field secretary, served as a featured speaker and remained in New Orleans to help with voter registration. The

NAACP branch also publicized its registration campaigns through the news media. And during this period the branch's political action committee established voter registration schools at five area churches. African Americans citizens received instruction on how to fill out registration forms, with emphasis on the several inevitable "trick" questions. To maximize the schools' effectiveness, Wilfred Aubert, chairman of the political action committee, developed another tactic. He realized that some African Americans would not go to the voter registration schools, so he decided to bring the schools to them. With assistance from the NAACP Youth Council, Aubert and his workers went door-to-door "to teach them at home."[22] In "teaching them at home" or at the schools, the branch received assistance from the League of Women Voters.

Many individuals continued to contribute to the black freedom agenda, and the expanding needs of the struggle brought additional activists into the arena. Some veteran activists, however, such as Virginia Collins, merely increased their level of protest activities. Collins worked with churches and fraternal organizations to provide voter registration information to the community. In addition, she operated a voter education school similar to the citizenship schools run by Highlander and the Southern Christian Leadership Conference. Yet Collins knew that voter education alone would not lead to black political empowerment. As a result, she organized and assisted in several protest demonstrations to dramatize the level of resistance black citizens encountered when they attempted to register. Despite the best efforts of leaders such as Aubert and Collins to increase the number of African American voters, progress was slow because some white resistance remained. And white politicians such as Victor Schiro still derived political capital from either distancing themselves from black voters or displaying outright hostility to them. As a result, African American leaders in New Orleans watched with keen interest the voter registration strategies and activities in other parts of the state and across the South. And like much of the nation in the spring of 1965, they paid particular attention to events in Selma, Alabama.[23]

The passage of the Voting Rights Act of 1965 necessitated a change from mostly protest to education and registration. Effectively barred from the political process for over seventy-five years, community leaders knew that African Americans would need some guidance and leadership to assist them in gaining sufficient political acumen to transform political potential into political influence and power. The local NAACP branch continued to conduct voter registration campaigns. With financial assistance from the national office, the local NAACP Youth Council implemented a registration drive in two of the city's seventeen wards during the summer of 1967. The Youth Council workers identified 1,741 unregistered African American voters in the two wards and through their efforts registered 331 new voters. An almost identical registration project conducted the next year, this time by the branch, yielded similar results. Project members, of course, wanted larger numbers but understood the need to build a political tradition among a people long denied meaningful political participation.[24]

After the passage of the Voting Rights Act a new group of African American leaders emerged to help usher in the new political order. Prominent among them were Israel Augustine Jr., Oretha Castle, Sherman Copelin, Nils Douglas, and Ernest "Dutch" Morial. The Institute of Politics at Loyola University also aided the development of black leaders through training in the practical aspects of modern politics. Expanded black voter registration and the efforts of political activists contributed to the formation of several black political organizations.[25] The most successful of the early organizations were the Black Organization for Leadership Development (BOLD), the Community Organization for Urban Politics (COUP), and the Southern Organization for Unified Leadership (SOUL). The voter registration projects and political organizations started to produce the intended political results. In 1967 Ernest Morial won a seat in the state legislature, becoming the first African American to join that body in the twentieth century. During the 1970s the increased black vote contributed to a rise in the number of black elected officials. Dr. Mack Spears won a seat on the school board, and Edwin Lombard was elected clerk of the criminal district court. Suffrage, office holding, and coalition politics began to replace protest, petition, and litigation as strategies for black community development.

Many African Americans found common cause — through professional, political, and civic involvement — with members of the white middle class. Perhaps the fullest expression of the political coalition between some middle-class blacks and whites began during Maurice "Moon" Landrieu's successful mayoral campaign in 1969 and 1970 and subsequent administrations. Landrieu included African Americans at all levels of his campaign and administration, appointing the city's first black chief administrative officer. The high profile of African Americans in the Landrieu administration and the continued rise in black voter registration helped Dutch Morial win election as the city's first black mayor in 1977.[26] Morial's election suggested that New Orleans, at Jim Crow's end, was making the transition from a largely race-conscious society to a society in which race and class both mattered. The civil rights movement ended legal racial segregation and, in doing so, also concluded a significant and distinct period in black New Orleans.

NOTES

1. The Rise and Decline of Black Equality

1. John Keegan, *The American Civil War: A Military History* (New York: Knopf, 2009), 42–43, 91–94; Russell F. Weigley, *A Great Civil War: A Military and Political History, 1861–1865* (Bloomington: Indiana University Press, 2000), 58–60; James M. McPherson, *Ordeal by Fire: The Civil War and Reconstruction,* 3rd ed. (New York: McGraw-Hill, 2001), 163–64, 179–84.

2. Keegan, *American Civil War,* 139, 280–84; Weigley, *Great Civil War,* 341–43; McPherson, *Ordeal by Fire,* 192–99; James M. Merrill, "Confederate Shipbuilding at New Orleans," *Journal of Southern History* 28, no. 1 (February 1962): 87–93.

3. Merrill, "Confederate Shipbuilding at New Orleans," 93.

4. David W. Blight, *Frederick Douglass' Civil War: Keeping Faith in Jubilee* (Baton Rouge: Louisiana State University Press, 1989), 107–21, 148–74; McPherson, *Ordeal by Fire,* 253–54; Keegan, *American Civil War,* 134; Chester G. Hearn, *The Capture of New Orleans, 1862* (Baton Rouge: Louisiana State University Press, 1995), 237–48.

5. Lincoln to Johnson, 26 March 1863, Lincoln to Conkling, 26 August 1863, in Michael P. Johnson, ed., *Abraham Lincoln, Slavery, and the Civil War: Selected Writings and Speeches* (Boston: Bedford / St. Martins, 2001), 223–24, 257; Harry S. Stout, *Upon the Altar of the Nation: A Moral History of the American Civil War* (New York: Viking, 2006), 167–68, 178–80; Gary W. Gallagher, *The Union War* (Cambridge, Mass.: Harvard University Press, 2011), 34–36, 75–78; James M. McPherson, *For Cause and Comrades: Why Men Fought in the Civil War* (New York: Oxford University Press, 1997), 117–30; Mary Francis Berry, *Military Necessity and Civil Rights Policy: Black Citizenship and the Constitution, 1861–1868* (Port Washington, N.Y.: National University Publications, 1977), 61–74.

6. Charles Vincent, "'Of Such Historical Importance . . .': The African American Experience in Louisiana," *Louisiana History* 50, no. 2 (Spring 2009): 145–46.

7. James G. Hollandsworth Jr., *The Louisiana Native Guards: The Black Military Experience during the Civil War* (Baton Rouge: Louisiana State University Press, 1995), 53–58.

8. Quoted in Noah Andre Trudeau, *Like Men of War: Black Troops in the Civil War, 1862–1865* (Boston: Little, Brown, 1998), 59.

9. Quoted in Joseph T. Glatthaar, *Forged in Battle: The Civil War Alliance of Black Soldiers and White Officers* (Baton Rouge: Louisiana State University Press, 1990), 45, 59.

10. Johnson, *Abraham Lincoln*, 274; David Goldfield, *America Aflame: How the Civil War Created a Nation* (New York: Bloomsbury Press, 2011), 418–19.

11. Goldfield, *America Aflame*, 419.

12. Eric Foner, *Free Soil, Free Labor, Free Men: The Ideology of the Republican Party Before the Civil War* (New York: Oxford University Press, 1971), 40, 50–52.

13. Caryn Cossé Bell, *Revolution, Romanticism, and the Afro-Creole Protest Tradition in Louisiana, 1718–1868* (Baton Rouge: Louisiana State University Press, 1997), 224–25, 250–55.

14. In Manning Marable and Leith Mullings, eds., *Let Nobody Turn Us Around: Voices of Resistance, Reform, and Renewal* (Lanham, Md.: Rowman and Littlefield, 2000), 126.

15. David C. Rankin, "The Forgotten People: Free People of Color in New Orleans, 1850–1870" (Ph.D. diss., John Hopkins University, 1976), 233.

16. Rankin, "Forgotten People," 226–27; William P. Connor, "Reconstruction Rebels: The New Orleans Tribune in Post-War Louisiana," *Louisiana History* 21, no. 2 (Spring 1980): 163–67; *New Orleans Tribune*, 16 November 1864.

17. Dale A. Somers, "Black and White in New Orleans: A Study in Urban Race Relations, 1865–1900," *Journal of Southern History* 40, no. 1 (1974): 22–24; Rankin, "Forgotten People," 226–27; Glatthaar, *Forged in Battle*, 248–50; Donald R. Shaffer, *After the Glory: The Struggle of Black Civil War Veterans* (Lawrence: University Press of Kansas, 2004), 67–73.

18. Edmonia G. Highgate to Rev. M. E. Strieby, in *We Are Your Sisters: Black Women in the Nineteenth Century*, edited by Dorothy Sterling (New York: Norton, 1984), 297.

19. Joseph Logsdon and Caryn Cossé Bell, "The Americanization of Black New Orleans, 1850–1900," in *Creole New Orleans: Race and Americanization*, edited by Arnold R. Hirsch and Joseph Logsdon (Baton Rouge: Louisiana State University Press, 1992), 204–9, 221–28.

20. Joe Gray Taylor, *Louisiana Reconstructed, 1863–1877* (Baton Rouge: Louisiana State University Press, 1974), 147; Ted Tunnell, *Crucible of Reconstruction: War, Radicalism, and Race in Louisiana, 1862–1877* (Baton Rouge: Louisiana State University Press, 1984), 113–14; Roger A. Fischer, *The Segregation Struggle in Louisiana, 1862–1877* (Urbana: University of Illinois Press, 1974), 48, 55; Charles Vincent, *Black Legislators in Louisiana during Reconstruction* (Baton Rouge: Louisiana State University Press, 1976), 49; Bell, *Revolution*, 276–80.

21. *Journal of the Convention for the Framing of a Constitution for the State of Louisiana* (New Orleans, 1867–68), 3–4; Charles Vincent, "Negro Leadership and Programs," *Louisiana History* 10, no. 4 (Fall 1969): 343–45; Fischer, *Segregation Struggle*, 48–49; Taylor, *Louisiana Reconstructed*, 342.

22. Vincent, "Negro Leadership and Programs," 350.

23. Rebecca J. Scott, *Degrees of Freedom: Louisiana and Cuba after Slavery* (Cambridge: Belknap Press of Harvard University Press, 2005), 44, 45.

24. *Journal of the Convention*, 13; Taylor, *Louisiana Reconstructed*, 136, 151–52; Vincent, "Negro Leadership and Programs," 342.

25. Ella Lonn, *Reconstruction in Louisiana after 1868* (New York: G. P. Putnam's Sons, 1918), 11; *New Orleans Tribune*, 27 December 1867.

26. Paul A. Kunkel, "Modifications in Louisiana Negro Legal Status under Louisiana Con-

stitutions, 1812–1957," *Journal of Negro History* 44, no. 1 (January 1959): 11–12; Melinda Meek Hennessey, "Race and Violence in Reconstruction New Orleans: The 1868 Riot," *Louisiana History* 20, no. 1 (Winter 1979): 82–87; Fischer, *Segregation Struggle*, 59.

27. In Marable and Mullings, *Let Nobody Turn Us Around*, 130.

28. *New Orleans Tribune*, 12 December 1867; Vincent, *Black Legislators*, 68–69; Fischer, *Segregation Struggle*, 57; Taylor, *Louisiana Reconstructed*, 156–57.

29. H. E. Sterkx, *The Free Negro in Ante-Bellum Louisiana* (Rutherford, N.J.: Fairleigh Dickinson University Press, 1972), 268; C. Peter Ripley, *Slaves and Freedmen in Civil War Louisiana* (Baton Rouge: Louisiana State University Press, 1976), 126–27; Charles B. Rousseve, *The Negro in Louisiana* (New Orleans: Xavier University Press, 1937), 43–44; John Blassingame, *Black New Orleans, 1860–1880* (Chicago: University of Chicago Press, 1973), 107–10.

30. Thomas L. Webber, *Deep Like the Rivers: Education in the Slave Quarter Community, 1831–1865* (New York: Norton, 1978), 131; Eugene D. Genovese, *Roll, Jordan Roll: The World the Slaves Made* (New York: Vintage Books, 1976), 563; Blassingame, *Black New Orleans*, 107.

31. Robert C. Morris, *Reading, 'Riting, and Reconstruction: The Education of Freedmen in the South* (Chicago: University of Chicago Press, 1981), 23; James D. Anderson, *The Education of Blacks in the South, 1860–1935* (Chapel Hill: University of North Carolina Press, 1988), 9; Elisabeth Doyle, "Nurseries of Treason: Schools in Occupied New Orleans," *Journal of Southern History* 26, no. 2 (May 1960): 176; Barry A. Crouch, "Black Education in Civil War and Reconstruction Louisiana: George T. Ruby, the Army, and the Freedmen's Bureau," *Louisiana History* 38, no. 3 (Summer 1997): 289–92.

32. B. Rush Plumly to G. N. Taylor, 21 September 1864, Records of the Superintendent of Education for the State of Louisiana, Bureau of Refugees, Freedmen, and Abandoned Lands, 1864–69, Record Group 105 (National Archives Microforms Publications, M 1026); hereafter cited as LA BRFAL.

33. Mortimer Warren, "Monthly Report," 30 October 1865, LA BRFAL.

34. J. H. Ford, "Weekly Report," 29 July 1864, LA BRFAL.

35. Howard A. White, *The Freedmen's Bureau in Louisiana* (Baton Rouge: Louisiana State University Press, 1970), 173; Crouch, "Black Education in Civil War and Reconstruction Louisiana," 303–8.

36. Board of School Directors of New Orleans Minutes, 4 December 1867. (In July 1864 the school board had been reorganized as the Board of School Directors of New Orleans and maintained that name or a variation of it until 1916. That year the name was changed to the Orleans Parish School Board. Hereafter references to minutes and reports generated and produced by the various boards will be cited as OPSB. Unless otherwise noted, the records are in the Louisiana and Special Collections Department, Earl K. Long Library, University of New Orleans.)

37. *New Orleans Tribune*, 12 May 1867; OPSB Meeting Minutes, 10 January 1868.

38. *New Orleans Times*, 1, 19 September 1867.

39. *Louisiana, Annual Report of the State Superintendent of Public Education, 1869* (New Orleans: A. E. Lee, 1870), 12.

40. James G. Hollandsworth, *An Absolute Massacre: The New Orleans Riot of July 30, 1866* (Baton Rouge: Louisiana State University Press, 2001); Donald E. Reynolds, "The New Orleans Riot of 1866 Reconsidered," *Louisiana History* 5, no. 1 (Winter 1964): 5–27.

41. *Southwestern Christian Advocate* (New Orleans), 18 June 1874, 23 September 1875;

New Orleans Weekly Louisianian, 15 February 1875; Mary Niall Mitchell, *Raising Freedom's Child: Black Children and Visions of the Future after Slavery* (New York: New York University Press, 2008), 207–24; Louis R. Harlan, "Desegregation in New Orleans Public Schools during Reconstruction," *American Historical Review* 67, no. 3 (April 1962): 663–75; Blassingame, *Black New Orleans*, 118–22.

42. C. Vann Woodward, *The Strange Career of Jim Crow*, 3rd ed. (New York: Oxford University Press, 1974), 29.

43. Blassingame, *Black New Orleans*, 26, 186.

44. T. Harry Williams, "The Louisiana Unification Movement of 1873," *Journal of Southern History* 11, no. 3 (August 1945): 350; Taylor, *Louisiana Reconstructed*, 277; *New Orleans Daily Picayune*, 16 June 1873; *New Orleans Times*, 17 June 1873.

45. Bell, *Revolution, Romanticism, and the Afro-Creole Protest Tradition*, 277–79; *New Orleans Republican*, 28 May, 1, 4 June 1873.

46. *New Orleans Times*, 17 June 1873; Taylor, *Louisiana Reconstructed*, 277.

47. Williams, "Louisiana Unification Movement," 359.

48. *New Orleans Times*, 16 July 1873; *New Orleans Daily Picayune*, 16 July 1873; Williams, "Louisiana Unification Movement," 363–67; Blassingame, *Black New Orleans*, 174.

49. Charles W. Calhoun, *Conceiving a New Republic: The Republican Party and the Southern Question, 1869–1900* (Lawrence: University Press of Kansas, 2006), 50.

50. *Weekly Louisianian*, 22 August 1874; *New Orleans Daily Picayune*, 8, 13, 15, 16, 18 September 1874; Taylor, *Louisiana Reconstructed*, 241–48.

51. C. Vann Woodward, *Reunion and Reaction: The Compromise of 1877 and the End of Reconstruction* (New York: Little, Brown, 1951), 235–41; Kenneth M. Stampp, *The Era of Reconstruction, 1865–1877* (New York: Vintage Books, 1965), 186–215; Tunnell, *Crucible of Reconstruction*, 170–71; Calhoun, *Conceiving a New Republic*, 47–49.

52. Louisiana Annual Report, 1877.

53. OPSB Meeting Minutes, 22 June 1877.

54. Bell, *Revolution, Romanticism, and the Afro-Creole Protest Tradition*, 280; *New Orleans Daily Picayune*, 27 June 1877; OPSB Meeting Minutes, 3 July 1877.

55. Fischer, *Segregation Struggle*, 142.

56. *New Orleans Tribune*, 26 April 1867; Richard Follett, "Legacies of Enslavement: Plantation Identities and the Problem of Freedom," in *Slavery's Ghost: The Problem of Freedom in the Age of Emancipation*, edited by Richard Follett, Eric Foner, and Walter Johnson (Baltimore: John Hopkins University Press, 2011), 53.

57. OPSB Meeting Minutes, 3 July 1877.

58. Louisiana, Constitution (1879), Art. 231; J. Morgan Kousser, *The Shaping of Southern Politics: Suffrage Restriction and the Establishment of the One-Party South, 1880–1910* (New Haven, Conn.: Yale University Press, 1974), 152; Henry C. Dethloff and Robert R. Jones, "Race Relations in Louisiana, 1877–1898," *Louisiana History* 9, no. 4 (Fall 1968): 308–23; Scott, *Degrees of Freedom*, 71–72.

59. *Weekly Louisianian*, 11 June 1881; Rodolphe Desdunes, *Our People and Our History: A Tribute to the Creole People of Color in Memory of the Great Men They Have Given Us and of the Good Works They Have Accomplished*, translated and edited by Sister Dorothea Olga McCants (Baton Rouge: Louisiana State University Press, 1973), 136–38.

60. Desdunes, *Our People and Our History*, 136–38.

61. Herbert Aptheker, ed., *A Documentary History of the Negro People in the United States* (New York: Carol Publishing, 1992), 2:741.

62. Joy J. Jackson, *New Orleans in the Gilded Age: Politics and Urban Progress, 1880–1896* (Baton Rouge: Louisiana State University Press, 1969), 32–37, 318–19.

63. Jackson, *New Orleans in the Gilded Age*, 98–110.

64. Leon F. Litwack, *Trouble in Mind: Black Southerners in the Age of Jim Crow* (New York: Knopf, 1999), 229, 230; William Ivy Hair, *Bourbonism and Agrarian Protest: Louisiana Politics, 1877–1900* (Baton Rouge: Louisiana State University Press, 1975), 170; Rayford W. Logan, *The Betrayal of the Negro from Rutherford B. Hayes to Woodrow Wilson*, rev. ed. (New York: Collier-Macmillan, 1972), 195–217; Dethloff and Jones, "Race Relations in Louisiana," 316–23.

65. Desdunes, *Our People and Our History*, 141.

66. Blair L. M. Kelley, *Right to Ride: Streetcar Boycotts and African American Citizenship in the Era of* Plessy v. Ferguson (Chapel Hill: University of North Carolina Press, 2010), 60–63; Arthe A. Anthony, "The Negro Creole Community in New Orleans, 1880–1920: An Oral History" (Ph.D. diss., University of California, Irving, 1978), 50–52.

67. Otto H. Olsen, ed., *The Thin Disguise: Turning Point in Negro History,* Plessy v. Ferguson (New York: Humanities Press, 1967), 47–49.

68. Keith W. Medley, *We as Freemen:* Plessy v. Ferguson (Gretna, La.: Pelican Publishing, 2003), 99–101; Olsen, *Thin Disguise*, 52–55; Fischer, *Segregation Struggle*, 153; Kelley, *Right to Ride*, 68.

69. J. Morgan Kousser, *Colorblind Injustice: Minority Voting Rights and the Undoing of the Second Reconstruction* (Chapel Hill: University of North Carolina Press, 1999), 323–24; Olsen, *Thin Disguise*, 112; Desdunes, *Our People and Our History,* 141.

70. Michael Perman, *Struggle for Mastery: Disfranchisement in the South, 1888–1908* (Chapel Hill: University of North Carolina Press, 2001), 125–36; Donna A. Barnes, *The Louisiana Populist Movement, 1881–1900* (Baton Rouge: Louisiana State University Press, 2011), 228–29; Henry C. Dethloff, "The Alliance and the Lottery: Farmers Try for the Sweepstakes," *Louisiana History* 6, no. 2 (Spring 1965): 158–59; Hair, *Bourbonism and Agrarian Protest*, 237–41; Philip D. Uzee, "The Republican Party in the Louisiana Election of 1896," *Louisiana History* 2, no. 3 (Summer 1961): 343–44; Kousser, *Shaping of Southern Politics*, 159–64.

71. *Official Journal of the Proceedings of the Constitutional Convention of the State of Louisiana, 1898* (New Orleans: H. J. Hearsey, 1898), 9–10; Perman, *Struggle for Mastery,* 137–39.

72. Booker T. Washington, "An Open Letter to the Louisiana Constitutional Convention," 19 February 1898, in *The Booker T. Washington Papers,* edited by Louis R. Harlan, Stuart B. Kaufman, Barbara S. Kraft, and Raymond W. Smock (Urbana: University of Illinois Press, 1975), 4:381–84.

73. Steven Hahn, *A Nation under Our Feet: Black Political Struggles in the Rural South from Slavery to the Great Migration* (Cambridge: Belknap Press of Harvard University Press, 2003), 442–43.

74. *Official Journal of the Proceedings of the Constitutional Convention of the State of Louisiana,* 9–10; R. Volney Riser, *Defying Disfranchisement: Black Voting Rights Activism in the Jim Crow South, 1890–1908* (Baton Rouge: Louisiana State University Press, 2010), 76–82; Londa L. Davis, "After Reconstruction: Black Politics in New Orleans, 1876–1900" (master's thesis, University of New Orleans, 1981), 179–80; Perman, *Struggle for Mastery,* 137–39, 144.

75. William Ivy Hair, *Carnival of Fury: Robert Charles and the New Orleans Race Riot of*

1900 (Baton Rouge: Louisiana State University Press, 1976), 137–200; Desdunes, *Our People and Our History*, 147; Litwack, *Trouble in Mind*, 239.

76. Woodward, *Strange Career of Jim Crow*, 108; Desdunes, *Our People and Our History*, 147.

2. Higher Education and Individual Initiative

1. W.E.B. Du Bois, *The Souls of Black Folk: Essays and Sketches by W. E. Burghardt Du Bois* (New York: Dodd, Mead, 1979), 2; W.E.B. Du Bois, "The Talented Tenth," in *The Negro Problem* (1903; repr., New York: Arno Press and New York Times, 1969), 59.

2. Booker T. Washington, "Industrial Education for the Negro," in *Negro Problem*, 16.

3. Murphy to Washington, 9 January 1900, in Harlan, *Booker T. Washington Papers*, 5:405–6.

4. Robert J. Norrell, *Up from History: The Life of Booker T. Washington* (Cambridge: Belknap Press of Harvard University Press, 2009), 189.

5. Southern Society for the Promotion of the Study of Race Conditions and Problems in the South [hereafter cited as Southern Society], *Race Problems of the South: Report of the Proceedings of the First Annual Conference Held under the Auspices of the Southern Society for the Promotion of the Study of Race Conditions and Problems in the South* (Montgomery, Ala., 1900), 88, 216.

6. Charles W. Chesnutt, "The Disfranchisement of the Negro," in *Negro Problem*, 81.

7. Southern Society, *Race Problems of the South*, 50, 44, 106.

8. Southern Society, *Race Problems of the South*, 58, 138–40.

9. MacCorkle to Washington, 14 May 1900, Harlan, *Booker T. Washington Papers*, 5:523.

10. *New Orleans Daily Picayune*, 4 December 1910.

11. Quoted in Clarence Mohr, "Minds of the New South: Higher Education in Black and White, 1880–1915," *Southern Quarterly* 46, no. 4 (Summer 2009): 20.

12. W.E.B. Du Bois, *The Education of Black People: Ten Critiques, 1906–1960*, edited by Herbert Aptheker (New York: Monthly Review Press, 1973), 37; Du Bois, "Talented Tenth," 74–75.

13. Shawn C. Comminey, "The Origin, Organization, and Progression of Straight University, 1869–1880," *Louisiana History* 51, no. 4 (Fall 2010): 411–14; Joe M. Richardson, "The American Missionary Association and Black Education in Louisiana, 1862–1878," in *Louisiana's Black Heritage*, edited by Robert Macdonald, John R. Kemp, and Edward Haas (New Orleans: Louisiana State Museum, 1979), 157–62; David C. Marshall, "A History of the Higher Education of Negroes in the State of Louisiana" (Ph.D. diss., Louisiana State University, 1956), 67–70; Blassingame, *Black New Orleans*, 125–30.

14. Comminey, "Origin, Organization, and Progression of Straight University," 431–33; Howard V. Young Jr., "James A. Garfield and Hampton Institute," in *Stony the Road: Chapters in the History of Hampton Institute*, edited by Keith L Schall (Charlottesville: University Press of Virginia, 1977), 34–50; Charles D. Walters, "Projections, Projects, and Finance: The Letters of Hollis Burke Frissell," in Schall, *Stony the Road*, 51–62.

15. Joe M. Richardson and Maxine D. Jones, *Education for Liberation: The American Missionary Association and African Americans, 1890 to the Civil Rights Movement* (Tuscaloosa: University of Alabama Press, 2009), 119–20; *Southwestern Christian Advocate*, 25 October 1877; Louisiana Annual Reports, 1872, 1873.

16. *Southwestern Christian Advocate*, 3 July 1873, 6 May 1875.

17. *Southwestern Christian Advocate,* 28 September 1876, 1 June 1882.
18. Janice Richard Johnson, "Leland University in New Orleans, 1870–1915" (Ph.D. diss., University of New Orleans, 1996), 7–9, 92–93; Marshall, "History of the Higher Education of Negroes," 127–31; Blassingame, *Black New Orleans,* 124.
19. Johnson, "Leland University," 102–3; Rousseve, *Negro in Louisiana,* 112.
20. Gloria T. Hull, ed., *Give Us Each Day: The Diary of Alice Dunbar-Nelson* (New York: Norton, 1984), 95, 178.
21. Marshall, "History of the Higher Education of Negroes," 74–77.
22. OPSB Meeting Minutes, 18 July 1900, 12 July 1901.
23. Charles Vincent, *A Centennial History of Southern University and A and M College, 1880–1980* (Baton Rouge, La.: Southern University, 1981), 7–62.
24. Anderson, *Education of Blacks in the South,* 244–47, 274–78.
25. Vincent, *Centennial History of Southern University,* 72–83.
26. *Crisis,* May 1919.
27. *Survey of Negro Colleges and Universities* (1929; repr., New York: Negro Universities Press, 1969), 390–93.
28. *Survey of Negro Colleges and Universities,* 394–96; Vincent, *Centennial History of Southern University,* 114–22.
29. Marshall, "History of the Higher Education of Negroes," 78.
30. *New Orleans University, Seventy-Five Years of Service* (New Orleans, 1935), 61–82; *Survey of Negro Colleges and Universities,* 2–4.
31. *Survey of Negro Colleges and Universities,* 20–22.
32. O'Brien, "A Series of Questions," Emile J. LaBranche Papers, box 1, folder 6, Amistad Research Center, Tulane University, New Orleans.
33. O'Brien, "Series of Questions."
34. Eric Anderson and Alfred A. Moss Jr., *Dangerous Donations: Northern Philanthropy and Southern Black Education, 1902–1930* (Columbia: University of Missouri Press, 1999), 14.
35. *Louisiana Weekly,* 23 February 1929.
36. Richardson and Jones, *Education for Liberation,* 132.
37. *Louisiana Weekly,* 16 November 1929, 1 March 1930; Marshall, "History of the Higher Education of Negroes," 116–17.
38. *Louisiana Weekly,* 8 March 1930.
39. *New Orleans Times-Picayune,* 20 June 1930.
40. *New Orleans Times-Picayune,* 27 June 1930.
41. Richardson and Jones, *Education for Liberation,* 148.
42. Joe M. Richardson, "Edgar B. Stern: A White New Orleans Philanthropist Helps Build a Black University," *Journal of Negro History* 82, no. 3 (Summer 1997): 336–37; Joe M. Richardson, "Albert W. Dent: A Black New Orleans Hospital and University Administrator," *Louisiana History* 37, no. 3 (Summer 1996): 317–18.
43. Brownlee to Stern, 26 September 1940, Brownlee to Williams, 23 September 1940, Williams to Brownlee, 29 October 1940, Albert Walter and Ernestine Jessie Covington Dent Papers, box 1, folder 3, Amistad Research Center; Richardson, "Edgar Stern," 337.
44. Brownlee to Stern, 26 September 1940, Dent Papers, box 1, folder 3.
45. Rousseve, *Negro in Louisiana,* 143–45.
46. Marshall, "History of the Higher Education of Negroes," 140–41; *Xavier University Bulletin,* 1926, 1927.

47. *Xavier University Bulletin*, 1928; *Louisiana Weekly*, 31 May 1930, 17 September 1932.
48. Fannie C. Williams Papers, box, 1, folder 2, Amistad Research Center.
49. Williams Papers, box 1, folder 2.
50. Spears to Williams, 22 September 1960, Williams Papers, box 1, folder 1.
51. Quoted in Adam Fairclough, *A Class of Their Own: Black Teachers in the Segregated South* (Cambridge: Belknap Press of Harvard University Press, 2007), 279.
52. George Longe Papers, box 1, folder 3, Amistad Research Center.
53. Carter G. Woodson, *The Mis-Education of the Negro* (1933; repr., Trenton, N.J.: Africa World Press, 1990), 22–23.
54. Longe Papers, box 1, folder 3, box 2, folders 4, 7.
55. George Longe Papers, box 1, folders 3, 7.
56. Woodson, *Mis-Education of the Negro*, 192.
57. Nicholas Bauer to Hutton, 27 May 1927, 23 June 1931, 29 June 1932, Lucille Hutton Papers, box 2, folder 1, Amistad Research Center; Al Kennedy, *Chord Changes on the Chalkboard: How Public School Teachers Shared Jazz and the Music of New Orleans* (Lanham, Md.: Scarecrow Press, 2002), 1–21.
58. H. W. Cargill, Oberlin treasurer, to Hutton, 26 May, 12 June 1936, Hutton Papers, box 5, folder 10.
59. Ferdinand Rousseve Papers, box 1, folders 1, 5, Amistad Research Center.
60. Rachel L. Emanuel and Alexander P. Tureaud Jr., *A More Noble Cause: A. P. Tureaud and the Struggle for Civil Rights in Louisiana* (Baton Rouge: Louisiana State University Press, 2011), 17–23.
61. Emanuel and Tureaud, *More Noble Cause*, 24–51.
62. Quoted in Emanuel and Tureaud, *More Noble Cause*, 47.

3. The Religious Dimensions of Community Development

1. Carter G. Woodson, *The Negro Professional Man and the Community* (1938; repr., New York: Negro Universities Press, 1969), 122.
2. C. Eric Lincoln and Lawrence H. Mamiya, *The Black Church in the African American Experience* (Durham, N.C.: Duke University Press, 1990), 11; C. Eric Lincoln, *Race, Religion, and the Continuing American Dilemma* (New York: Hill and Wang, 1984), 72–73, 95; William E. Montgomery, *Under Their Own Vine and Fig Tree: The African-American Church in the South, 1865–1900* (Baton Rouge: Louisiana State University Press, 1993), 136–39, 156, 190, 307; Albert J. Raboteau, *Slave Religion: The "Invisible Institution" in the Antebellum South* (New York: Oxford University Press, 1978), 320–21.
3. Lincoln, *Race, Religion, and the Continuing American Dilemma*, 79.
4. Dolores Egger Labbe, *Jim Crow Comes to Church: The Establishment of Segregated Catholic Parishes in South Louisiana* (Lafayette: Center for Louisiana Studies, 1971), 2–7.
5. James B. Bennett, *Religion and the Rise of Jim Crow in New Orleans* (Princeton, N.J.: Princeton University Press, 2005), 145.
6. Annemarie Kasteel, *Francis Janssens, 1843–1897: A Dutch-American Prelate* (Lafayette: Center for Louisiana Studies, 1992), 293–99; Rousseve, *Negro in Louisiana*, 138–41; John B. Alberts, "Black Catholic Schools: The Josephite Parishes during the Jim Crow Era," *U.S. Catholic Historian* 12, no. 1 (Winter 1994): 82–85; *New Orleans Times Democrat*, 20 May 1895.

7. Joseph G. Tregle, "Creoles and Americans," in Hirsch and Logsdon, *Creole New Orleans*, 165–74; Alberts, "Black Catholic Schools," 83.

8. Bambra (Barb) Pitman, "Culture, Caste, and Conflict in New Orleans Catholicism: Archbishop Francis Janssens and the Color Line," *Louisiana History* 49, no. 4 (Fall 2008): 443–49; Rousseve, *Negro in Louisiana*, 139.

9. Kasteel, *Francis Janssens*, 310–11; *New Orleans Times Democrat*, 20 May 1895.

10. Bennett, *Religion and the Rise of Jim Crow in New Orleans*, 151; Labbe, *Jim Crow Comes to Church*, 23.

11. Kasteel, *Francis Janssens*, 293.

12. Stephen J. Ochs, *Desegregating the Altar: The Josephites and the Struggle for Black Priests, 1871–1960* (Baton Rouge: Louisiana State University Press, 1990), 36–44; Labbe, *Jim Crow Comes to Church*, 23–25, 37.

13. Labbe, *Jim Crow Comes to Church*, 63.

14. Quoted in Kasteel, *Francis Janssens*, 297.

15. Alberts, "Black Catholic Schools," 85–94; Rousseve, *Negro in Louisiana*, 140.

16. Labbe, *Jim Crow Comes to Church*, 63–84; Alberts, "Black Catholic Schools," 90–92.

17. Ochs, *Desegregating the Altar*, 43–44, 456–60.

18. Cyprian Davis, *The History of Black Catholics in the United States* (New York: Crossroad Publishing, 1990), 206.

19. Davis, *History of Black Catholics*, 202–3.

20. Ochs, *Desegregating the Altar*, 164–65; Labbe, *Jim Crow Comes to Church*, 66–67.

21. Ralph E. Luker, *The Social Gospel in Black and White: American Racial Reform, 1885–1912* (Chapel Hill: University of North Carolina Press, 1991), 115.

22. Ochs, *Desegregating the Altar*, 165–67.

23. Ochs, *Desegregating the Altar*, 164.

24. Labbe, *Jim Crow Comes to Church*, 66; Ochs, *Desegregating the Altar*, 168–74.

25. Rousseve, *Negro in Louisiana*, 141.

26. James M. O'Toole, *The Faithful: A History of Catholics in America* (Cambridge: Belknap Press of Harvard University Press, 2008), 157–58.

27. Robert Elijah Jones Papers, box 1, folder 12, Amistad Research Center.

28. Phil Zuckerman, ed., *Du Bois on Religion* (Walnut Creek, Calif.: AltaMira Press, 2000), 21.

29. Bennett, *Religion and the Rise of Jim Crow in New Orleans*, 38.

30. Jones to Rev. T. B. Neely, 1 November 1901, Jones Papers, box 1, folder 2; Montgomery, *Under Their Own Vine and Fig Tree*, 307.

31. Jones Papers, box 1, folder, 2; box 3, folder 3.

32. Jones Papers, box 3, folder 8.

33. Jones Papers, box 3, folder 9.

34. Lincoln and Mamiya, *Black Church in the African American Experience*, 11.

35. Zuckerman, *Du Bois on Religion*, 145–46; Barbara Dianne Savage, *Your Spirits Walk behind Us: The Politics of Black Religion* (Cambridge: Belknap Press of Harvard University Press, 2008), 40–44.

36. Jones Papers, box 3, folder 11.

37. Jones Papers, box 3, folder 6.

38. Lincoln and Mamiya, *Black Church*, 14.

39. Beecher Memorial United Church of Christ Records, Amistad Research Center.

NOTES TO PAGES 78-87

40. Beecher Memorial Records; Lincoln, *Race, Religion, and the Continuing American Dilemma*, 72.
41. Central Congregational United Church of Christ Records, Amistad Research Center.
42. Central Records.
43. Trustees Board Minutes Book, 1912-20, Central Congregational Church Records Book, 1913-22, Central Records.
44. Lucille Hutton, "History of Central Congregational Church," Hutton Papers, box 8, folders 1, 3.
45. Quoted in Milton C. Sernett, ed., *African American Religious History: A Documentary Witness* (Durham, N.C.: Duke University Press, 1999), 552.
46. Trustees Board Minutes Book, 1912-20, Central Records.
47. Andrew Billingsley, *Mighty Like a River: The Black Church and Social Reform* (New York: Oxford University Press, 1999), 174.
48. Trustees Board Minutes Book, 1912-20; Central Records Book, 1913-22, Central Records.
49. Board of Trustees Meeting, 5 May 1919, Central Trustees Board Minutes Book, 1912-20, Central Records.
50. Board of Trustees Meeting, 19 July 1919, Central Trustees Board Minutes Book, 1912-20, Central Records.
51. See, e.g., various issues of the *Crisis* magazine for 1919 and 1920.
52. Board of Trustees Meeting, 1 December 1919, 5 January 1920, Central Trustee Board Minutes Book, Central Records.
53. Henry H. Mitchell, "Toward a Theology of Black Preaching," in *African American Religious Studies: An Interdisciplinary Anthology*, edited by Gayraud Wilmore (Durham, N.C.: Duke University Press, 1989), 361-71; Lincoln and Mamiya, *Black Church*, 13-14.
54. Emmett J. Scott, *Negro Migration during the War* (1920; repr., New York: Arno Press and the New York Times, 1969), 3-25; Gilbert Osofsky, *Harlem: The Making of a Ghetto; Negro New York, 1890-1930*, 2nd ed. (New York: Harper and Row, 1971), 92-123.
55. Central Trustees Board Minutes Book, 1912-20, Central Records.
56. Central Records Book, 1913-22, Central Records.
57. Central Records Book, 1913-22, Central Records.
58. Secretary of Board of Trustee Minutes Book, 1920-24, Central Records.
59. Savage, *Your Spirits Walk behind Us*, 66-67.
60. Central Records Book, 1913-22; Secretary of Board of Trustees Minutes Book, 1920-24, Central Records.
61. Secretary of Board of Trustees Minutes Book, 1920-24, Central Records.
62. Board of Trustees Minutes Book, 1920-24, Central Records; Marcus Christian, "Churches, 1900-1942," 3, Marcus Christian Papers, Louisiana and Special Collections Department, Earl K. Long Library, University of New Orleans.
63. Board of Trustees Minutes Book, 1920-24, Central Records.
64. Board of Trustees Minutes Book, 1920-24, Central Records.
65. Second Church Register and Minutes of Central Congregational Church, 1922-46, Central Records.
66. Secretary of Board of Trustees Minutes Book, 1920-24; Second Church Register and Minutes Book, 1922-46, Central Records.
67. Second Church Register and Minutes Book, 1922-46, Central Records.
68. Board of Trustees Minutes Book, 1924-30, Central Records.

69. Second Church Register and Minutes Book, 1922–46, Central Records.
70. Howard N. Rabinowitz, *Race Relations in the Urban South, 1865–1890* (Urbana: University of Illinois Press, 1980), 204.
71. Board of Trustees Minutes Book, 1924–30, Central Records.
72. Board of Trustees Minutes Book, 1924–30, Central Records.
73. Board of Trustees Minutes Book, 1924–30, Central Records.
74. Second Church Register and Minutes Book, 1922–46, Central Records.
75. Second Church Register, 1922–46, Central Records.
76. Elouise A. Thornhill to Fred Brownlee, 14 May 1929, Central Records.
77. Second Church Register and Minutes Book, 1922–46, Central Records.
78. Board of Trustees Minutes Book, 1924–30, Central Records.
79. Second Church Register and Minutes Book, 1922–46, Central Records.
80. Second Church Register, 1922–46, Central Records.

4. The Secular Dimensions of Community Development

1. Manfred Berg, *"The Ticket to Freedom": The NAACP and the Struggle for Black Political Integration* (Gainesville: University Press of Florida, 2005), 10–14; Minnie Finch, *The NAACP: Its Fight for Justice* (Metuchen, N.J.: Scarecrow Press, 1981), 3–27; Charles Flint Kellogg, *NAACP: A History of the National Association for the Advancement of Colored People*, vol. 1: *1909–1920* (Baltimore: John Hopkins Press, 1967), 31–57; Langston Hughes, *Fight for Freedom: The Story of the NAACP* (New York: Berkley Publishing, 1962), 19–25; August Meier and John H. Bracey Jr., "The NAACP as a Reform Movement, 1909–1965: 'To Reach the Conscience of America,'" *Journal of Southern History* 59, no. 1 (February 1993): 3.
2. Adam Fairclough, *Race and Democracy: The Civil Rights Struggle in Louisiana, 1915–1972* (Athens: University of Georgia Press, 1995), 18–20; Lee Sartain, *Invisible Activists: Women of the Louisiana NAACP and the Struggle for Civil Rights, 1915–1945* (Baton Rouge: Louisiana State University Press, 2007), 50–56; Berg, *"Ticket to Freedom,"* 21–22; Kellogg, *NAACP,* 119–20.
3. Arnold H. Taylor, *Travail and Triumph: Black Life and Culture in the South since the Civil War* (Westport, Conn.: Greenwood Press, 1976), 194.
4. Grace Elizabeth Hale, *Making Whiteness: The Culture of Segregation in the South, 1890–1940* (New York: Pantheon Books, 1998), 22.
5. Barbara Ransby, *Ella Baker and the Black Freedom Movement: A Radical Democratic Vision* (Chapel Hill: University of North Carolina Press, 2003), 106.
6. William I. Hair, "Henry J. Hearsey and the Politics of Race," *Louisiana History* 17, no. 4 (Fall 1976): 400.
7. Hale, *Making Whiteness,* 5.
8. Eugene Levy, *James Weldon Johnson: Black Leader, Black Voice* (Chicago: University of Chicago Press, 1973), 228.
9. E. M. Dunn to NAACP National Office, 14 July, 23 August 1917, Papers of the NAACP, Branch Records, New Orleans, pt. 12, reel 14; Sharlene S. DeCuir, "Attacking Jim Crow: Black Activism in New Orleans, 1925–1941" (Ph.D. diss., Louisiana State University, 2009), 123–25.
10. Souvenir Program, 16 December 1917, Papers of the NAACP, Branch Records, New Orleans, pt. 12, reel 14.

11. New Orleans NAACP Membership Report, 22 December 1917, Papers of the NAACP Branch Records, New Orleans, pt. 12, reel 14.

12. Walter F. White to E. W. Kinchen, 14 May 1918, Kinchen to White, 20 May 1918, Papers of the NAACP, Branch Records, New Orleans, pt. 12, reel 14.

13. E. M. Dunn to John R. Shillady, 22 May 1918, New Orleans NAACP Membership Drive Program, 19 May 1918, Membership Drive Announcement, 3 December 1918, Papers of the NAACP, Branch Records, New Orleans, pt. 12, reel 14.

14. Papers of the NAACP, Branch Records, New Orleans, pt. 12, reel 14.

15. Archie Perkins, *Who's Who in Colored Louisiana* (Baton Rouge: Douglas Loan Co., 1930), 113; *Louisiana Weekly,* 24 December 1927, 17 January 1931.

16. Woodson, *Negro Professional Man,* 126; Thomas J. Ward Jr., *Black Physicians in the Jim Crow South* (Fayetteville: University of Arkansas Press, 2003), 282–83.

17. Pickens to Lucas, 17 July 1925, Papers of the NAACP, Branch Records, New Orleans, pt. 12, reel 14.

18. Pickens to Lucas, 17 July 1925, Lucas to Pickens, 20 January 1926, Papers of the NAACP, Branch Records, New Orleans, pt. 12, reel 14.

19. Pickens to Lucas, 23 January 1926, Papers of the NAACP, Branch Records, New Orleans, pt. 12, reel 14.

20. "N.O. Branch NAACP Makes Appeal for Members," *Houston Informer,* 13 March 1926, Lucas to Bagnall, 21 May 1926, Papers of the NAACP, Branch Records, New Orleans, pt. 12, reel 14.

21. Lucas to Bagnall, 10 March 1928, Papers of the NAACP, Branch Records, New Orleans, pt. 12, reel 14.

22. Lucas to Johnson, 8 June 1928, Papers of the NAACP, Branch Records, New Orleans, pt. 12, reel 14.

23. Lucas to Bagnall, 19, 23 March, 15, 27, 30 April 1929, Bagnall to Lucas, 25 March, 15 April, 6 May 1929, Papers of the NAACP, Branch Records, New Orleans, pt. 12, reel 14.

24. Lucas to Bagnall, 11 December 1929, 5 June 1930, Papers of the NAACP, Branch Records, New Orleans, pt. 12, reel 14; Berg, *"Ticket to Freedom,"* 109–10.

25. Ward, *Black Physicians in the Jim Crow South,* 283–85.

26. James B. Lafourche to Walter White, 4 January 1933, White to Lafourche, 16 January 1933, Papers of the NAACP, Branch Records, New Orleans, pt. 12, reel 15.

27. Ward, *Black Physicians in the Jim Crow South,* 265; DeCuir, "Attacking Jim Crow," 94–97.

28. DeCuir, "Attacking Jim Crow," 111–15; Ward, *Black Physicians in the Jim Crow South,* 277–87.

29. Joseph Hardin Papers, box 1, folders 4, 8, Amistad Research Center.

30. Dunn-Landry Papers, box 10, folders 19, 21, Amistad Research Center.

31. Donald E. DeVore and Joseph Logsdon, *Crescent City Schools: Public Education in New Orleans, 1841–1991* (Lafayette: Center for Louisiana Studies, 1991), 179–82.

32. *New Orleans Herald,* 19 September 1925.

33. James Weldon Johnson, *Writings* (New York: Library of America, 2004), 607.

34. "That Theatre Fiasco," *Louisiana Weekly,* 12 April 1930, 6a.

35. "Carnival Season," *Louisiana Weekly,* 1 March 1930, 6.

36. *Louisiana Weekly,* 13 August 1938.

37. *Louisiana Weekly,* 19 March 1927.

38. Jackson, *New Orleans in the Gilded Age,* 183–85; Darlene Clark Hine, *Black Women*

in White: Racial Conflict and Cooperation in the Nursing Profession, 1890–1950 (Bloomington: Indiana University Press, 1989), 19–20, 65–66.

39. Hine, *Black Women in White,* 66; Abraham Flexner, *Medical Education in the United States and Canada: Report to the Carnegie Foundation for the Advancement of Teaching* (New York, 1910), 11, 13.

40. Flexner, *Medical Education,* 180–81.

41. Flexner, *Medical Education,* 181; Hine, *Black Women in White,* 66.

42. "Dr. T. Restin Heath, Flint-Goodridge Supt., to Quit," *Louisiana Weekly,* 20 March 1926, 1.

43. Ward, *Black Physicians in the Jim Crow South,* 83–84.

44. "It Is Done," *Louisiana Weekly,* 29 March 1930; Marcus Christian Papers, subseries 13.1, box 10, Louisiana and Special Collections Department, Earl K. Long Library, University of New Orleans; Hine, *Black Women in White,* 66–68.

45. *New Orleans Times-Picayune,* 3 February 1932.

46. Richardson, "Edgar B. Stern," 334–35.

47. *Louisiana Weekly,* 28 November 1931.

48. Dent to Stern, 15 October 1938, Dent Papers, box 1, folder 2.

49. Nida Vital, "Dr. Rivers Frederick and the History of Black Medicine in New Orleans" (master's thesis, University of New Orleans, 1978), 60–61.

50. *Saturday Evening Post,* 2 September 1939.

51. Vital, "Dr. Rivers Frederick," 40–45.

52. *Modern Hospital,* April 1937, 3–8.

53. Claude Francis Jacobs, "Strategies of Neighborhood Health-Care among New Orleans Blacks: From Voluntary Association to Public Policy" (Ph.D. diss., Tulane University, 1980), 65–66; *Modern Hospital,* 3–8.

54. Richardson, "Albert W. Dent," 316–17; *Modern Hospital,* 3–8.

55. Kevin K. Gaines, *Uplifting the Race: Black Leadership, Politics, and Culture in the Twentieth Century* (Chapel Hill: University of North Carolina Press, 1996), 234.

56. *Louisiana Weekly,* 12 March 1938.

57. Longe Papers, box 1, folder 3; *Louisiana Weekly,* 12 March 1938.

58. *New Orleans Times-Picayune,* 16 November 1938.

59. Pam Tyler, *Silk Stockings and Ballot Boxes: Women and Politics in New Orleans, 1920–1963* (Athens: University of Georgia Press, 1996), 221–25; Longe Papers, box 5, folder 1.

60. Michelle Cliff, ed., *The Winner Names the Age: A Collection of Writings by Lillian Smith* (New York: Norton, 1978), 24.

61. *Louisiana Weekly,* 19 November 1938.

62. Louis Harlan, *Booker T. Washington: The Making of a Black Leader, 1856–1901* (New York: Oxford University Press, 1972), 217–20.

63. Longe Papers, box 1, folder 3; box 2, folder 4; box 4, folders 17–20.

5. Public Education

1. DeVore and Logsdon, *Crescent City Schools,* 179–215; Meyer Weinberg, *A Chance to Learn: The History of Race and Education in the United States* (Cambridge: Cambridge University Press, 1977), 1–7.

2. Anderson, *Education of Blacks in the South*, 80–81.
3. OPSB Meeting Minutes, 9 March, 29 June 1900; *Southwestern Christian Advocate*, 5 July 1900.
4. *Southwestern Christian Advocate*, 25 September 1902.
5. OPSB Meeting Minutes, 29 June 1900, 6 January 1916, 12 January 1923.
6. New Orleans, Annual Reports, 1900–1910; OPSB Meeting Minutes, 13 January 1911.
7. OPSB Meeting Minutes, 13 January 1911; New Orleans, Annual Reports, 1911, 1912.
8. OPSB Meeting Minutes, 10 November 1925; *Louisiana Weekly*, 9 April 1927.
9. OPSB Meeting Minutes, 17 April, 10 November 1911, 10 February 1928, 8 May 1936; Horace Mann Bond, *The Education of the Negro in the American Social Order* (New York: Prentice-Hall, 1934), 225–26.
10. OPSB Meeting Minutes, 12 January 1923.
11. OPSB Meeting Minutes, 11 November 1910; DeVore and Logsdon, *Crescent City Schools*, 199–204.
12. OPSB Meeting Minutes, 12 January, 16 February 1914.
13. *New Orleans Times-Picayune*, 21 September 1914, 30 September, 1, 2, 4 October, 11 November 1915, 23 March 1917; OPSB Meeting Minutes, 1 April, 14 May, 15 June, 9 July 1914.
14. OPSB Meeting Minutes, 28 July 1928.
15. OPSB Meeting Minutes, 12 January 1923.
16. Roger L. Rice, "Residential Segregation by Law, 1910–1917," *Journal of Southern History* 34, no. 2 (May 1968): 189–99; OPSB Meeting Minutes, 12 January 1923.
17. OPSB Meeting Minutes, 12 January 1923.
18. OPSB Meeting Minutes, 18, 26 January 1926.
19. *New Orleans Times-Picayune*, 27 January, 9, 10 February 1923.
20. OPSB Meeting Minutes, 9 February 1923; Robert R. Moton, *What the Negro Thinks* (New York: Doubleday Doran, 1940), 5–9.
21. OPSB Meeting Minutes, 9 February 1923.
22. New Orleans, Annual Reports, 1910–11.
23. OPSB Meeting Minutes, 13 March 1903; New Orleans, Annual Report, 1920–21.
24. See, e.g., OPSB Meeting Minutes, 1 February 1907, 17 April 1911, 13 August 1914, 11 May 1923, 22 August 1924, 16 November 1934, 9 January 1937; DeCuir, "Attacking Jim Crow," 99–106.
25. Ullin W. Leavell, *Philanthropy in Negro Education* (Nashville: Cullon and Ghertner, 1930), 80–82; Bullock, *History of Negro Education in the South*, 158–59.
26. *Louisiana Weekly*, 18 February 1928; OPSB Meeting Minutes, 14 February, 3 June, 12 September 1913.
27. *Louisiana Weekly*, 8 May 1926, 23 April 1927, 21 January 1928; OPSB Meeting Minutes, 13 January 1928.
28. OPSB Meeting Minutes, 7 August 1928; *Louisiana Weekly*, 2 November 1929.
29. OPSB Meeting Minutes, 12 April 1907, 11 November 1910, 11 March 1915, 9 November 1916, 27 October 1922, 28 September 1923, 13 January 1928, 9 October 1931, 9 October 1938.
30. Vincent, *Centennial History of Southern University and A and M College*, 63–72.
31. OPSB Meeting Minutes, 2 July, 8 August 1913, 26 January 1926.
32. Louis Harlan, *Separate and Unequal*, 264–65; Anderson, *Education of Blacks in the South*, 186–87; Bond, *Education of the Negro*, 114–16.
33. OPSB Meeting Minutes, 11 June, 8 October 1909, 12 May 1911, 9 February 1917; New

Orleans, Annual Report, 1912–13, 1914–15; Samuel C. Shepherd, "In Pursuit of Louisiana Progressives," *Louisiana History* 46, no. 4 (Fall 2005): 389–95.

34. Thomas Sowell, *Education: Assumption versus History* (Stanford, Calif.: Hoover Institution Press, 1986), 9, 18–21; OPSB Meeting Minutes, 24 August, 14, 28 September 1917.

35. New Orleans, Annual Report, 1917–18, 1920–21; *Louisiana Weekly*, 19 March 1927.

36. New Orleans, Annual Report, 1917–18.

37. U.S. Department of Commerce, Bureau of Census, *Abstract of the Fourteenth Census of the United States, 1920* (Washington, D.C.: U.S. Government Printing Office, 1923); OPSB Meeting Minutes, 10 July, 3 November 1903, 13 May 1904, 10 November 1905, 14 August 1908, 13 October 1911; New Orleans, Annual Report, 1903–4, 1905–6, 1911–12.

38. *Southwestern Christian Advocate*, 9 January 1908; OPSB Meeting Minutes, 13 November 1908.

39. *Southwestern Christian Advocate*, 9 November 1911.

40. Lawrence A. Cremin, *American Education: The Metropolitan Experience, 1876–1980* (New York: Harper and Row, 1988), 231; Myrtle Banks, "The Education of the Negro in New Orleans" (master's thesis, Xavier University, 1935), 280–81; New Orleans, Annual Report, 1918–19; OPSB Meeting Minutes, 22 November 1918.

41. August Meier, *Negro Thought in America, 1880–1915: Racial Ideologies in the Age of Booker T. Washington* (Ann Arbor: University of Michigan Press, 1978), 166–255.

42. New Orleans, Annual Report, 1904–5; OPSB Meeting Minutes, 14 June 1901, 9 June 1905, 8 March 1907, 13 May 1910, 14 May 1914.

43. U.S. Department of Commerce, Bureau of the Census, *Fourteenth Census of the United States, 1920*, vol. 4: *Population* (Washington, D.C.: U.S. Government Printing Office, 1923); *U.S. Census of Population: 1950, Detailed Characteristics, Louisiana* (Washington, D.C.: U.S. Government Printing Office, 1952).

44. New Orleans, Annual Report, 1911–12.

45. OPSB Meeting Minutes, 13 April, 19 June 1916, 1 November, 27 December 1918; *Louisiana Weekly*, 19 March, 9, 16, 23 April 1927.

46. *Louisiana Weekly*, 22 February 1930.

47. OPSB Meeting Minutes, 26 January 1923, 12 February 1930; *Louisiana Weekly*, 22 February 1930.

48. *Louisiana Weekly*, 7 February 1931.

49. *Louisiana Weekly*, 7 February 1931.

50. *New Orleans Times-Picayune*, 1 February 1931.

51. *Louisiana Weekly*, 26 September 1931.

52. OPSB Meeting Minutes, 16 November 1934, 12 March 1937, 12 May 1939; *Louisiana Weekly*, 3 November 1934, 13 August 1938, 13 September 1940.

6. Business and Labor

1. Paul K. Edwards, *The Southern Urban Negro as a Consumer* (1932; repr., College Park, Md.: McGrath Publishing, 1969), 138.

2. John N. Ingham, "Building Businesses, Creating Communities: Residential Segregation and the Growth of African American Business in Southern Cities, 1880–1915," *Business History Review* 77, no. 4 (Winter 2003): 639–42; U.S. Department of Commerce and Labor Bu-

reau of the Census, *Thirteenth Census of the United States Taken in the Year 1910, Abstract of the Census with Supplement for Louisiana;* U.S. Department of Commerce, *Negroes in the United States, 1920–1932* (Washington, D.C.: U.S. Government Printing Office, 1935).

3. Harlan, *Booker T. Washington,* 266–71; Norrell, *Up from History,* 229.

4. Robert L. Boyd, "Racial Segregation and Insurance Enterprise among Black Americans in Northern Cities," *Sociological Quarterly* 39, no. 2 (Spring 1998): 337–38.

5. Colored Civic League of New Orleans, *Colored New Orleans: High Points of Negro Endeavor, 1922–1923* (1923), 6.

6. Jacobs, "Strategies of Neighborhood Health-Care among New Orleans Blacks," 51–52; *Louisiana Weekly,* 28 April 1934.

7. *Woods' Directory: Being a Colored Business, Professional and Trades Directory of New Orleans, Louisiana* (New Orleans, 1912).

8. Claude F. Jacobs, "Benevolent Societies of New Orleans Blacks during the Late Nineteenth and Early Twentieth Centuries," *Louisiana History* 29, no. 1 (Winter 1988): 22–24.

9. Juliet E. K. Walker, *The History of Black Business in America: Capitalism, Race, Entrepreneurship* (New York: Macmillan, 1998), 187–91; Walter B. Weare, *Black Business in the New South: A Social History of the North Carolina Mutual Life Insurance Company* (Durham, N.C.: Duke University Press, 1993), 16–28.

10. Jesse O. Sheffield Papers, box 1, Amistad Research Center.

11. Sheffield Papers, box 1.

12. Sheffield Papers, box 2.

13. Sheffield Papers, box 2.

14. *Woods' Directory,* 1912; *Colored New Orleans;* Sheffield Papers, box 2.

15. Walker, *History of Black Business in America,* 213–17; Edwards, *Southern Urban Negro as a Consumer,* 139–45.

16. Christian, "History of the Negro in Louisiana," Marcus Christian Papers, subseries 13.1, box 10.

17. Leedell W. Neyland, "The Negro in Louisiana since 1900: An Economic and Social Study" (Ph.D. diss., New York University, 1959), 55; "Negroes in the United States, 1920–1932."

18. *Louisiana Weekly,* 27 August 1938.

19. *Colored New Orleans.*

20. Scott Family Papers (the processing of this collection is not complete), Amistad Research Center.

21. Scott Family Papers.

22. Christian, "History of the Negro in Louisiana."

23. Paula Giddings, *When and Where I Enter: The Impact of Black Women on Race and Sex in America* (New York: Bantam Books, 1984), 187–89.

24. Tiffany M. Gill, *Beauty Shop Politics: African American Women's Activism in the Beauty Industry* (Urbana: University of Illinois Press, 2010), 35.

25. *Woods' Directory,* 1912; Christian, "History of the Negro in Louisiana."

26. Gill, *Beauty Shop Politics,* 77.

27. Walker, *History of Black Business in America,* 208–11.

28. *Woods' Directory,* 1912; *Colored New Orleans.*

29. Vital, "Dr. Rivers Frederick," 60–61.

30. Hine, *Black Women in White,* 63–84.

31. Perkins, *Who's Who in Colored Louisiana,* 90–96; U.S. Department of Commerce, Bu-

reau of the Census, *Fifteenth Census of the United States, 1930,* vol. 4: *Population; Negroes in the United States, 1920–1932.*

32. *U.S. Census of Population: 1950, Detailed Characteristics, Louisiana;* Anderson, *Education of Blacks in the South,* 110–14; Bond, *Education of the Negro,* 264–68; OPSB Meeting Minutes, 29 June 1906, 9 August 1907, 8 July, 19 September 1910.

33. *Southwestern Christian Advocate,* 9 February 1911; OPSB Meeting Minutes, 8, 26 April, 13 May 1915, 13 January 1916, 25 June 1919; Banks, "Education of the Negro in New Orleans," 267.

34. U.S. Department of Commerce, *Negroes in the United States.*

35. Charles B. Rousseve, *Negro in Louisiana,* 126–51; Christian, "History of the Negro in Louisiana."

36. *U.S. Census of Population: 1950, Detailed Characteristics, Louisiana;* U.S. Department of Commerce, Bureau of the Census, Abstract of the Fourteenth Census of the United States, 1920.

37. Eric Arnesen, *Waterfront Workers of New Orleans: Race, Class, and Politics, 1863–1923* (Urbana: University of Illinois Press, 1991), 114–18, 125–45, 244–52; Abram L. Harris and Sterling D. Spero, *The Black Worker: The Negro and the Labor Movement* (New York: Columbia University Press, 1931), 183; Herbert R. Northrup, "The New Orleans Longshoremen," *Political Science Quarterly* 57, no. 4 (December 1942): 527–29; Neyland, "Negro in Louisiana since 1900," 46.

38. David Wells, "The ILWU in New Orleans: CIO Radicalism in the Crescent City, 1937–1957" (master's thesis, University of New Orleans 1979), 5.

39. *Louisiana Weekly,* 31 July 1937.

40. *Louisiana Weekly,* 16 October 1937.

41. Wells, "ILWU in New Orleans," 6–7.

42. Wells, ILWU in New Orleans," 7–8.

43. *Louisiana Weekly,* 16 July 1938.

44. Northrup, "New Orleans Longshoremen," 538; Wells, "ILWU in New Orleans," 7–9.

45. U.S. Department of Commerce, U.S. Bureau of the Census, *Sixteenth Census of the United States, 1940,* vol. 3: *Housing,* pt. 2: *Characteristics by Monthly Rent or Value; Louisiana Weekly,* 8 October 1932.

46. *Sixteenth Census,* 1940: *Housing,* pt. 2: *Characteristics.*

7. Jim Crow Attacked

1. *New Orleans Times-Picayune,* 10, 17 September 1924.

2. New Orleans, "An Ordinance Relative to Negro and White Communities" (1924).

3. *New Orleans Times-Picayune,* 19 September 1924, 9 May, 6 June, 15 August 1925.

4. *Louisiana Weekly,* 24 October 1925; *New Orleans Times-Picayune,* 16 October 1925.

5. *Louisiana Weekly,* 14 November 1925; *New Orleans Times-Picayune,* 8 November 1925.

6. *Louisiana Weekly,* 14 November 1925; *New Orleans Times-Picayune,* 10 November 1925.

7. *New Orleans Times-Picayune,* 19 February 1926: *Louisiana Weekly,* 20 February, 15 May 1926.

8. "New Orleans NAACP Wins Suit against City Segregation Ordinance," Papers of the

NAACP, Branch Files, New Orleans, pt. 12, reel 14; *New Orleans Times-Picayune*, 31 October 1924.

9. *Tyler v. Harmon, Louisiana Reports,* vol. 158: *1924–25,* 446.
10. *Tyler v. Harmon,* 458.
11. *New Orleans Times-Picayune,* 4 March 1925.
12. *Louisiana Weekly,* 1, 15 May 1926; *New Orleans Times-Picayune,* 3 March 1925.
13. *Louisiana Weekly,* 6 November 1926.
14. *Louisiana Weekly,* 12, 20 November 1926
15. George Lucas to Walter White, 19 January 1927, Papers of the NAACP, Branch Files, New Orleans, pt. 12, reel, 14; *Louisiana Weekly,* 11 December 1926, 5 March 1927; *New Orleans Times-Picayune,* 1 March 1926.
16. *New Orleans Times-Picayune,* 1 March 1926.
17. Fairclough, *Race and Democracy,* 19; *Louisiana Weekly,* 19 March 1927.
18. W.E.B. Du Bois, *The Autobiography of W.E.B. Du Bois* (New York: International Publishers, 1986), 250.
19. *Louisiana Weekly,* 12 November 1927.
20. Hair, *Bourbonism and Agrarian Protest,* 234–79.
21. Robert N. and Lillian Dunn Perry Papers, box 7, folder 8, Amistad Research Center.
22. Richard B. Sherman, *The Republican Party and Black America from McKinley to Hoover, 1896–1933* (Charlottesville: University Press of Virginia, 1973), 47–48, 71–72, 153–54; Vincent DeSantis, *Republicans Face the Southern Question: The New Departure Years, 1877–1897* (Baltimore, Md.: John Hopkins Press, 1959), 11–13.
23. Perkins, *Who's Who in Colored Louisiana,* 113; Philip D. Uzee, "Republican Politics in Louisiana, 1877–1900" (Ph.D. diss., Louisiana State University, 1950), 170–74; *Louisiana Weekly,* 3 January 1931.
24. *Louisiana Weekly,* 26 December 1925, 20 February 1926.
25. Hardin Papers, box 1, folders 1, 4; *Louisiana Weekly,* 19 November 1933.
26. Sherman, *Republican Party and Black America,* 88–89, 230–52.
27. *Louisiana Weekly,* 4 September 1926.
28. Uzee, "Republican Politics in Louisiana," 139; *Louisiana Weekly,* 4, 6 September 1926.
29. *Louisiana Weekly,* 5, 12 November, 24 December 1927.
30. *Louisiana Weekly,* 29 January, 4, 11, 18 February, 9, 16 June 1928.
31. *Louisiana Weekly,* 9 June 1928.
32. *Louisiana Weekly,* 22 September 1928.
33. George Reynolds, *Machine Politics in New Orleans, 1897–1926* (New York: Columbia University Press, 1936), 74.
34. *Louisiana Weekly,* 12 November 1927.
35. *New Orleans Times-Picayune,* 30 October 1929; *Louisiana Weekly,* 2, November 1929.
36. William T. Andrews to George Labat, 30 June 1931, Papers of the NAACP, Branch Files, New Orleans, pt. 12, reel 14; *Louisiana Weekly,* 19 April 1930, 11 July, 7 November 1931; Fairclough, *Race and Democracy,* 19; Hirsch, "Simply a Matter of Black and White," 268–70.
37. Emanuel and Tureaud, *More Noble Cause,* 63–64; *Louisiana Weekly,* 10 October 1931.
38. *Trudeau v. Barnes,* 1 F. Supp. *453* (E. D. La, 1932); *New Orleans Times-Picayune,* 7 January 1932.
39. *Trudeau v. Barnes,* 65 F.2d 563 (5th Cir. 1933).

40. *Louisiana Weekly*, 18 November 1933.

41. Michele Grigsby Coffey, "*The State of Louisiana v. Charles Guerand:* Interracial Sexual Mores, Rape Rhetoric, and Respectability in 1930s New Orleans," *Louisiana History* 54, no. 1 (Winter 2013): 47–48.

42. Althea Hart to W.E.B. Du Bois, 11 February 1930, Papers of the NAACP, Branch Files, New Orleans, pt. 12, reel 14; Coffey, "*State of Louisiana v. Charles Guerand,*" 52–54.

43. Walter White to Hart, 17 February 1930, Papers of the NAACP, Branch Files, New Orleans, pt. 12, reel, 14; Walter White, *A Man Called White: The Autobiography of Walter White* (New York: Viking Press, 1948), 11–12, 56–59.

44. "Murder," *Louisiana Weekly*, 15 February 1930, 6.

45. "To Prosecute Murderer of Young Girl," *Louisiana Weekly*, 22 February 1930, 1, "McCray Defense Fund Growing Very Rapidly," *Louisiana Weekly*, 1 March 1930, 1; George Lucas to Walter White, 21 February 1930, Papers of the NAACP, Branch Files, New Orleans, pt. 12, reel 14.

46. "A Just Verdict," *New Orleans Times-Picayune*, 5 April 1930.

47. "The Guerand Verdict," *New Orleans States*, 5 April 1930.

48. "A Just Verdict," *Louisiana Weekly*, 12 April 1930, 6; Fairclough, *Race and Democracy*, 19; Coffey, "*State of Louisiana v. Charles Guerand*," 78–80.

49. Lucas to White, 4 April 1930, Papers of the NAACP, Branch Files, New Orleans, pt. 12, reel 14; Coffey, "*State of Louisiana v. Charles Guerand*," 86–93.

50. OPSB Meeting Minutes, 28 September 1900, 27 September 1920.

51. Horace Mann Bond, *Education of the Negro*, 267–74; Bullock, *History of Negro Education in the South*, 216–17; Sartain, *Invisible Activists*, 94–96.

52. *Louisiana Weekly*, 28 August 1937.

53. Raphael Cassimere Jr., "Equalizing Teachers' Pay in Louisiana," *Integrateducation* (July–August 1977): 5; Fairclough, *Race and Democracy*, 62–63.

54. Richard Kluger, *Simple Justice: The History of* Brown v. Board of Education *and Black America's Struggle for Equality* (New York: Knopf, 1976), 179–82, 197; Cassimere, "Equalizing Teachers' Pay in Louisiana," 5; Sartain, *Invisible Activists*, 96–97.

55. Bullock, *History of Negro Education in the South*, 219; Bond, *Education of the Negro*, 88–115; Cassimere, "Equalizing Teachers' Pay in Louisiana," 5; OPSB Meeting Minutes, 9 May 1941.

56. Emanuel and Tureaud, *More Noble Cause*, 102–3; OPSB Minutes, 17 June 1941.

57. Tureaud to Marshall, 4 September 1941, Marshall to Tureaud, 8 September 1941, Tureaud Papers, box 49, folder 22.

58. Tureaud to Marshall, 14 June 1942, Marshall to Tureaud, 19 June 1942, Tureaud Papers, box 49, folder 23.

59. Tureaud to Marshall, 3 July 1942, Marshall to Tureaud, 6 July 1942, Tureaud Papers, box 49, folder 23; Emanuel and Tureaud, *More Noble Cause*, 104–5.

60. Marshall to Tureaud, 6 July 1942, Tureaud Papers, box 49, folder 23; OPSB Meeting Minutes, 11 September 1942; Cassimere, "Equalizing Teachers' Pay in Louisiana," 6; Mark V. Tushnet, *The NAACP's Legal Strategy against Segregated Education, 1925–1950* (Chapel Hill: University of North Carolina Press, 1987), 97–99; *Louisiana Weekly*, 3 October 1942.

61. Berg, "*Ticket to Freedom*," 88–91; Kousser, *Colorblind Injustice;* 53; Fairclough, *Race and Democracy*, 102–3; Keyssar, *Right to Vote*, 198–99.

62. Patricia Sullivan, *Days of Hope: Race and Democracy in the New Deal Era* (Chapel

Hill: University of North Carolina Press, 1996), 133–37, 166–68; White, *Man Called White*, 329–33.

63. Richard English Papers, box 2, Amistad Research Center.

64. Kluger, *Simple Justice*, 136–38.

65. Petition dated 3 May 1946, OPSB to Daniel Byrd, 9 May, 16 June 1946, Byrd to OPSB, 10 July, 15 August 1946, Tureaud Papers, box 43, folder 3, 13.

66. Samson P. Bordelon, "The New Orleans Public Schools under the Superintendency of Lionel John Bourgeois" (Ph.D. diss., University of Southern Mississippi, 1966), 7, 89–95, 236; Juliette Landphair, "Sewerage, Sidewalks, and Schools: The New Orleans Ninth Ward and Public School Desegregation," *Louisiana History* 40, no. 1 (Winter 1999): 44–48; OPSB Meeting Minutes, 12 March 1948.

67. OPSB Meeting Minutes, 12 March, 21 May, 7, 11 June 1948.

68. *Louisiana Weekly*, 15 May 1948.

69. Byrd to Bourgeois, 21 April 1948, Tureaud Papers, box 43, folder 4.

70. Horace Mann Bond, "The Role of History of Education in Understanding the Struggle for Equalizing Educational Opportunity," *History of Education Journal* 1, no. 3 (Spring 1950): 106; Finch, *NAACP*, 20–27.

71. Landphair, "Sewerage, Sidewalks, and Schools," 49.

72. Byrd to Marshall, 12 September 1951, Daniel Byrd Papers, box 1, folder 1, Amistad Research Center; OPSB Meeting Minutes, 12 November 1951; Landphair, "Sewerage, Sidewalks, and Schools," 49–50.

73. A copy of the petition is in Tureaud Papers, box 43.

74. Typescript of interview in Robert and Lillian Perry Papers, box 7, folder 8.

75. Emanuel and Tureaud, *More Noble Cause*, 155–58; Fairclough, *Race and Democracy*, 108; OPSB Minutes, 12 September 1952.

76. Tushnet, *NAACP's Legal Strategy*, 138–43.

77. Kluger, *Simple Justice*, 540.

78. Kluger, *Simple Justice*, 782.

79. *Louisiana Weekly*, 22 May 1954.

80. Louisiana, Acts of the State Legislature, Regular Session, 1954, Acts 555, 556; Mary Lee Muller, "New Orleans Public School Desegregation," *Louisiana History* 17, no. 1 (Winter 1976): 71–72.

81. *Southern School News*, 8 June 1955.

82. A copy of the "Declaration" is located in the Byrd Papers, box 5, folder 2.

83. Fairclough, *Race and Democracy*, 253; David Alan Horowitz, "White Southerners' Alienation and Civil Rights: The Response to Corporate Liberalism, 1956–1965," *Journal of Southern History* 54, no. 2 (May 1988): 173–80; *Southern School News*, 4 November, 1 December 1954.

84. Earleen Mary McCarrick, "Louisiana's Official Resistance to Segregation" (Ph.D. diss., Vanderbilt University, 1964), 26–44, 105–31; Neil McMillen, *The Citizens' Council: Organized Resistance to the Second Reconstruction, 1954–1964* (Urbana: University of Illinois Press, 1971), 59, 64, 67; Muller, "New Orleans Public School Desegregation," 71–75.

85. OPSB Meeting Minutes, 26 September 1955.

86. *Southern School News*, April, June 1956.

87. R. Bentley Anderson, *Black White and Catholic: New Orleans Interracialism, 1947–1956* (Nashville: Vanderbilt University Press, 2005), 153–89; Jason Sokol, *There Goes My*

Everything: White Southerners in the Age of Civil Rights (New York: Knopf, 2006), 124–48; Tyler, *Silk Stockings and Ballot Boxes*, 222–29; OPSB Meeting Minutes, 12 and 26 September 1955; *Southern School News*, April 1956.

88. *Southern School News*, September 1955.
89. New Orleans Branch NAACP Papers, folder 211, Louisiana and Special Collections Department, Earl K. Long Library, University of New Orleans.
90. New Orleans Branch NAACP Papers, folder 70.
91. Quoted in Emanuel and Tureaud, *More Noble Cause*, 195.
92. *Southern School News*, August 1959.
93. OPSB Meeting Minutes, 24 May 1960.
94. *Louisiana Weekly*, 7, 14 May 1960.
95. New Orleans Branch NAACP Papers, folder 70.
96. Emanuel and Tureaud, *More Noble Cause*, 205; Muller, "New Orleans Public School Desegregation," 83–84; Landphair, "Sewerage, Sidewalks, and Schools," 56–60.
97. *New Orleans Times-Picayune*, 15, 16, 18, 19 November 1960; *Louisiana Weekly*, 19, 26 November 1960; *Southern School News*, December 1960; Liva Baker, *The Second Battle of New Orleans* (New York: HarperCollins, 1996), 400–404; Fairclough, *Race and Democracy*, 234–49.
98. Responses are located in the New Orleans Branch NAACP Papers, box 71.
99. Ruby Bridges, *Through My Eyes* (New York: Scholastic Press, 1999), 4, 9, 20.
100. Emanuel and Tureaud, *More Noble Cause*, 229–34.

8. Freedom Now

1. *Louisiana Weekly*, 19 March 1960.
2. Chapital to Wilkins, New Orleans Branch NAACP Papers, folder 70.
3. Wilkins to Chapital, New Orleans Branch NAACP Papers, folder 70.
4. *Louisiana Weekly*, 5 March 1960.
5. Fairclough, *Race and Democracy*, 267; New Orleans Branch NAACP Papers, folder 70.
6. Morrison to Chapital, 18 April 1960, New Orleans Branch NAACP Papers, folder 70.
7. Hirsch, "Simply a Matter of Black and White," 283–88; *Louisiana Weekly*, 16 April 1960.
8. Chapital to Consumers' League of Greater New Orleans, 5 May 1960, New Orleans Branch NAACP Papers, folder 70.
9. August Meier and Elliot Rudwick, *CORE: A Study in the Civil Rights Movement, 1942–1968* (New York: Oxford University Press, 1973), 166–67; Kim Lacy Rogers, *Righteous Lives: Narratives of the New Orleans Civil Rights Movement* (New York: New York University Press, 1993), 77–109.
10. New Orleans Branch NAACP Papers, folder 71.
11. Edward F. Haas, *DeLesseps S. Morrison and the Image of Reform* (Baton Rouge: Louisiana State University Press, 1974), 260; Meier and Rudwick, *CORE*, 114–15.
12. *Louisiana Weekly*, 17 September 1960.
13. Haas, *DeLesseps S. Morrison*, 262; New Orleans Branch NAACP Papers, folder 182; Emanuel and Tureaud, *More Noble Cause*, 238, 243–44.
14. Meier and Rudwick, *CORE*, 115, 191.

15. Kim Lacy Rogers, "Humanity and Desire: Civil Rights Leaders and the Desegregation of New Orleans, 1954–66" (Ph.D. diss., University of Minnesota, 1982), 330–31; *Louisiana Weekly*, 5 October 1963.

16. Gerda Lerner, ed., *Black Women in White America: A Documentary History* (New York: Vintage Books, 1973), 553–58.

17. *Louisiana Weekly*, 7 September 1963.

18. *Louisiana Weekly*, 7 September 1963; Emanuel and Tureaud, *More Noble Cause*, 243–44.

19. Fairclough, *Race and Democracy*, 335–37; *Louisiana Weekly*, 11 July, 28 November 1964.

20. New Orleans NAACP Papers, folder 192.

21. Louisiana, Report(s) of the Secretary of State, 1960, 1964.

22. New Orleans Branch NAACP Papers, folder 52.

23. Edward F. Haas, "The Expedient of Race: Victor H. Schiro, Scott Wilson, and the New Orleans Mayoralty Campaign of 1962," *Louisiana History* 42, no. 1 (Winter 2001): 16–27; Adam Fairclough, *To Redeem the Soul of America: The Southern Christian Leadership Conference and Martin Luther King, Jr.* (Athens: University of Georgia Press, 1987, 2001), 225–51.

24. New Orleans NAACP Papers, folder 52.

25. George L. Amedee, "The Origins of African American Political Empowerment in New Orleans, Louisiana: The Role of the Trailblazer in Leadership and Organizational Development" (Ph.D. diss., Northern Illinois University, 1993), 63–74; *New Orleans States-Item*, 12, 15 February 1973.

26. Hirsch, "Simply a Matter of Black and White," 288–319; Addison Carey, "Black Political Participation in New Orleans" (Ph.D. diss., Tulane University, 1974), 87–89, 174; James M. Vanderleeuw, "A City in Transition: The Impact of Changing Racial Composition on Voting Behavior" (Ph.D. diss., University of New Orleans, 1988), 49–51; Allen Rosenzweig, "The Influence of Class and Race on Political Behavior in New Orleans" (master's thesis, University of New Orleans, 1967), 119; *New Orleans States-Item*, 16, 19, 20 February 1973.

BIBLIOGRAPHY

Primary Sources

Amistad Research Center, Tulane University, New Orleans

Beecher Memorial United Church of Christ Records
Byrd, Daniel E., Papers
Central Congregational United Church of Christ Records
Dent, Albert Walter and Jessie Covington, Papers
Dunn-Landry Family Papers
English, Richard W., Papers
Frederick, Rivers, Papers
Hardin, Joseph A., Papers
Holmes, Norman A., Papers
Hutton, Lucile L., Papers
Jones, Robert Elijah, Papers
Keller, Rosa Freeman, Papers
LaBranche, Emile J., Papers
Longe, George, Papers
National Association for the Advancement of Colored People (NAACP), Office of Field Director of Louisiana Records
Perry, Lillian Dunn and Robert N., Papers
Rousseve, Charles B., Papers
Rousseve, Ferdinand L., Papers
Save Our Schools Records
Scott Family Papers
Sheffield, Jesse O., Papers
Tureaud, Alexander P., Papers
Williams, Fannie C., Papers

BIBLIOGRAPHY

Louisiana and Special Collections Department, Earl K. Long Library, University of New Orleans, New Orleans

Christian, Marcus, Papers
Community Services Council of New Orleans, Inc.
Orleans Parish School Board Collection.
Records of the National Association for the Advancement of Colored People, New Orleans Branch

Government Documents

Annual Report(s) of the State of Louisiana Superintendent of Public Education, 1867–79
Biennial Report(s) of the State of Louisiana Superintendent of Public Education, 1880–1901
Louisiana, Acts of the State Legislature, Regular Session, 1954
Louisiana Constitution of 1879
Official Journal of the Proceedings of the Constitutional Convention of the State of Louisiana, 1898
Official Journal of the Proceedings of the Convention for the Framing of a Constitution for the State of Louisiana, 1867–68
Survey of Negro Colleges and Universities. Washington, D.C.: U.S. Government Printing Office, 1929. Reprint. New York: Negro Universities Press, 1969.
U.S. Department of Commerce. Bureau of the Census. *Abstract of the Fourteenth Census of the United States, 1920.* Washington, D.C.: U.S. Government Printing Office, 1923.
———. *Negroes in the United States, 1920–1932.* Washington, D.C.: U.S. Government Printing Office, 1935.
———. *U.S. Census of Population: 1920.* Vol. 4: *Population.* Washington, D.C.: U.S. Government Printing Office, 1923.
———. *U.S. Census of Population: 1950, Detailed Characteristics, Louisiana.* Washington, D.C.: U.S. Government Printing Office, 1952.
U.S. Department of Commerce and Labor. Bureau of the Census. *Thirteenth Census of the United States Taken in the Year 1910. Abstract of the Census with Supplement for Louisiana.*

Microfilm

Papers of the National Association for the Advancement of Colored People, Branch Records, New Orleans. Pt. 12, reels 14 and 15.
Records of the Superintendent of Education for the State of Louisiana. Bureau of Refugees, Freedmen, and Abandoned Lands, 1864–1869. Record Group 105.

Newspapers

Louisiana Weekly (New Orleans), 1925–66
New Orleans Daily Picayune, 1862, 1873–74, 1877–79
New Orleans Republican, 1873–75

New Orleans States-Item, 1973
New Orleans Times, 1873–74, 1877
New Orleans Times-Picayune, 1915, 1923, 1929–32, 1954–66
New Orleans Tribune, 1865–67
Southern School News (Nashville), 1954–62
Southwestern Christian Advocate (New Orleans), 1873–1926
Weekly Louisianian (New Orleans), 1870–82

Secondary Sources

Books

Anderson, Eric, and Alfred A. Moss Jr. *Dangerous Donations: Northern Philanthropy and Southern Black Education, 1902–1930*. Columbia: University of Missouri Press, 1999.

Anderson, James D. *The Education of Blacks in the South*. Chapel Hill: University of North Carolina Press, 1988.

Anderson, James D., and Vincent P. Franklin, eds. *New Perspectives on Black Educational History*. Boston: G. K. Hall, 1978.

Anderson, R. Bentley. *Black, White, and Catholic: New Orleans Interracialism, 1947–1956*. Nashville, Tenn.: Vanderbilt University Press, 2005.

Aptheker, Herbert, ed. *A Documentary History of the Negro People in the United States*. Vol. 2. New York: Carol Publishing, 1992.

Arnesen, Eric. *Waterfront Workers of New Orleans: Race, Class, and Politics, 1863–1923*. Urbana: University of Illinois Press, 1991.

Ashmore, Harry S. *The Negro and the Schools*. Chapel Hill: University of North Carolina Press, 1954.

Baker, Liva. *The Second Battle of New Orleans*. New York: HarperCollins, 1996.

Barnes, Donna A. *The Louisiana Populist Movement, 1881–1900*. Baton Rouge: Louisiana State University Press, 2011.

Bartley, Numan V. *The Rise of Massive Resistance: Race and Politics in the South during the 1950s*. Baton Rouge: Louisiana State University Press, 1969.

Bell, Caryn Cossé. *Revolution, Romanticism, and the Afro-Creole Protest Tradition in Louisiana, 1718–1868*. Baton Rouge: Louisiana State University Press, 1997.

Bennett, James B. *Religion and the Rise of Jim Crow in New Orleans*. Princeton, N.J.: Princeton University Press, 2005.

Berg, Manfred. *"The Ticket to Freedom": The NAACP and the Struggle for Black Political Integration*. Gainesville: University Press of Florida, 2005.

Berry, Mary Francis. *Military Necessity and Civil Rights Policy: Black Citizenship and the Constitution, 1861–1868*. Port Washington, N.Y.: National University Publications, 1977.

Billingsley, Andrew. *Mighty Like a River: The Black Church and Social Reform*. New York: Oxford University Press, 1999.

BIBLIOGRAPHY

Blassingame, John W. *Black New Orleans, 1860–1880.* New York: Oxford University Press, 1973.

Blight, David W. *Frederick Douglass' Civil War: Keeping Faith in Jubilee.* Baton Rouge: Louisiana State University Press, 1989.

Bond, Horace Mann. *The Education of the Negro in the American Social Order.* New York: Prentice-Hall, 1934.

Bridges, Ruby. *Through My Eyes.* New York: Scholastic Press, 1999.

Bullock, Henry A. *A History of Negro Education in the South: From 1819 to the Present.* Cambridge: Harvard University Press, 1967.

Butchart, Ronald E. *Northern Schools, Southern Blacks, and Reconstruction: Freedmen's Education, 1862–1875.* Westport, Conn.: Greenwood Press, 1980.

Calhoun, Charles W. *Conceiving a New Republic: The Republican Party and the Southern Question, 1869–1900.* Lawrence: University Press of Kansas, 2006.

Carter, Hodding, ed. *The Past as Prelude: New Orleans, 1718–1968.* New Orleans: Tulane University, 1968.

Cliff, Michelle, ed. *The Winner Names the Age: A Collection of Writings by Lillian Smith.* New York: Norton, 1978.

Coles, Robert. *Children of Crisis: A Study of Courage and Fear.* Boston: Little, Brown, 1967.

Cremin, Lawrence A. *American Education: The Metropolitan Experience, 1876–1980.* New York: Harper and Row, 1988.

Davis, Cyprian. *The History of Black Catholics in the United States.* New York: Crossroad Publishing, 1990.

Dawson, Joseph G. *Army Generals and Reconstruction: Louisiana, 1862–1877.* Baton Rouge: Louisiana State University Press, 1982.

De Jong, Greta. *A Different Day: African American Struggles for Justice in Rural Louisiana.* Chapel Hill: University of North Carolina Press, 2002.

De Santis, Christopher C., ed. *Langston Hughes and the Chicago Defender: Essays on Race, Politics, and Culture, 1942–62.* Urbana: University of Illinois Press, 1995.

DeSantis, Vincent. *Republicans Face the Southern Question: The New Departure Years, 1877–1897.* Baltimore, Md.: John Hopkins Press, 1959.

Desdunes, Rodolphe L. *Our People and Our History: A Tribute to the Creole People of Color in Memory of the Great Men They Have Given Us and of the Good Works They Have Accomplished.* Translated and edited by Dorothea Olga McCants. Baton Rouge: Louisiana State University Press, 1973.

DeVore, Donald E., and Joseph Logsdon. *Crescent City Schools: Public Education in New Orleans, 1841–1991.* Lafayette: Center for Louisiana Studies, 1991.

Du Bois, W.E.B. *The Autobiography of W.E.B. Du Bois.* New York: International Publishers, 1986.

———. *The Education of Black People: Ten Critiques, 1906–1960.* Edited by Herbert Aptheker. New York: Monthly Review Press, 1973.

———. *The Souls of Black Folk: Essays and Sketches by W. E. Burghardt Du Bois.* New York: Dodd, Mead, 1979.
Edwards, Paul K. *The Southern Urban Negro as a Consumer.* New York: Prentice-Hall, 1932.
Emanuel, Rachel L., and Alexander P. Tureaud Jr. *A More Noble Cause: A. P. Tureaud and the Struggle for Civil Rights in Louisiana.* Baton Rouge: Louisiana State University Press, 2011.
Fairclough, Adam. *A Class of Their Own: Black Teachers in the Segregated South.* Cambridge: Belknap Press of Harvard University Press, 2007.
———. *Race and Democracy: The Civil Rights Struggle in Louisiana, 1915–1972.* Athens: University of Georgia Press, 1995.
———. *To Redeem the Soul of America: The Southern Christian Leadership Conference and Martin Luther King, Jr.* Athens: University of Georgia Press, 1987.
Finch, Minnie. *The NAACP: Its Fight for Justice.* Metuchen, N.J.: Scarecrow Press, 1981.
Fischer, Roger A. *The Segregation Struggle in Louisiana, 1862–1877.* Urbana: University of Illinois Press, 1974.
Flexner, Abraham. *Medical Education in the United States and Canada: Report to the Carnegie Foundation for the Advancement of Teaching.* New York, 1910.
Follett, Richard, Eric Foner, and Walter Johnson, eds. *Slavery's Ghost: The Problem of Freedom in the Age of Emancipation.* Baltimore, Md.: John Hopkins University Press, 2011.
Foner, Eric. *Free Soil, Free Labor, Free Men: The Ideology of the Republican Party before the Civil War.* New York: Oxford University Press, 1971.
Gaines, Kevin K. *Uplifting the Race: Black Leadership, Politics, and Culture in the Twentieth Century.* Chapel Hill: University of North Carolina Press, 1996.
Gallagher, Gary W. *The Union War.* Cambridge: Harvard University Press, 2011.
Genovese, Eugene D. *Roll, Jordan, Roll: The World the Slaves Made.* New York: Vintage Books, 1976.
Germany, Kent B. *New Orleans after the Promises: Poverty, Citizenship, and the Search for the Great Society.* Athens: University of Georgia Press, 2007.
Giddings, Paula. *When and Where I Enter: The Impact of Black Women on Race and Sex in America.* New York: Bantam Books, 1984.
Gill, Tiffany M. *Beauty Shop Politics: African American Women Activism in the Beauty Industry.* Urbana: University of Illinois Press, 2010.
Glatthaar, Joseph T. *Forged in Battle: The Civil War Alliance of Black Soldiers and White Officers.* Baton Rouge: Louisiana State University Press, 1990.
Goldfield, David. *America Aflame: How the Civil War Created a Nation.* New York: Bloomsbury Press, 2011.
Grace, Alonzo G. *Tomorrow's Citizens: A Study and Program for the Improvement of the New Orleans Public Schools.* New Orleans: Citizens' Planning Committee, 1939.

BIBLIOGRAPHY

Haas, Edward F. *DeLesseps S. Morrison and the Image of Reform*. Baton Rouge: Louisiana State University Press, 1974.

Hahn, Steven. *A Nation under Our Feet: Black Political Struggles in the Rural South from Slavery to the Great Migration*. Cambridge: Belknap Press of Harvard University, 2003.

Hair, William I. *Bourbonism and Agrarian Protest: Louisiana Politics, 1877–1900*. Baton Rouge: Louisiana State University Press, 1975.

———. *Carnival of Fury: Robert Charles and the New Orleans Race Riot of 1900*. Baton Rouge: Louisiana State University Press, 1976.

Hale, Grace Elizabeth. *Making Whiteness: The Culture of Segregation in the South, 1890–1940*. New York: Pantheon Books, 1998.

Harlan, Louis. *Booker T. Washington: The Making of a Black Leader, 1856–1901*. New York: Oxford University Press, 1972.

———. *Separate and Unequal: Public School Campaigns and Racism in the Southern Seaboard States, 1901–1915*. New York: Atheneum, 1968.

Harlan, Louis R., Stuart B. Kaufman, Barbara S. Kraft, and Raymond W. Smock, eds. *The Booker T. Washington Papers*. Vols. 4, 5, 6, 10, and 13. Urbana: University of Illinois Press, 1975, 1976, 1977, 1981, and 1984.

Harris, Abram L., and Sterling D. Spero. *The Black Worker: The Negro and the Labor Movement*. New York: Columbia University Press, 1931.

Hearn, Chester G. *The Capture of New Orleans, 1862*. Baton Rouge: Louisiana State University Press, 1995.

Higginbotham, Evelyn Brooks. *Righteous Discontent: The Women's Movement in the Black Baptist Church, 1880–1920*. Cambridge: Harvard University Press, 1993.

Hine, Darlene Clark. *Black Women in White: Racial Conflict and Cooperation in the Nursing Profession, 1890–1950*. Bloomington: Indiana University Press, 1989.

Hirsch, Arnold R., and Joseph Logsdon, eds. *Creole New Orleans: Race and Americanization*. Baton Rouge: Louisiana State University Press, 1992.

Hollandsworth, James G., Jr. *An Absolute Massacre: The New Orleans Riot of July 30, 1866*. Baton Rouge: Louisiana State University Press, 2001.

———. *The Louisiana Native Guards: The Black Military Experience during the Civil War*. Baton Rouge: Louisiana State University Press, 1995.

Hughes, Langston. *Fight for Freedom: The Story of the NAACP*. New York: Berkley Publishing, 1962.

Hull, Gloria T., ed. *Give Us Each Day: The Diary of Alice Dunbar-Nelson*. New York: Norton, 1984.

Inger, Morton. *Politics and Reality in a Southern City: The New Orleans School Crisis of 1960*. New York: Center for Urban Education, 1969.

Jackson, Joy J. *New Orleans in the Gilded Age: Politics and Urban Progress, 1880–1896*. Baton Rouge: Louisiana State University Press, 1969.

Jeansonne, Glen S. *Race, Religion, and Politics: The Gubernatorial Elections of 1959–60*. Lafayette: University of Southwestern Louisiana, 1977.

Johnson, James Weldon. *Writings*. New York: Library of America, 2004.
Johnson, Michael P., ed. *Abraham Lincoln, Slavery, and the Civil War: Selected Writings and Speeches*. Boston: Bedford/St. Martins, 2001.
Kasteel, Annemarie. *Francis Janssens, 1843–1897: A Dutch-American Prelate*. Lafayette: Center for Louisiana Studies, 1992.
Keegan, John. *The American Civil War: A Military History*. New York: Knopf, 2009.
Kelley, Blair L. M. *Right to Ride: Streetcar Boycotts and African American Citizenship in the Era of Plessy v. Ferguson*. Chapel Hill: University of North Carolina Press, 2010.
Kellogg, Charles Flint. *NAACP: A History of the National Association for the Advancement of Colored People. Vol. 1: 1909–1920*. Baltimore, Md.: John Hopkins Press, 1967.
Kennedy, Al. *Chord Changes on the Chalkboard: How Public School Teachers Shaped Jazz and the Music of New Orleans*. Lanham, Md.: Scarecrow Press, 2002.
Kluger, Richard. *Simple Justice: The History of Brown v. Board of Education and Black America's Struggle for Equality*. New York: Knopf, 1976.
Kousser, J. Morgan. *Colorblind Injustice: Minority Voting Rights and the Undoing of the Second Reconstruction*. Chapel Hill: University of North Carolina Press, 1999.
———. *The Shaping of Southern Politics: Suffrage Restriction and the Establishment of the One-Party South, 1880–1910*. New Haven, Conn.: Yale University Press, 1974.
Labbe, Dolores Egger. *Jim Crow Comes to Church: The Establishment of Segregated Catholic Parishes in South Louisiana*. Lafayette: Center for Louisiana Studies, 1971.
Leavell, Ullin W. *Philanthropy in Negro Education*. Nashville: Cullon and Ghertner Co., 1930.
Levy, Eugene. *James Weldon Johnson: Black Leader, Black Voice*. Chicago: University of Chicago Press, 1973.
Lincoln, C. Eric. *Race, Religion, and the Continuing American Dilemma*. New York: Hill and Wang, 1984.
Lincoln, C. Eric, and Lawrence H. Mamiya. *The Black Church in the African American Experience*. Durham, N.C.: Duke University Press, 1990.
Lerner, Gilda, ed. *Black Women in White America: A Documentary History*. New York: Vintage Books, 1973.
Litwack, Leon F. *Trouble in Mind: Black Southerners in the Age of Jim Crow*. New York: Knopf, 1999.
Logan, Rayford W. *The Betrayal of the Negro from Rutherford B. Hayes to Woodrow Wilson*. Rev. and enl. ed. New York: Collier-Macmillan, 1972.
Lonn, Ella. *Reconstruction in Louisiana after 1868*. New York: G. P. Putnam's Sons, 1918.

Luker, Ralph E. *The Social Gospel in Black and White: American Racial Reform, 1885–1912*. Chapel Hill: University of North Carolina Press, 1991.

Macdonald, Robert R., John R. Kemp, and Edward F. Haas, eds. *Louisiana's Black Heritage*. New Orleans: Louisiana State Museum, 1979.

Marable, Manning, and Leith Mullings, eds. *Let Nobody Turn Us Around: Voices of Resistance, Reform, and Renewal*. Lanham, Md.: Rowman and Littlefield, 2000.

McMillen, Neil. *The Citizens' Council: Organized Resistance to the Second Reconstruction, 1954–64*. Urbana: University of Illinois Press, 1971.

McPherson, James M. *For Cause and Comrades: Why Men Fought in the Civil War*. New York: Oxford University Press, 1997.

———. *Ordeal by Fire: The Civil War and Reconstruction*. 3rd ed. New York: McGraw-Hill, 2001.

Medley, Keith W. *We as Freemen:* Plessy v. Ferguson. Gretna, La.: Pelican Publishing, 2003.

Meier, August. *Negro Thought in America, 1880–1915: Racial Ideologies in the Age of Booker T. Washington*. Ann Arbor: University of Michigan Press, 1978.

Meier, August, and Elliot Rudwick. *CORE: A Case Study in the Civil Rights Movement, 1942–1968*. New York: Oxford University Press, 1993.

Messner, William F. *Freedmen and the Ideology of Free Labor: Louisiana, 1862–1865*. Lafayette: Center for Louisiana Studies, 1978.

Middleton, Ernest J. *The History of the Louisiana Education Association*. Washington, D.C.: National Education Association, 1984.

Mitchell, Mary Niall. *Raising Freedom's Child: Black Children and Visions of the Future after Slavery*. New York: New York University Press, 2008.

Montgomery, William E. *Under Their Own Vine and Fig Tree: The African-American Church in the South, 1865–1900*. Baton Rouge: Louisiana State University Press, 1993.

Morris, Robert C. *Reading, 'Riting, and Reconstruction: The Education of Freedmen in the South*. Chicago: University of Chicago Press, 1981.

Newby, I. A. *Jim Crow's Defense: Anti-Negro Thought in America, 1900–1930*. Baton Rouge: Louisiana State University Press, 1965.

New Orleans University: Seventy-Five Years of Service. New Orleans: New Orleans University, 1935.

Norrell, Robert J. *Up from History: The Life of Booker T. Washington*. Cambridge: Belknap Press of Harvard University Press, 2009.

Ochs, Stephen J. *Desegregating the Altar: The Josephites and the Struggle for Black Priests, 1871–1960*. Baton Rouge: Louisiana State University Press, 1990.

Olsen, Otto, ed. *The Thin Disguise: Turning Point in Negro History:* Plessy v. Ferguson, *A Documentary Presentation (1864–1896)*. New York: Humanities Press, 1967.

Osofsky, Gilbert. *Harlem: The Making of a Ghetto: Negro New York, 1890–1930*. 2nd ed. New York: Harper and Row, 1971.

BIBLIOGRAPHY

O'Toole, James M. *The Faithful: A History of Catholics in America.* Cambridge: Belknap Press of Harvard University Press, 2008.
Parker, Joseph H. *The Morrison Era: Reform Politics in New Orleans.* Gretna, La.: Pelican Publishing, 1974.
Perkins, Archie. *Who's Who in Colored Louisiana.* Baton Rouge: Douglas Loan Co., 1930.
Perman, Michael. *Struggle for Mastery: Disfranchisement in the South, 1888–1908.* Chapel Hill: University of North Carolina Press, 2001.
Rabinowitz, Howard N. *Race Relations in the Urban South, 1865–1890.* Urbana: University of Illinois Press, 1980.
Raboteau, Albert J. *Slave Religion: The "Invisible Institution" in the Antebellum South.* New York: Oxford University Press, 1978.
Ransby, Barbara. *Ella Baker and the Black Freedom Movement: A Radical Democratic Vision.* Chapel Hill: University of North Carolina Press, 2003.
Reynolds, George. *Machine Politics in New Orleans, 1897–1926.* New York: Columbia University Press, 1936.
Richardson, Joe M. *Christian Reconstruction: The American Missionary Association and Southern Blacks, 1861–1890.* Athens: University of Georgia Press, 1986.
Richardson, Joe M., and Maxine D. Jones. *Education for Liberation: The American Missionary Association and African Americans, 1890 to the Civil Rights Movement.* Tuscaloosa: University of Alabama Press, 2009.
Ripley, Peter C. *Slaves and Freedmen in Civil War Louisiana.* Baton Rouge: Louisiana State University Press, 1976.
Riser, R. Volney. *Defying Disfranchisement: Black Voting Rights Activism in the Jim Crow South, 1890–1908.* Baton Rouge: Louisiana State University Press, 2010.
Roediger, David R. *Working toward Whiteness: How America's Immigrants Became White.* New York: Basic Books, 2005.
Rogers, Kim Lacy. *Righteous Lives: Narratives of the New Orleans Civil Rights Movement.* New York: New York University Press, 1993.
Rosenberg, Daniel. *New Orleans Dockworkers: Labor and Unionism, 1892–1923.* Albany: State University of New York Press, 1988.
Rousseve, Charles B. *The Negro in Louisiana.* New Orleans: Xavier University Press, 1937.
Sartain, Lee. *Invisible Activists: Women of the Louisiana NAACP and the Struggle for Civil Rights, 1915–1945.* Baton Rouge: Louisiana State University Press, 2007.
Savage, Barbara Dianne. *Your Spirits Walk behind Us: The Politics of Black Religion.* Cambridge: Belknap Press of Harvard University Press, 2008.
Schall, Keith L., ed. *Stony the Road: Chapters in the History of Hampton Institute.* Charlottesville: University Press of Virginia, 1977.
Scott, Emmett J. *Negro Migration during the War.* 1920. Reprint. New York: Arno Press and the New York Times, 1969.

BIBLIOGRAPHY

Scott, Rebecca J. *Degrees of Freedom: Louisiana and Cuba after Slavery.* Cambridge: Belknap Press of Harvard University Press, 2005.

Sernett, Milton C., ed. *African American Religious History: A Documentary Witness.* Durham, N.C.: Duke University Press, 1999.

Shaffer, Donald R. *After the Glory: The Struggle of Black Civil War Veterans.* Lawrence: University Press of Kansas, 2004.

Sherman, Richard B. *The Republican Party and Black America from McKinley to Hoover, 1896–1933.* Charlottesville: University Press of Virginia, 1973.

Sokol, Jason. *There Goes My Everything: White Southerners in the Age of Civil Rights, 1945–1975.* New York: Knopf, 2006.

Southern Society for the Promotion of the Study of Race Conditions and Problems in the South. *Race Problems of the South: Report of the Proceedings of the First Annual Conference Held under the Auspices of the Southern Society for the Promotion of the Study of Race Conditions and Problems in the South.* Montgomery, Ala., 1900.

Sowell, Thomas. *Education: Assumption versus History.* Stanford, Calif.: Hoover Institution Press, 1986.

Spivey, Donald. *Schooling for the New Slavery: Black Industrial Education, 1868–1915.* Westport, Conn.: Greenwood Press, 1978.

Stampp, Kenneth M. *The Era of Reconstruction, 1865–1877.* New York: Vintage Books, 1965.

Sterkx, H. E. *The Free Negro in Ante-Bellum Louisiana.* Rutherford, N.J.: Fairleigh Dickinson University Press, 1972.

Sterling, Dorothy, ed. *We Are Your Sisters: Black Women in the Nineteenth Century.* New York: Norton, 1984.

Stout, Harry S. *Upon the Altar of the Nation: A Moral History of the American Civil War.* New York: Viking, 2006.

Sullivan, Patricia. *Days of Hope: Race and Democracy in the New Deal Era.* Chapel Hill: University of North Carolina Press, 1996.

Taylor, Arnold H. *Travail and Triumph: Black Life and Culture in the South since the Civil War.* Westport, Conn.: Greenwood Press, 1976.

Taylor, Joe Gray. *Louisiana Reconstructed, 1863–1877.* Baton Rouge: Louisiana State University Press, 1974.

The Negro Problem. 1903. Reprint. New York: Arno Press and the New York Times, 1969.

Trudeau, Noah Andre. *Like Men of War: Black Troops in the Civil War, 1862–1865.* Boston: Little, Brown, 1998.

Tunnell, Ted. *Crucible of Reconstruction: War, Radicalism, and Race in Louisiana, 1862–1877.* Baton Rouge: Louisiana State University Press, 1984.

Tushnet, Mark V. *The NAACP's Legal Strategy against Segregated Education, 1925–1950.* Chapel Hill: University of North Carolina Press, 1987.

Tyler, Pamela. *Silk Stockings and Ballot Boxes: Women and Politics in New Orleans, 1920–1963.* Athens: University of Georgia Press, 1996.

Vincent, Charles. *Black Legislators in Louisiana during Reconstruction.* Baton Rouge: Louisiana State University Press, 1976.

———. *A Centennial History of Southern University and A and M College.* Baton Rouge: Southern University, 1981.

Walker, Juliet E. K. *The History of Black Business in America: Capitalism, Race, Entrepreneurship.* New York: Macmillan, 1998.

Ward, Thomas J. *Black Physicians in the Jim Crow South.* Fayetteville: University of Arkansas Press, 2003.

Weare, Walter B. *Black Business in the New South: A Social History of the North Carolina Mutual Life Insurance Company.* Durham, N.C.: Duke University Press, 1993.

Webber, Thomas L. *Deep Like the Rivers: Education in the Slave Quarter Community, 1831–1865.* New York: Norton, 1978.

Weigley, Russell F. *A Great Civil War: A Military and Political History, 1861–1865.* Bloomington: Indiana University Press, 2000.

Weinberg, Meyer. *A Chance to Learn: The History of Race and Education in the United States.* Cambridge: Cambridge University Press, 1977.

White, Howard A. *The Freedmen's Bureau in Louisiana.* Baton Rouge: Louisiana State University Press, 1970.

White, Walter. *A Man Called White: The Autobiography of Walter White.* New York: Viking Press, 1948.

Wilmore, Gayraud, ed. *African American Religious Studies: An Interdisciplinary Anthology.* Durham, N.C.: Duke University Press, 1989.

Woodson, Carter G. *The Mis-Education of the Negro.* 1933. Reprint. Trenton, N.J.: Africa World Press, 1990.

———. *The Negro Professional Man and the Community.* 1938. Reprint. New York: Negro Universities Press, 1969.

Woodward, C. Vann. *Reunion and Reaction: The Compromise of 1877 and the End of Reconstruction.* Rev. ed. Garden City, N.Y.: Doubleday, 1956.

———. *The Strange Career of Jim Crow.* 3rd ed. New York: Oxford University Press, 1974.

Zuckerman, Phil, ed. *Du Bois on Religion.* Walnut Creek, Calif.: AltaMira Press, 2000.

Articles

Alberts, John B. "Black Catholic Schools: The Josephite Parishes during the Jim Crow Era." *U.S. Catholic Historian* 12, no. 1 (Winter 1994): 77–98.

Bond, Horace Mann. "The Role of History of Education in Understanding the Struggle for Equalizing Educational Opportunity." *History of Education Journal* 1, no. 3 (Spring 1950): 101–7.

Boyd, Robert L. "Racial Segregation and Insurance Enterprise among Black Americans in Northern Cities." *Sociological Review* 39, no. 2 (Spring 1998): 337–49.

BIBLIOGRAPHY

Cassimere, Raphael, Jr. "Equalizing Teachers' Pay in Louisiana." *Integrateducation* (July–August 1977): 3–8.
Coffey, Michele Grisby. "*The State of Louisiana v. Charles Guerand*: Interracial Sexual Mores, Rape Rhetoric, and Respectability in 1930s New Orleans." *Louisiana History* 54, no. 1 (Winter 2013): 47–93.
Comminey, Shawn C. "The Origin, Organization, and Progression of Straight University, 1869–1880." *Louisiana History* 51, no. 4 (Fall 2010): 404–41.
Connor, William P. "Reconstruction Rebels: The New Orleans Tribune in Post-War Louisiana." *Louisiana History* 21, no. 2 (Spring 1980): 159–81.
Crouch, Barry A. "Black Education in Civil War and Reconstruction Louisiana: George T. Ruby, the Army, and the Freedmen's Bureau." *Louisiana History* 38, no. 3 (Summer 1997): 287–308.
Dethloff, Henry C. "The Alliance and the Lottery: Farmers Try for the Sweepstakes." *Louisiana History* 6, no. 2 (Spring 1965): 141–59.
Dethloff, Henry C., and Robert R. Jones. "Race Relations in Louisiana, 1877–98." *Louisiana History* 9, no. 4 (Fall 1968): 301–23.
Doyle, Elisabeth. "Nurseries of Treason: Schools in Occupied New Orleans." *Journal of Southern History* 26, no. 2 (May 1960): 161–79.
Haas, Edward F. "The Expedient of Race: Victor H. Schiro, Scott Wilson, and the New Orleans Mayoralty Campaign of 1962." *Louisiana History* 42, no. 1 (Winter 2001): 5–29.
Hair, William Ivy. "Henry J. Hearsey and the Politics of Race." *Louisiana History* 17, no. 4 (Fall 1976): 393–400.
Hall, Jacquelyn Hall. "The Long Civil Rights Movement and the Political Uses of the Past." *Journal of American History* 91, no. 4 (March 2005): 1233–63.
Harlan, Louis R. "Desegregation in New Orleans Public Schools during Reconstruction." *American Historical Review* 67, no. 3 (April 1962): 663–75.
Hennessey, Melinda Meek. "Race and Violence in Reconstruction New Orleans: The 1868 Riot." *Louisiana History* 20, no. 1 (Winter 1979): 77–91.
Horowitz, David Alan. "White Southerners' Alienation and Civil Rights: The Response to Corporate Liberalism, 1956–1965." *Journal of Southern History* 54, no. 2 (May 1988): 173–200.
Ingham, John N. "Building Businesses, Creating Communities: Residential Segregation and the Growth of African American Business in Southern Cities, 1880–1915." *Business History Review* 77, no. 4 (Winter 2003): 639–65.
Jacobs, Claude F. "Benevolent Societies of New Orleans Blacks during the Late Nineteenth and Early Twentieth Centuries." *Louisiana History* 29, no. 1 (Winter 1988): 21–33.
Kunkel, Paul. "Modifications in Louisiana Negro Legal Status under Louisiana Constitutions, 1812–1957." *Journal of Negro History* 44, no. 1 (January 1959): 1–25.
Landphair, Juliette. "Sewerage, Sidewalks, and Schools: The New Orleans Ninth Ward and Public School Desegregation." *Louisiana History* 40, no. 1 (Winter 1999): 35–62.

Meier, August, and John H. Bracey Jr. "The NAACP as a Reform Movement, 1909–1965: 'To Reach the Conscience of America.'" *Journal of Southern History* 59, no. 1 (February 1993): 3–30.
Merrill, James M. "Confederate Shipbuilding at New Orleans." *Journal of Southern History* 28, no. 1 (February 1962): 87–93.
Mohr, Clarence. "Minds of the New South: Higher Education in Black and White, 1880–1915." *Southern Quarterly* 46, no. 4 (Summer 2009): 8–34.
Muller, Mary Lee. "New Orleans Public School Desegregation." *Louisiana History* 17, no. 1 (Winter 1976): 69–88.
Northrup, Herbert R. "The New Orleans Longshoremen." *Political Science Quarterly* 57, no. 4 (December 1942): 526–44.
O'Kelly, Charlotte G. "Black Newspapers and the Black Protest Movement, 1946–1972." *Phylon* 41, no. 4 (1980): 313–24.
Pitman, Bambra (Barb). "Culture, Caste, and Conflict in New Orleans Catholicism: Archbishop Francis Janssens and the Color Line." *Louisiana History* 49, no. 4 (Fall 2008): 423–62.
Porter, Betty. "The History of Negro Education in Louisiana." *Louisiana Historical Quarterly* 25 (July 1942): 728–821.
Reynolds, Donald E. "The New Orleans Riot of 1866 Reconsidered." *Louisiana History* 5, no. 1 (Winter 1964): 5–27.
Rice, Roger L. "Residential Segregation by Law, 1910–1917." *Journal of Southern History* 34, no. 2 (May 1968): 179–99.
Richardson, Joe M. "Albert W. Dent: A Black New Orleans Hospital and University Administrator." *Louisiana History* 37, no. 3 (Summer 1996): 309–23.
———. "Edgar B. Stern: A White New Orleans Philanthropist Helps Build a Black University." *Journal of Negro History* 82, no. 3 (Summer 1997): 328–42.
Shepherd, Samuel C. "In Pursuit of Louisiana Progressives." *Louisiana History* 46, no. 4 (Fall 2005): 389–406.
Somers, Dale. "Black and White in New Orleans: A Study in Urban Race Relations, 1865–1900." *Journal of Southern History* 40, no. 1 (February 1974): 19–43.
Uzee, Philip D. "The Republican Party in the Louisiana Election of 1896." *Louisiana History* 2, no. 3 (Summer 1961): 332–44.
Vincent, Charles. "Negro Leadership and Programs in the Louisiana Constitutional Convention of 1868." *Louisiana History* 10, no. 4 (Fall 1969): 339–51.
———. "'Of Such Historical Importance . . .': The African American Experience in Louisiana." *Louisiana History* 50, no. 2 (Spring 2009): 133–58.
Wieder, Alan. "The New Orleans School Crisis of 1960: Causes and Consequences." *Phylon* 48, no. 2 (1987): 122–31.
Williams, T. Harry. "The Louisiana Unification Movement of 1873." *Journal of Southern History* 11, no. 3 (August 1945): 349–69.

Theses and Dissertations

Amedee, George L. "The Origins of African American Political Empowerment in New Orleans, Louisiana: The Role of the Trailblazer in Leadership and Organizational Development." Ph.D. diss., Northern Illinois University, 1993.

Anthony, Arthe A. "The Negro Creole Community in New Orleans, 1880–1920: An Oral History." Ph.D. diss., University of California, Irving, 1978.

Banks, Myrtle. "The Education of the Negro in New Orleans." Master's thesis, Xavier University, 1935.

Bordelon, Samson P. "The New Orleans Public Schools under the Superintendency of Lionel John Bourgeois." Ph.D. diss., University of Southern Mississippi, 1966.

Carey, Addison. "Black Political Participation in New Orleans." Ph.D. diss., Tulane University, 1974.

Davis, Londa L. "After Reconstruction: Black Politics in New Orleans, 1876–1900." Master's thesis, University of New Orleans, 1981.

DeCuir, Sharlene S. "Attacking Jim Crow: Black Activism in New Orleans, 1925–1941." Ph.D. diss., Louisiana State University, 2009.

DeJan, Marie. "Education for Negroes in New Orleans prior to 1915." Master's thesis, Xavier University, 1941.

DeVore, Donald E. "Race Relations and Community Development: The Education of Blacks in New Orleans, 1862–1960." Ph.D. diss., Louisiana State University, 1989.

———. "The Rise from the Nadir: Black New Orleans between the Wars, 1920–1940." Master's thesis, University of New Orleans, 1983.

Jacobs, Claude Francis. "Strategies of Neighborhood Health-Care among New Orleans Blacks: From Voluntary Association to Public Policy." Ph.D. diss., Tulane University, 1980.

Johnson, Janice Richard. "Leland University in New Orleans, 1870–1915." Ph.D. diss., University of New Orleans, 1996.

Marshall, David C. "A History of the Higher Education of Negroes in the State of Louisiana." Ph.D. diss., Louisiana State University, 1956.

McCarrick, Earlean M. "Louisiana's Official Resistance to Segregation." Ph.D. diss., Vanderbilt University, 1964.

Muller, Mary L. "The Orleans Parish School Board and Negro Education, 1940–1960." Master's thesis, University of New Orleans, 1975.

Neyland, Leedell W. "The Negro in Louisiana since 1900: An Economic and Social Study." Ph.D. diss., New York University, 1959.

Rankin, David C. "The Forgotten People: Free People of Color in New Orleans, 1850–1870." Ph.D. diss., John Hopkins University, 1976.

Rogers, Kim Lacy. "Humanity and Desire: Civil Rights Leaders and Desegregation of New Orleans, 1954–1966." Ph.D. diss., University of Minnesota, 1982.

Rosenzweig, Allen. "The Influence of Class and Race on Political Behavior in New Orleans." Master's thesis, University of New Orleans, 1967.

Uzee, Philip D. "Republican Politics in Louisiana, 1877–1900." Ph.D. diss., Louisiana State University, 1950.

Vanderleeuw, James M. "A City in Transition: The Impact of Changing Racial Composition on Voting Behavior." Ph.D. diss., University of New Orleans, 1988.

Vital, Nida H. "Dr. Rivers Frederick and the History of Black Medicine in New Orleans." Master's thesis, University of New Orleans, 1978.
Wells, David. "The ILWU in New Orleans: CIO Radicalism in the Crescent City, 1937–1957." Master's thesis, University of New Orleans, 1979.
Worthy, Barbara Ann. "The Travail and Triumph of a Southern Black Civil Rights Lawyer: The Legal Career of Alexander Pierre Tureaud, 1899–1972." Ph.D. diss., Tulane University, 1984.

INDEX

Act 111 (railroad car bill, 1890), 25–27
Acts 555 and 556 (school segregation, 1954), 205
Ainsworth, Robert A., Jr., 206
Albert, A.E.P., 26, 38
Albert, Fr. John, 69–70
Alexander, Avery, 218, 221
Alexander, Will W., 50
Allain, T. T., 22
American Missionary Association (AMA), 36–37, 44, 50–51, 78–79, 83, 90
Anderson, James D., 124
Antoine, Caesar C., 17, 19, 37
Armstrong, Samuel, 37
Article 231 (La. Constitution, 1879), 21–22
Associated Negro Press, 107
Atlanta Declaration (NAACP), 206
attorneys as black professionals, 164
Aubert, Wilfred, 226
Augustine, Israel, Jr., 227

baby contest (NAACP), 99–100
Bagnall, Robert, 98, 101, 102
Bailey, Thomas, 93–94
Baker, Ella, 94
Ballard, Marshall, Sr., 118–19
Banks, Nathaniel P., 12
Baptist denominations, 39
Barnes, Charles, 188–89
Bauer, Nicholas, 127–28, 137, 150
Baumgartner, Mrs. Arthur, 133, 134

Bayou Road Elementary School, 60, 129–35
Beauregard, Pierre G. T., 9, 16, 17
beauty salons, 161–63
Beck, Anna, 176
Beecher Memorial Congregational Church, 76–78
Bell, Caryn Cossé, 6
Bennett, James B., 64, 73
Best, Blanche, 119
Bingaman, James, 185–86
Black and Tan movement, 183–84
black churches. *See* religious dimensions of community development
Black Codes, 5
Blassingame, John, 17
Blenk, Archbishop James H., 52, 66–67, 70
Blessed Sacrament, 67
bombings, 179
Bond, Horace Mann, 50, 51, 203–4
Borah, Wayne, 188–89, 197–99
Bourgeois, Lionel J., 201
Braden, Henry E., 179, 185
Bradley, Phillips, 50–51
Brazier, Aaron, 103
Bridges, Harry, 172
Bridges, Ruby, 211–12
Broussard, Albert, 88
Brown, A. Angold, 84–86
Brown, Mayme O., 166
Brown, William G., 19

INDEX

Brownlee, Fred, 50–51, 89
Brown v. Board of Education, 205–13
Buchanan v. Warley, 131, 175, 178, 179, 180
building trades, 167
Bulloch, James D., 2
Bureau of Refugees, Freedmen, and Abandoned Lands (Freedmen's Bureau), 13, 36, 39
Burke, Fr. John E., 69
Bush, Oliver, 204–5
businesses, black-owned: discrimination patterns and, 157, 164–69; factors affecting, 151, 169; funeral homes, 157–58; insurance companies, 153–57; retail, 158–61; segregation and, 151, 153; service businesses, 161–63; urbanization and, 152; Washington and Du Bois on, 152. *See also* employment
Byrd, Daniel, 202–4, 206, 214, 220
Byrd, Mildred, 208

Canal Street picketers, 222–24
Carnival, 107–8
Carter, Robert, 204
Cash, W. L., 86–87, 88
Cassimere, Raphael, 223, 224
Castle, Oretha, 218–19, 220–21, 227
Central Congregational Church, 78–91
Chamberlain, Holbrook, 39
Chapelle, Archbishop Placide, 66
Chapital, Arthur, 208–12, 215, 218, 220, 221, 225
Chapman-Catt, Carrie, 28
Charbonnet, Loys, 179, 180
Charity Hospital, 113
Chasse, Louis A., 65
Chesnutt, Charles W., 33
churches. *See* religious dimensions of community development
Citizens' Committee (1890s), 25
Citizens' Committee (1960s), 221–23
citizens' councils (white), 207–8
city council, 13, 48–49
Civil Rights Act (1964), 224–25
civil rights campaigns. *See* direct action campaigns
Civil War, 1–4
Clark, Joseph Samuel, 42–43, 140

clerical workers, 167
Cockran, W. Bourke, 28
Cohen, Walter, 93–94, 133, 153–54, 157, 181, 182–85, 187
colleges. *See* education, higher
Collins, Virginia Y., 221–22, 226
Colored Educational Alliance, 54–55, 83, 105–6, 133, 135, 136, 150, 164–65, 202
Committee of One Hundred, 17
Committee on Elementary Schools, 195
Community Chest drives, 121
community development. *See* religious dimensions of community development
Confederacy, 1–4
Congress of Industrial Organizations (CIO), 170–71
Congress of Racial Equality (CORE), 219, 220–21
constitutions and constitutional conventions (Louisiana), 8–11, 21–23, 28–29
Consumers League of Greater New Orleans, 217–18
Conway, Thomas W., 14–15
Copelin, Sherman, 227
Corpus Christi church, 67
Council of Social Agencies, 117
court cases and lawsuits: *Brown v. Board of Education,* 205–13; *Buchanan v. Warley,* 131, 175, 178, 179, 180; Bush case, 204–5, 207; *Guinn and Beal v. United States,* 188–89; *Myers vs. Anderson,* 188–89; *Plessy v. Ferguson,* 27, 64, 189, 201; rail car bill and, 27; in Reconstruction, 16; *Smith v. Allwright,* 199; *Trudeau v. Barnes,* 186–89; *Tyler v. Harmon,* 177–80
Couvent, Madame Maria, 11
Couvent School, 67
Craig, Joseph A., 20–21, 134
Crisis, 42, 93
Crusader, 25, 106
Current, Gloster B., 215
Curry, J.L.M., 33, 34

Dana, Charles, 4
Danizer, A. D., 47
Davis, A. L., 214
Davis, Henry, 5
Davis, Robert C., 23

death rates, 109
Dejoie, Constant C., Sr., 80–81, 84, 87–88, 90, 94, 106, 107, 111, 119
Dejoie, Prudhomme, 153, 157
Demas, Henry, 41, 182
Democratic-Conservative Party, 23
demonstration tactic. *See* direct action campaigns
Dent, Albert W., 50, 51–52, 113–16, 117
Desdunes, Rodolphe L., 25
desegregated schools. *See* school segregation and desegregation
Dillard, James H., 48
Dillard University, 47–52, 164, 216
direct action campaigns: Canal Street demonstrations and hiring negotiations, 222–24; Citizens Committee and, 221–23; CORE, 219, 220–21; Dryades Street campaign, 217–19; "friendly" competition among civil rights groups, 215; lunch counter sit-ins, 219–20; NAACP and, 214–16, 219, 224–26; NAACP Youth Council and, 220, 222–24, 227; political participation and, 227–28; Sept. 1963 protest march (largest in New Orleans), 221; as strategy, 214–15; student-led demonstrations and white responses, 216–17; Title VII and, 224–25; voter registration and education, 225–27
discrimination. *See specific topics, such as* employment
Dorsey, Willie, 171–72
Douglas, Nils, 227
Douglass, Frederick, 3, 6, 10, 76, 181
dressmakers, 163
Drexel, Katherine, 52
Dryades Street campaign, 217–19
dry cleaners, 161
Du Bois, W. E. B.: on black churches, 72, 75; Dillard commencement speech (1936), 50; on economic development, 152; on education, 31, 35–36, 142, 145; Hart letter to, 191; liberation ideology of, 76; NAACP and, 93; Pinchback compared to, 22; on rights, 180–81
Dumas, Francis E., 11
Dunbar, Paul Laurence, 40, 57
Dunn, Alberta, 98

Dunn, Emmanuel, 93, 95, 96, 100
Dunn, Henderson H., 78–84, 94, 105, 120, 136, 165–66
Dunn, James, 49
Dunn, Lillian, 91
Dunn, Oscar J., 11

Easton, Warren, 126–27, 144, 145–46
economic subordination, 108–9, 172–73, 177–78. *See also* employment
education, higher: African American leaders on, 31–32, 35–36; college graduates, lives of, 54–61; Dillard University, 47–52, 164, 216; enrollments, 37, 39–40, 43, 46, 50, 53–54; faculty, 45–46; Flint Medical College, 109–10, 114, 163; growth factors, 43–44; Hampton Institute (VA), 37, 40, 122; industrial education, 33, 40; Leland University, 39; New Orleans University, 38, 43, 44, 47–48, 109–10; in Reconstruction and post-Reconstruction, 22–23; Southern Society conference (Montgomery, 1900), 32–35; Southern University, 22–23, 41–43, 139–40; standards, maintenance of, 46; Straight College/University, 36–37, 39–40, 43, 45–48, 79, 89–90, 140; teacher training, 40–41, 56; Tuskegee Institute, 28, 32, 40, 122; World War I and, 42; Xavier University, 52–54, 59
education, primary and secondary: aims of black protest, 123; all-black teaching corps campaign, 165–66; Bayou Road School, case of, 129–35; on college campuses, 43–44, 140; conversion of schools from white to black, 128–29, 201–2; curriculum committee, 57–58; discrimination petition (1946), 201; enrollment statistics, 138–39, 143; evening schools, 143–45, 146; Freedmen's Bureau teachers, 13; high school facilities, 139–43; industrial and vocational approach, 122, 125–27, 142, 145–50; music education, 58–59; need for additional black schools, 135–37; number, condition, and value of black vs. white schools, 135; overcrowding and part-time classes, 137, 139; philosophy of limitation and exclusion, 122–24, 145; primary-only policy,

INDEX

education, primary and secondary (*continued*)
125–26; racist ideology and, 123–24; in Reconstruction and post-Reconstruction, 12–14; school support clubs, 106; secondary, declining support for, 37; segregation of teachers meetings, 127; slaves and, 11–12; superintendent philosophies and policies, 126–28; teacher salaries equalization campaign, 194–98; teachers and principals, 54–61; trade school project, 148–50. *See also* school segregation and desegregation
employment: building and skilled trades, 167, 168; hiring practices campaigns, 217–19, 221, 222–25; professional categories, 163–64, 165; public employment, 166–67; teachers, 164–66; women and, 161–63, 168–69. *See also* businesses, black-owned
English, Richard, 200
Esplanade High School, 140–41
Etienne, Gail, 211–12

Fairclough, Adam, 207
Farragut, David G., 2
Fayerweather, George H., 20
Federation of Civic Leagues, 104–5, 150, 193, 202
Fifteenth Amendment, 27, 34, 189
First African Baptist Church, 185–86
Fischer, Roger, 8–9
Fisk Elementary School, 54
Fitzgerald, John, 28
Flexner report, 109–10
Flint-Goodridge Hospital, 109–16
Flint Medical College, 109–10, 114, 163
Flott, N. B., 96
Flower, Walter C., 28
Floyd, Raymond, 217, 218
Follett, Richard, 21
Fortier, James, 124, 126, 131–32, 133–34, 145
Foster, Murphy J., 27–28
Fourteenth Amendment, 27, 34, 177–78, 199, 201, 203
Fourth Ward Civic League, 128
Fourth Ward Poll Tax Association, 104
Francis Nicholls High School, 140–41

Frazier, E. Franklin, 116
Frederick, Rivers, 94, 111, 114–15
free blacks, 6, 7–8
Freedmen's Bureau (Bureau of Refugees, Freedmen, and Abandoned Lands), 13, 36, 39
French culture, 64–65
French language, 7
Frissell, Hollis Burke, 28
funeral homes, 157–58

Gaines, Kevin K., 116
Garrett, John, 206, 207
Gayle, James E., 93, 111, 176, 183, 184
Geddes, George, 153, 158
General Education Board, 47, 48
Genovese, Eugene, 12
Goldfinch, Sydney, 220
Grace Methodist Episcopal Church, 97
Graves, John Temple, 33–34
Great Depression, 159, 160, 190
Green, Samuel, 153, 183
Guerand, Charles, 190–91, 192–93
Guidry, Deborah, 98, 100, 176, 181, 192
Guillaume, John, 148
Guinn and Beal v. United States, 188–89
Gwinn, Joseph, 127, 132–33, 140, 147

Hahn, Steven, 29
Hair, William I., 95
Hale, Grace Elizabeth, 94
Hampton Institute (VA), 37, 40, 122
Handy, W. Talbot, 118
Harder, William C., 184
Hardin, Joseph, 104, 136, 137, 176–77, 181, 183, 184
Harlan, John M., 27
Harmon, Benjamin, 177–78, 180
Harrison, Hubert H., 116
Hart, Althea, 191–92
Hartman, Chester W., 212
Hearsey, Henry J., 95
Heath, T. Restin, 111
Heller, Isaac, 137, 149, 150
Heller, Max, 96
Henley, Mrs. A. M., 96
Highgate, Edmonia, 7, 13
Hildebrand, Mrs. J., 49

270

INDEX

hiring practices campaigns, 217–19, 221, 222–25. *See also* employment
Hoffman, John, 58, 141–42
Holland, David, 79
Holmes, Norman, 89, 91, 117
housing segregation, 174–80
housing stock, 172–73
Houston, Charles, 201, 214
Hughes, Langston, 57
Hutton, Lucille, 54, 58–59, 91
Hutton, Robert E. L., 79, 84

industrial education, 33, 40
institutional development. *See* secular organizations and community development
insurance companies, 153–57
International Longshoremen Association (ILA), 171
International Longshoremen's and Warehousemen's Unions (ILWU), 170–72
Irwin, Emmett Lee, 207

James, Joseph, 159–60
Janssens, Archbishop Francis, 64–67
Jim Crow, onset of, 25, 30. *See also* education; school segregation and desegregation; segregation; suffrage and voting rights
Johnson, Charles S., 51, 52
Johnson, James Weldon, 102, 107
Johnson, Mrs. Ida, 94
Joint Legislative Committee on Segregation, 205
Jones, Donald, 196
Jones, Maxine, 47–48
Jones, Robert Elijah, 47, 56, 72–76, 91, 120
Jones, William, 80, 81, 84
Josephites, 68–71

Katie Beauty School, 162–63
Kearny, Warren, 49, 51
Keller, Franklin, 148–49
Kinchen, E. W., 97
Knights of St. Peter Claver, 71–72
Kohn, Joseph, 145, 147
Kousser, J. Morgan, 27
Kriege, Otto E., 44

Kruttschnitt, Ernest B., 28
Kuntz, Emile, 184–85

Labat, George, 103, 187
labor solidarity, 169–72
LaBranche, Emile, 86, 88, 91, 120, 133
Landix, Paul A., 93, 94
Landphair, Juliette, 204
Landrieu, Maurice "Moon," 227
Larsen, Ludwig T., 45–46
Lawless, Alfred, 153
Lawless, Alfred, Jr., 77, 84
Laws, Clarence, 119
lawsuits. *See* court cases and lawsuits
LeBeau, Fr. Pierre, 66, 70
Legier, John, 49
Leland University, 39
Lele, Victor, 225
Lenfant, Howard, 197
Lewis, James, 25, 153
lily-white movement, 183–85
Lincoln, Abraham, 1–6
Lincoln, C. Eric, 63, 75
Litwack, Leon, 25
Loke, Emily, 16
Lombard, Edwin, 227
Lombard, Rudolph "Rudy," 219, 220
Longe, George, 54, 56–58, 120–21
Longshoremen Protective Union Benevolent Association, 169–70
Louisianan, 106
Louisiana Weekly: about, 106–8; editorials, 148, 149, 150, 179, 180, 182, 185, 192, 195, 199, 214, 216; McCray case and, 192, 193, 194
Lucas, George, 94, 98–103, 176, 177, 181, 183, 187, 192, 194
Luke, Leontine, 211–12
Luker, Ralph, 70
lunch counter sit-ins, 219–20
Lusher, Robert M., 19
lynchings, 29, 187, 192. *See also* violence

MacCorkle, William A., 34–35
machine politics, 23
Mallory, Stephen R., 2
Mamiya, Lawrence, 63, 75
Mardi Gras, 107–8
Margold, Nathan, 201

INDEX

Marks, Isaac N., 16, 17–18
Marshall, Thurgood, 196–99, 200, 202, 204, 208
Martinet, Louis A., 20, 25–26, 106
Mary, Aristide, 17, 20, 23
McCray, Hattie, 190–94
McDonogh No. 5 School, 128
McDonogh No. 13 School, 141
McDonogh No. 19 School, 211
McDonogh No. 35 High School, 141–43, 147–48
McKelpin, Joseph, 196–97
McShane, Andrew J., 175
Meine, Emile, 87
Methodist Episcopal Church, 38, 44, 54, 72–76, 110, 112
middle class, black, 79
midwifery, 164
migration: to New Orleans, 23, 83, 152, 190; out-migration from South, 82–83, 149; urbanization, 152, 190
Milliken's Bend, Battle of, 3–4
Mitchell, Archibald, 19, 20
Moise, Percy, 132
Mollay, Alex, 104
Montanot, J. P., 6
Montgomery, William, 73
Moore, Alice Ruth, 40
Morial, Ernest Nathan "Dutch," 220, 221, 227–28
Morris Brown Congregational Church, 77
Morrison, deLesseps Story "Chep," 217, 219–20
Mothers' Clubs, 106
Moton, Robert, 57
Murphy, Daniel, 131, 132
Murphy, Edgar Gardner, 32–33
music education, 58–59
Myers vs. Anderson, 188–89
Myrdal, Gunnar, 200

NAACP (National Association for the Advancement of Colored People): about, 92–104; Atlanta Declaration, 206; direct action strategy and, 214–16, 219; education and, 133, 135, 150, 200–204, 208–13; Hattie McCray case and, 191–93; lunch counter sit-ins, 219–20; residential segregation and, 177, 179; suspension of operations (1959–1960), 216; Title VII coordinator, 224–25; Voter Registration Committee, 225–27; voting rights and, 187–88, 199; Youth Council, 214–15, 220, 222–24, 227
National Negro Business League, 152
National Progressive Association for Negroes, 133
National Urban League, 116–18
"Negro Question" or "Problem," 18, 24, 27, 32
neighborhood improvement campaigns, 105. *See also* residential segregation
Nelson, William Stuart, 50
New Orleans: battle for political control of (1870s), 18–19; black population and migration to, 23, 83; fall of, in Civil War, 2; free blacks during Civil War, 6; migration to, 23, 83, 152; population trends, 152; residential segregation ordinance, 174–80; strikes, 170. *See also specific topics,* such as education
New Orleans Citizens' Committee for Equalizing Educational Opportunities, 195, 196
New Orleans Colored Hospital Association, 111–12
New Orleans Republican, 17
New Orleans Times, 14
New Orleans Times-Picayune, 133, 178, 180, 193
New Orleans Tribune, 7, 9–10, 14, 21, 25
New Orleans University, 38, 43, 44, 47–48, 109–10
newspapers: as communication network, 106; *Crisis,* 42, 93; *Crusader,* 25, 106; *Louisianan,* 106; *Louisiana Weekly,* 106–8, 148, 149, 150; *New Orleans Republican,* 17; *New Orleans Times,* 14; *New Orleans Times-Picayune,* 133; *New Orleans Tribune,* 7, 9–10, 14, 21, 25; *Southwestern Christian Advocate,* 73–74, 91, 106, 125; *L'Union,* 6
Nicholls, Francis T., 19, 20, 21
Ninth Ward Civic and Improvement League, 106, 202, 204
Norrell, Robert J., 27–28

INDEX

North Carolina Mutual Life Insurance Co., 154
nursing, 164

O'Brien, James P., 45
Oertling, Gus, 184
O'Niell, Charles A., 178
organizations and institutions. *See* religious dimensions of community development; secular organizations and community development

Patrons' Clubs, 106
Pelican Republican Club, 184
Peoples Benevolent Industrial Life, 153–54
Perez, Leander, 206
Perkins, Mrs. B. A., 96
Perman, Michael, 28
Perry, Robert, 181
Petty, B. N., 95, 96, 98
Phillips, Edward H., 77
Phillis Wheatley Club, 109
Phillis Wheatley Sanitarium and Training School for Nurses, 109
Pickens, William, 98, 99–100
Pierson, Victoria, 86, 88
Pinchback, P.B.S., 16, 19, 22–23, 25, 37, 41, 182
Plantevigne, Albert, 69, 70
Plantevigne, John J., 69–71
Plessy v. Ferguson, 27, 64, 189, 201
Plumbly, B. Rush, 12
political participation by African Americans: in civil rights era, 227–28; in Reconstruction and post-Reconstruction, 8–9, 16–19, 23–24. *See also* suffrage and voting rights
poll tax campaigns, 104, 120
Porterie, Louis, 207
Port Hudson, battle at, 3
Prevost, Tessie, 211–12
Proclamation of Amnesty and Reconstruction, 4–5
professional category of businesses, 163–64, 165
protest campaigns. *See* direct action campaigns
public employment, 166–67

racial uplift. *See* uplift ideology
railroad car bill (Act 111, 1890), 25–27
Rainach, William, 207
Reconstruction and post-Reconstruction (to 1900): Civil War and Confederacy, 1–4; constitutions and conventions, state, 8–11, 21–23, 28–29; dreams and aspirations, white and black, 5–6, 30; education, access to, 11–14, 22–23; free blacks and former slaves, alliance between, 7–8; Freedmen's Bureau, 13; Lincoln's Proclamation of Amnesty and Reconstruction, 4–5; machine politics, 23–24; northern critique of the South and Black Codes, 5; political participation by African Americans, 8–9, 16–19, 23–24; race relations, character of, 16, 21; railroad car bill (Act 111), 25–27; school segregation and desegregation, 14–16, 19–22; suffrage during, 4, 6–7, 9, 27–29; Unification Movement, 16–18; violence during, 18; Wade-Davis Bill, 5
religious dimensions of community development: Beecher Memorial Congregational Church, 76–78; beliefs, traits, and behaviors, 63; Catholic parishes, segregated, 63–67; Central Congregational Church, 78–91; critiques of black clergy, 74–75; denominational affiliation and religious interracialism, 73; Josephites and black priests, 68–71; Knights of St. Peter Claver, 71–72; Methodist Episcopal Church and Rev. Robert E. Jones, 72–76; role of the black church, 62–63, 80, 91; school integration and faith, 212; variety of denominations, 63
Republican Party: black participation in, 17, 181–86; local leaders in, 153; Louisiana constitutional convention and, 8; Reconstruction and, 11, 14, 18, 19; school segregation and, 14; Unification Movement and, 17
residential segregation, 174–80
retail businesses, black-owned, 158–61
Rhodes, Duplain, 158
Ricau, Jackson, 207
Richards, Charlotte, 96
Richardson, Joe, 47–48

INDEX

rights discourse, 9
Rittner, Lloyd, 210
Robertson, Bob, 170–72
Robinson, Henry W., 188
Robinson, William, 153
Rogers, William, 13
Roosevelt, Franklin D., 90
Rosenwald Fund, 47, 48, 148
Roudanez, Louis Charles, 6–7, 10, 11, 16
Rousseve, Ferdinand, 54, 59–60
Rousseve, Maurice, 71
Ruby, George T., 13
Rudolphe, William A., 25
Rummell, Archbishop Joseph F., 208

salaries equalization campaign for teachers, 194–98
sales workers, 167
Sarre, A. J., 119
Sauvinet, C. S., 16
Scheps, Clarence, 204
School Board, Orleans Parish. See education, primary and secondary
school segregation and desegregation: Acts 555 and 556 (Louisiana, 1954), 205–6; antisegregation in white community, 208; black community meetings, 208–9, 210–11; *Brown v. Board of Education,* 205–6; Bush lawsuit, 204–5, 207; first four students to integrate, 211–12; implementation of *Brown,* 206–13; interpretations of, 21; NAACP and postwar shift toward judicial action, 202–4; petitions, 204, 208; in Reconstruction and post-Reconstruction, 14–16, 19–22; school conversion and case of Bayou Road School, 128–35; survey of parents on, 210; white citizens' councils and, 207–8; white threats over, 209. See also education, primary and secondary
Scott, Rebecca J., 9
Scott, Winfield, 1
Screwmen's Benevolent Association No. 1, 169–70
secular organizations and community development: Colored Educational Alliance, 105–6; Community Chest drives, 121; economic subordination and, 108–9; Flint-Goodridge Hospital, 109–16; Hardin and Federation of Civic Leagues, 104–5; *Louisiana Weekly,* 106–8; multiple functions of, 92; NAACP, 92–104; poll tax campaigns, 120; Urban League, 116–19; Washington's philosophy and, 119–20
segregation: black-owned businesses and, 151, 153; churches and, 63–67; Jim Crow, onset of, 25, 30; railroad car bill, 25–27; residential, 174–80; of teacher meetings, 127. See also school segregation and desegregation
self-help tradition, black, 62, 76, 108. See also uplift ideology
Semmes, Raphael, 2
separate-but-equal doctrine, 136. See also *Plessy v. Ferguson*
service businesses, black-owned, 161–63
Seventh Ward Civic League, 55, 104, 137
Seventh Ward Educational League, 106
Shakspeare, Joseph, 23–24
Sheffield, Jesse O., 155–57, 158
Shields, Wilmer, 117
Simmons, Arthur, 84
Sisters of the Blessed Sacrament, 52
skilled trades, 167, 168
skin color, 8
Slattery, John R., 34
slaves and education, 11–12
Smith, Frank, 164, 179, 180
Smith, Lillian, 119
Smith, William, 16
Smith, William Benjamin, 35
Smith v. Allwright, 199
soldiers, African American, 2–4, 199–200
Sophie Wright High School, 140–41
The Souls of Black Folk (Du Bois), 31
South, out-migration from, 82–83, 149
Southern Society for the Promotion of the Study of Race Conditions and Problems in the South, 32–35
Southern University, 22–23, 41–43, 139–40
Southwestern Christian Advocate, 73–74, 91, 106, 125
Spalding, Martin J., 68
Spaulding, Charles, 154
Spears, Mack, 56, 227
Spotts, Mrs. M. J., 162

Spriggens, Edward, 166
St. Dominic Church, 66, 70
Stephens, Mrs. L. E., 174–75
Stern, Edgar B., 47–52, 113, 114, 119
Stern, Edith, 113
St. Francis Xavier Church, Baltimore, 71
St. John Berchman's Industrial Life Insurance Co., 155–57
St. Joseph Society of the Sacred Heart (Josephites), 68–71
St. Katherine's Church, 65, 66, 67, 70
St. Mary's Benevolent Association, 158
Stone, Valaria G., 36–37
Straight, Seymour, 36
Straight College/University, 36–37, 39–40, 43, 45–48, 79, 89–90, 140
strikes, 170
student-led demonstrations, 216
suffrage and voting rights: Du Bois on, 180–81; grandfather clauses, 29; literacy requirements and poll taxes, 186; number of registrations, 181; number of voters, 28, 29; during Reconstruction and post-Reconstruction, 4, 6–7, 9, 27–29; registration and education campaigns, 225–27; "understanding clause" and *Trudeau v. Barnes*, 186–89; Waddell on, 34; women's suffrage, 28
Supreme Court. *See* court cases and lawsuits
Survey of Negro Colleges and Universities, 44

"Talented Tenth," 36, 58, 121
Tate, Leona, 211–12
Taylor, O.C.W., 166
teachers' salaries equalization campaign, 194–98
teacher training, 40–41, 52–53, 56
Tete, August J., 198
Third Ward Educational Association, 106
Thomas, Jesse O., 117
Thompson, Charles, 78
Thomy Lafon School, 60, 120, 137, 147
Thornhill, Elouise, 86, 90, 118
Thurman, Howard, 80
Title VII, Civil Rights Act (1964), 224–25
Tourné, Pascal M., 20
Treadwell, George, 197

Trudeau v. Barnes, 186–89
Truman, Harry, 200
Tureaud, Alexander P., 54, 60–61, 164, 187–88, 196–98, 201–2, 204, 206, 209, 220
Tuskegee Institute (AL), 28, 32, 40, 122
Tyler, Joseph, 177–78, 180
Tyler v. Harmon, 177–80

"understanding clause," 186–89
Unification Movement, 16–18
L'Union, 6
unions and labor, 169–72
Unity Industrial Life Insurance Co., 153, 158
universities. *See* education, higher
unskilled laborers, 147
uplift ideology: black churches and, 63, 74, 76; Du Bois on, 36; education and, 56; Flint-Goodridge Hospital and, 113, 115; Urban League and, 116–17; Washington on, 76. *See also* self-help tradition, black
urbanization, 152, 190
Urban League of Greater New Orleans, 116–19

Valena C. Jones School, 55–56, 134, 137
Vaughn, Herbert, 68
Vigne, L. B., 96
Villard, Oswald Garrison, 97
violence: bombings, 179; lynchings, 29, 187, 192; murder of Albert Plantevigne, 70; NAACP and, 92–93; in Reconstruction and post-Reconstruction, 18, 29; rural vs. urban, 190; sexual, and Hattie McCray case, 190–94; threats over school integration, 209
Volz, Julia, 128
voting rights. *See* suffrage and voting rights
Voting Rights Act (1965), 225, 226

Waddell, Alfred M., 33, 34
Wade, Benjamin, 5
Wade-Davis Bill (1864), 5
Walker, Alice, 163
Walker, Madame C. J. (born Sarah Breedlove), 161–62, 163
Walker, O. Perry, 205
Walmsley, T. Semmes, 175–76

INDEX

Ward, Thomas, 99
Warmoth, Henry Clay, 11, 37
Warren, Mortimer, 12
Warren Easton High School, 134, 140–41
Washington, Booker T.: "Atlanta Compromise" speech, 30, 119–20; on economic development, 152; education and, 31–33, 35, 57, 126, 142, 145; on suffrage, 28–29; uplift ideology of, 76
Weaver, Robert, 51
Wegmann, John, 129–30
Wexler, Sol, 126
"What the Black Man Wants" (Douglass), 10
Wheatley, Phillis, 57
White, E. W., 96, 98
White, Walter, 98, 103–4, 191–92, 200
White League, 18
Wicker, Albert, 153
Wickham, Katie, 162–63
Wilkinson, Hugh, 188
Williams, Arthur, 153
Williams, Daniel Hale, 114
Williams, Fannie C., 50, 51, 52, 54–56, 91, 137
William T. Frantz School, 211, 212
Wilson, Woodrow, 42
women and business, 161–63, 168–69
women's suffrage, 28
Woodson, Carter G., 57, 62
Woodward, C. Vann, 16, 30
World War I, 42, 130, 149, 199
World War II, 90, 199–200
Wright, J. Skelly, 209–10

Xavier University, 52–54, 59

Young, Andrew J., 56
Young Men's Democratic Association, 23

Zengel, Fred, 133, 134

www.ingramcontent.com/pod-product-compliance
Lightning Source LLC
Chambersburg PA
CBHW030611230426
43661CB00053B/1940